ADROS VERSE EDUCATION S.R.L.

Learn & Retain

Italian

with Spaced Repetition

700+ Anki Notes for Level I

with Vocabulary, Grammar, & Audio Pronunciation

Bucharest - 2023

Published by ADROS VERSE EDUCATION S.R.L.

website: https://www.adrosverse.com/

e-mail: info@adrosverse.com

Table of Contents

I. Introduction to Spaced Repetition

Remember all the times that you learned something just to forget it when you get rusty after not practicing for a while? Now imagine that there is some way to remind yourself of only the things that you are about to forget before you forget them, without boring yourself with the ones that you have already memorized. You may think that this would be convenient but also impossible, when in fact, it is possible using *spaced repetition*. Spaced repetition is a method of learning new material and then reviewing and memorizing that material over *spaced* intervals. Spaced repetition is often carried out using *flashcards*. The cards that you memorize successfully (i.e., *easy* material) will be reviewed less often, whereas the cards that you stumble over and struggle to memorize (i.e., *hard* material) will be shown more often.

In essence, spaced repetition is an enhancement of the old technique of learning by flashcards. Flashcards rely on cramming the material into the learner's memory regardless of how many times the learner successfully memorizes the material. This makes the learning process inefficient and exhausting. Spaced repetition addresses this flaw by presenting the material to the learner with a frequency that is inversely proportional to his or her ability to memorize it. This way, the learner will ideally be presented with the learned material right before he or she is about to forget it. As you can guess, this technique comes in handy when used to learn new vocabulary.

There has been a lot of research on the usefulness of the spaced repetition of learned material since its first proposal by C. A. Mace in 1932. Since then, it has remained a subject of interest for many researchers and people who seek to improve their memory. In any case, we believe that the improvement that spaced repetition adds to old flashcard techniques, especially in the context of learning a new language, is substantial.

ANKI: THE MOST POPULAR SPACED REPETITION SOFTWARE

To apply spaced repetition to flashcards, we need to decide on many parameters, such as the interval between reviews and whether the interval is fixed or graduated. Many software programs use algorithms to implement spaced-repetition learning. We will not delve into the details of each software and the algorithms they use. Instead, we will pick the most popular software among students and language learners, and that is *Anki*. The word "Anki" in Japanese means "memorization." It is an application developed by Damien Elmes in 2006 that uses an algorithm called SM-2, developed by SuperMemo. The software seems to offer many features while maintaining a reasonable level of simplicity.

In the next chapter, we will walk you briefly through the basics of Anki, how to install it, and how to use the basic features. The Anki software can be used on a desktop device (AnkiWeb) or a smartphone using Android (AnkiDroid) or iOS (AnkiMobile). The use of AnkiWeb and AnkiDroid is free. AnkiMobile, unfortunately, is paid and can be purchased from the Apple Store. Alternatively, if you use an iPhone or iPad, you could install AnkiWeb on your computer and test it for a few days. If you like it, you can continue to use AnkiWeb or purchase AnkiMobile—if you deem it worthwhile. If you create an account using your Anki software, you can synchronize your account on different devices, including multiple desktops and mobile phones.

USING ANKI FOR LANGUAGE LEARNING

There are many studies out there that try to answer the question: "How many words do I need to know to understand X% of a language?" Stuart Webb, professor of linguistics at the University of Western Ontario, asserts that a typical native speaker knows 15,000 to 20,000 word families. A word family is the base form, or root, of a word (e.g., break, breaker, broken, broke, etc., all count as one word family). A language learner who learns only 800 of the most common words in English can understand 75% of the daily-spoken language.

Research done by Francis and Kucera in 1982 found that having a vocabulary size of 2,000 word families is sufficient to cover nearly 80% of a written English text.

To understand dialogue in a movie or on TV, Professor Webb asserts that you need to know 3,000 of the most common word families. A similar assertion has been made by famous linguist Paul Nation, who defines 3,000 as the reasonable threshold of high-frequency words needed by a second-language learner.

With over 5,000 flashcards of verbs, nouns, and adjectives, as well as detailed grammar lessons, this book aims at getting you to that level where you can converse, understand, and speak Italian in everyday settings.

A lot of Anki cards are available online. Some are free, and many others are on the costlier side. However, the issue with many of the available products is that they simply do not have progressive guidelines that go hand-in-hand with the cards. After all, memorization is different from knowledge acquisition, which requires an understanding of the material you are learning. We attempt to solve this missing piece of the puzzle by providing the proper introduction, learning progression, and grammar knowledge to make sense of the information you are trying to memorize.

We truly hope that many learners will find this technique and this book useful and that learning Italian and other languages will find its way to as many people as possible to help us understand and recognize each other in a way that serves humanity as a whole.

HOW TO USE THIS BOOK

First and foremost, make sure that you read Chapter II of this book following this introduction. This chapter will help you set up Anki on your desktop computer and mobile device(s). It is essential that you do that successfully to gain the maximum benefit of this book. The coupon code to obtain the flashcards for Level I, available for free for a limited time, can be found in **Appendix A**. Once you download the cards and back them up with the Anki account you create, the cards do not expire.

As you go through each level's introductory topics and grammar, we recommend that you use this book to read the levels and lessons in the order that they are presented. You can, of course, go quickly over the lessons that you find familiar. Nevertheless, we do not recommend that you skip any lesson. The best way to study using this book is to start with reading Level I, Lesson 1 in the book, then go to your Anki app and activate the cards of that lesson. If the lesson is easy compared to your level, you will be able to answer most of the cards as *easy*. As a result, you will see these cards less often in the future as they *fade away* in the memory of the app.

There may be some lessons that you find useful to return to for further review or reference. We try to point these out throughout the book. The appendix also contains some cheat sheets that summarize some of these rules. You can use those if you find them useful. The Anki app will help you through this process because it will keep repeating the concepts that slip your memory.

In the vocabulary-building section, we cover basic verbs and adjectives; then, we go over nouns from different categories. Nouns constitute more than 80% of all words in the Italian language. Thus, we try to cover a wide variety of categories. The vocabulary-building section of each level in this book is meant to serve as a reference. The Anki flashcards are preferred to take away the dull and boring part of that process.

In case you want to look up a word, you will find an Italian index, followed by an English index at the end of the book.

Finally, in the appendix, you will find two useful cheat sheets that give you an overall perspective of most moods and verb tenses in Italian. The first cheat sheet is the Verb Conjugation Chart, which is structured as a comprehensive reference for the reader. The second sheet dives deeper into the irregular verbs of each tense where necessary.

We recommend that you keep these two sheets handy by printing them out or having them available separately on your desk or electronic device.

II. Setting Up Anki

This is an important chapter that you should NOT skip if you want to use the Anki flashcards that accompany the book, which is highly recommended for your maximum benefit.

In this chapter, we cover how to download the Anki software, import the ADROS VERSE EDUCATION Italian Anki package, and activate the cards associated with the lessons in the book as you read through it.

If you prefer video instructions, go to our YouTube page at https://www.youtube.com/watch?v=kLlWwhFmMHM or simply search for **ADROS VERSE EDUCATION** channel on YouTube and look for the title: **Setting up Anki and Importing the ADROS VERSE Package - All Languages**.

The video in the link above goes through the same steps explained in this chapter.

Download Anki Software

The first step is to download the latest version of Anki compatible with your desktop, Android, or iOS device(s). You can download Anki on different devices and synchronize all of them to the latest study review that you have completed. It is highly recommended that you download a desktop version first to use it as a master copy and then synchronize any other mobile devices you have. However, you can choose to use Anki on your mobile device only.

Windows Desktop

1. Go to https://apps.ankiweb.net/ and download the latest Anki version for Windows. The procedure is similar for Mac and Linux if you use a different operating system.
2. Run the ".exe" file, and open the program by double-clicking on the Anki icon.

3. A default window will open under the username "**User 1.**" It is recommended that you create an account to have a backup of your data in the cloud and synchronize it with other devices. To create an account, click on "**Sync.**" A window that says "**Account Required**" will pop up. Click on "**Sign Up.**" This will take you to a web page where you can complete the signup process.

Android or iOS

1. If you have an Android device, go to "**Google Play**" and download "**AnkiDroid Flashcards,**" available for free. If you have an iOS device, go to "**Apple Store**" and download "**AnkiMobile Flashcards.**" Unfortunately, at the time of writing this book, the app is not free and is sold by "**Apple Store**" for $24.99. Alternatively, you can choose to use the desktop version for free.
2. Open the app from your mobile device.
3. If you have created an account on desktop Anki, you can simply synchronize to your account.

❖ On Android: Tap the three horizontal lines at the top left of the screen. Then, select **Settings** > **General Settings** > **AnkiWeb** account. Enter the same email from the account you created on desktop Anki.

❖ On iOS: Tap **"Synchronize"** at the bottom right of the screen and enter the same email from the account you created on desktop Anki.

4. If you have not created an account on desktop Anki, you can continue to use Anki on your mobile device without creating an account. However, you will not have any backup online if you lose the data on your phone.

Download & Import The Italian Anki Package

After downloading the Anki software on your device, you need to download the Anki package (.apkg) created specifically for this book.

Windows Desktop

1. Go to https://www.adrosverse.com/books-and-flashcards/, and download the **"Italian: Level I - Basic"** package. At the check-out, use the discount code provided to you in **Appendix A**. If you purchased the book, you should get the Level I Anki package for FREE for a limited time. Once you download the cards, the cards do not expire.

2. After downloading the package, take note of the folder in which it was downloaded.

3. Go to your Anki app, and in the menu bar, go to **"File,"** then select **"Import"** from the list of options and navigate to where the package was downloaded.

4. If you have not done so already, you can still create an account to save a backup copy online and synchronize it with other devices by clicking on the **"Sync"** button; this is highly recommended.

Android or iOS

If you have created an account on a desktop device, you only need to log in to your account on the mobile Anki app and synchronize it with the backup copy online.

If you want to continue without creating an account, you can still download and import the package on Android. This is a little more difficult on iOS because you may need to create a download link.

ACTIVATE CARDS

As you successfully import the Anki package with the lessons, you may realize that all the cards are suspended. This is done intentionally because you do not want to be presented with cards from all levels before you even start reading the book.

You are expected to start reading Level 1, Lesson 1. After you finish, you want to activate or *unsuspend* the cards associated with that lesson. To do this, follow the simple steps described here.

Windows Desktop

1. On the main Anki page where decks are presented, click on "**Browse**."

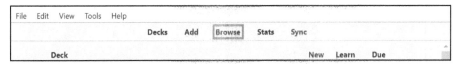

2. Highlight Lesson 1 from the menu on the left.

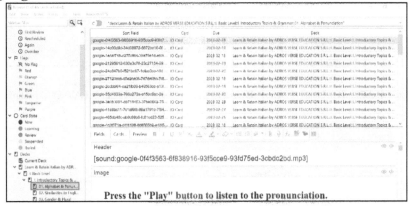

3. Highlight all the cards (shown on the right) in Lesson 1 using CTRL+A. Alternatively, you can click on **Edit** > **Select All**.

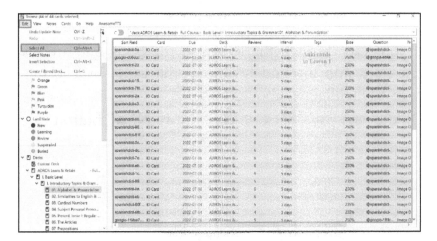

4. After highlighting all the cards from Lesson 1, activate them by clicking on **Cards** > **Toggle Suspend** to unsuspend the cards.

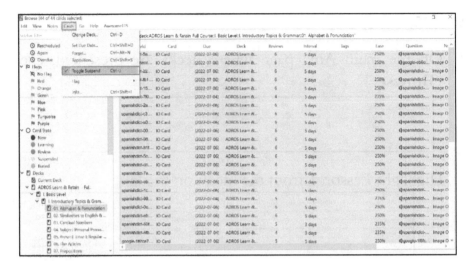

5. Go back to the decks page. You will notice now that there are a few cards that are due from Lesson 1.

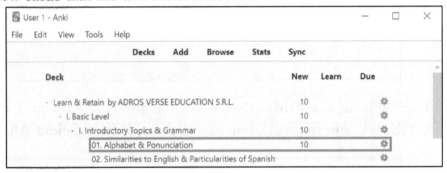

6. If you read through the lesson in the book and are ready, you can start studying and reviewing the cards by clicking on the deck, as highlighted above.

7. On the next page, click on the "**Study Now**" button.

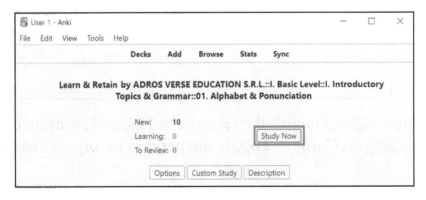

8. The first card will appear, and you will test your knowledge of the information presented on the card. Notice that you may see a different card than the one shown below. That is okay.

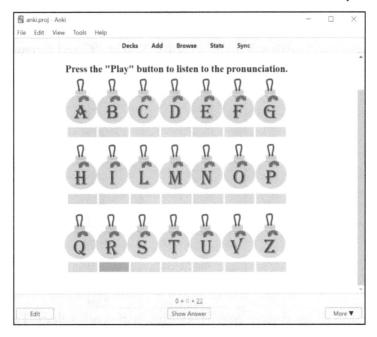

9. Once you are satisfied with your answer, click on the "**Show Answer**" button at the bottom of the page. The answer will appear with four options: "**Again**," "**Hard**," "**Good**," and "**Easy**." You will select the button that represents the difficulty you encountered in answering the card. This will determine how frequently you see the card in the future.

10. The next card will be shown after each answer until you finish all the cards due for the day.

Android

If you have activated the cards from the desktop app, you simply need to synchronize your phone version to see them activated. If you want to activate the cards from your mobile device, follow the steps below:

1. On the main AnkiDroid app page, where decks are presented, tap the three horizontal lines at the top left of the page. You will be presented with a list of options. Select **"Card browser."**

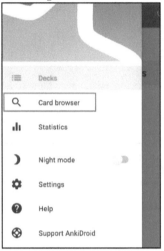

2. Tap the drop-down menu at the top and select Lesson 1 of Level I.

3. A list of cards will appear. Tap the three dots at the top right corner and select **"Select all"** to highlight all the cards.

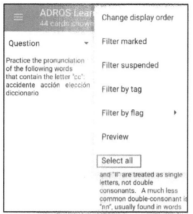

4. Tap the three dots at the top right corner again and select **"Unsuspend cards"** to activate all the cards in the lesson. If you make a mistake, go back to step 2, select all decks, select all cards, and suspend them. Then unsuspend only Lesson 1 of Level I.Go back to the main page where the decks are presented. You will notice now that there are a few cards that are due from Lesson 1.

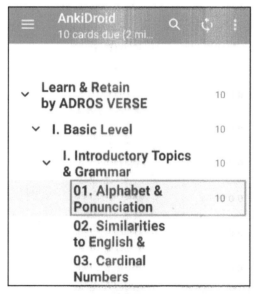

5. If you read through the lesson in the book and are ready, you can start studying and reviewing the cards by tapping on the deck, as highlighted above.

6. The first card will appear, and you will test your knowledge of the information presented on the card. Notice that you may see a different card than the one shown below. That is okay.

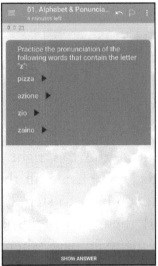

7. Once you have thought your answer through, tap the **"Show Answer"** button at the bottom of the page. The answer will appear with four options: **"Again,"** **"Hard,"** **"Good,"** and **"Easy."** You will select the button that represents the difficulty you encountered in answering the card. This will determine how frequently you see the card in the future.

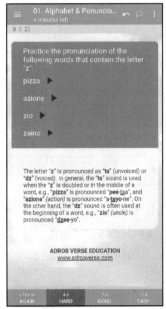

8. The next card will be shown after each answer until you finish all the cards due for today.

IMPORTANT:

If the cards appear too small or too large on your mobile device, as shown below, for example:

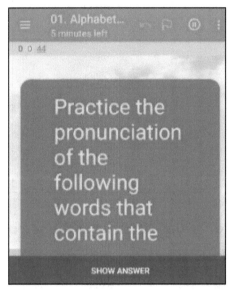

Tap on the three horizontal lines on the top left, then tap on: **Settings > Reviewing > Card Zoom**, and adjust the zoom until the font and card size fit your needs.

iOS

For iOS, replace the first four steps in the Android instructions with the following:

1. On the main AnkiMobile app page, where decks are presented, tap on Lesson 1 from Level I. You will be presented with the first card.

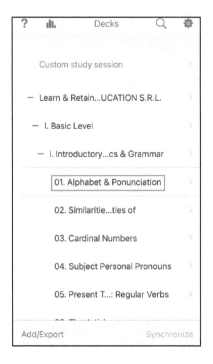

2. Tap on **"Browse"** at the top right of the screen.

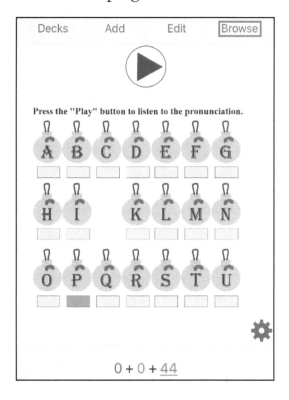

3. Tap on **"Select"** at the top right of the screen, then tap on **"Select All."**

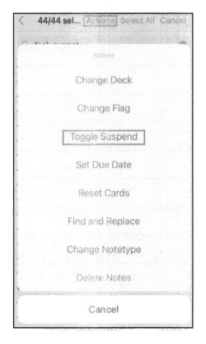

4. Tap on **"Actions,"** and from the drop-down menu, tap on **"Toggle Suspend"** to activate the cards in this lesson.

Follow the same remaining steps from 5 to 9 in the Android instructions.

MORE SETTINGS

You can always tweak your Anki settings based on how often you forget your cards. These settings can be accessed by clicking on the settings icon on your deck page, as shown below.

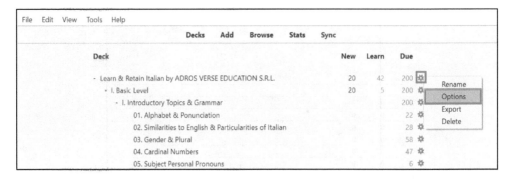

We recommend that you switch off the automatic audio play and keep the other default settings. However, feel free to experiment with the settings for a better personal experience.

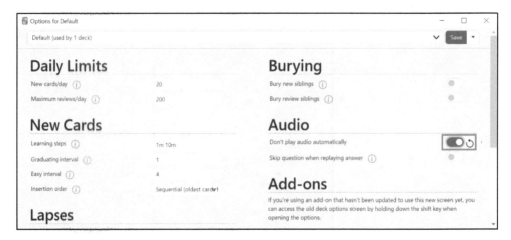

You can add your custom cards and even decks. To add a note (that is an Anki card), go to your **"Browse"** page and click on **Notes > Add Notes**.

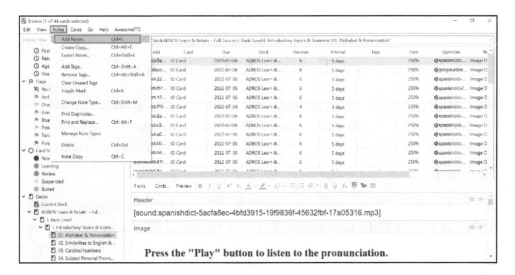

You can choose your preferred note type and add it to your learning deck.

It is not a requirement to know how to use Anki beyond the basics that we have covered in this introduction. However, if you are interested, we encourage you to learn from the plethora of resources online that teach you how to create and edit decks and notes on Anki.

I. Introductory Topics & Grammar

Start your journey with Italian by familiarizing yourself with the introductory topics in this section. We will cover grammar and basic knowledge that you need to equip yourself with to make the learning process easier, such as the alphabet, numbers, etc.

Do not worry if you do not absorb all of the information. Your Anki cards will help you memorize the material in a non-boring way until you master what you have learned. Ensure that you did not skip the introductory Chapter II of this book on setting up Anki.

1. ALPHABET & PRONUNCIATION

Luckily, Italian uses the Latin letters used in English with only a few differences in pronunciation. Italian, unlike English, is a phonetic language, meaning that you should be able to pronounce most written words without the need for a dictionary, with some exceptions with regard to syllable stress.

Start with the Italian alphabet in the table below, and use your Anki cards to anchor what you learned via spaced-repetition exercises.

Italian Letter		English Pronunciation[1]	Notes
A	a	ah	like "a" in "father"
B	b	bee	equivalent to English "b"
C	c	chee	sounds like English "k" and like "ch" in "cheese" only before "e" or "i"
D	d	dee	equivalent to English "d"
E	e	e	like "e" in "bet" but can sometimes be more closed
F	f	ef-fe	equivalent to English "f"
G	g	jee	sounds like "g" in "gab," and like "j" in "job" only before "e" or "i." In addition, "gn" sounds like "ny" in "canyon," and "gli" sounds like "lli" in "million"
H	h	ak-ka	silent letter like "h" in "hour"
I	i	ee	like "ee" in "see" or "i" in "marine"

L	l	**el**-le	equivalent to English "**l**" but softer
M	m	**em**-me	equivalent to English "**m**"
N	n	**en**-ne	equivalent to English "**n**"
O	o	o	equivalent to English "**o**," but sometimes more open
P	p	pee	equivalent to English "**p**"
Q	q	koo	always followed by "**u**" to form "**qu**" which sounds like "**kw**," e.g., "**quando**" pronounced "**kwan**-do"
R	r	**er**-re	like English "**r**" but rolled with a single flap against the upper palate
S	s	**es**-se	can sound like English "**s**" or "**z**"
T	t	tee	like "**t**" in "table" but strongly pronounced
U	u	oo	like "**oo**" in "**food**"
V	v	voo/vee	equivalent to English "**v**"
Z	z	**tse**-ta	pronounced like "**ts**" (unvoiced) or "**dz**" (voiced)

[1] The stressed syllable in the English pronunciation is in bold.

Further Notes on Italian Alphabet

❖ There are only 21 letters (five vowels and 16 consonants) in the official Italian alphabet compared to 26 in the English alphabet. Notice the absence of the letters "**j**," "**k**," "**w**," "**x**," and "**y**."

❖ The letters "**j**," "**k**," "**w**," "**x**," and "**y**" can still be encountered in some loanwords and acronyms in Italian. Below are the Italian names of these letters with examples:

Letter		Name in Italian	English Pronunciation	Example
J	j	i lunga	ee **loon**-ga	"**jacuzzi**" pronounced "ja-**koo**-tsee"
K	k	kappa	**kap**-pa	"**kiwi**" pronounced "**kee**-wee"
W	w	vu doppia	voo **dop**-pia	"**wafer**" pronounced "**wa**-fer"
X	x	ics	eeks	"**xeno**" *(xenon)* pronounced "**kse**-no"
Y	y	ipsilon/ i greca	ee-psee-lon/ ee **gre**-ka	"**yogurt**" pronounced "**yo**-goort"

❖ The letter "**c**" in Italian is used to form the equivalents of the sounds "**k**" (*hard* "**c**") and "**ch**" (*soft* "**c**") in English. The way this is achieved is as follows:

1. If the letter "**c**" is followed by "**e**" or "**i**," it is considered a soft "**c**" and is pronounced like *"ch"* in *"cheese."*

2. Otherwise, the letter "c" is considered a hard "c" and is pronounced like *"k"* in *"kit."*

The letter "h" is used to change the pronunciation of "c" from soft to hard if the "c" precedes an "e" or "i." For instance, "ci," meaning *"there,"* is pronounced "**chee**" (soft "c"), whereas "**chi**," meaning *"who,"* is pronounced "**kee**" (hard "c"). From the perspective of an English speaker, this explains how to produce the "**k**" sound before an "**e**" or "**i**" in Italian despite the absence of the letter "**k**" from the Italian alphabet.

The letter "i" is used to change the pronunciation of "c" from hard to soft if the "c" precedes a letter that is not "e" or "i." For instance, "**cane**" *(dog)* is pronounced "**ka**-ne," i.e., hard "c," whereas "**ciano**" *(cyan)* is pronounced "**cha**-no," i.e., soft "c." Remember that, in Italian, "**ch**" can only sound like "**k**" and never like *"ch"* in *"cheese."* The equivalent "**ch**" sound in English is formed only when the "**c**" with is followed by an "**i**" or "**e**." To summarize:

c	+	"e" or "i"	soft "c"	"**cena**" *(dinner)* pronounced "**che**-na"
ci	+	"a," "o," or "u"	soft "c"	"**ciao**" *(bye)* pronounced "**chaw**"
c	+	any letter other than "e" or "i"	hard "c"	"**cane**" *(dog)* pronounced "**ka**-ne" "**crudo**" *(raw)* pronounced "**kroo**-do"
ch	+	"e" or "i"	hard "c"	"**chi**" *(who)* pronounced "**kee**"

❖ The letter "g" can also have a *hard* sound like *"g"* in *"gab"* or a *soft* sound like *"j"* in *"jam."* The two basic rules are:

1. If the letter "g" is followed by "e" or "i," it is considered a soft "g" and is pronounced like *"j"* in *"jam,"* e.g., "**gelato**" *(ice cream)* is pronounced "je-**la**-to."

2. If the letter "g" is not followed by "e," "i," "n," or "li," it is considered a hard "g" and is pronounced like *"g"* in *"gab,"* e.g., "**gatto**" *(cat)* is pronounced "**gat**-to."

In addition to the two aforementioned rules, the letter "g" can precede "n" or "li" to form the following two distinctive sounds in Italian:

1. The letter "**g**" can precede the letter "**n**" to form "**gn**," pronounced like *"ny"* in *"ca<u>ny</u>on."* For example, "**gnocchi**" is pronounced as "**<u>ny</u>ok**-kee."

2. The letter "**g**" can precede "**li**" to form "**gli**," pronounced like *"lli"* in *"mi<u>lli</u>on."* [1] For example, "**figlia**," meaning *"daughter,"* is pronounced as "**fee**-<u>ly</u>a."

The letter "**h**" is used to change the pronunciation of "**g**" from soft to hard if the "**g**" precedes an "**e**" or "**i**." For instance, "**spaghetti**" is pronounced "spa-**get**-tee" (hard "**g**").

The letter "**i**" is used to change the pronunciation of "**g**" from hard to soft if the "**g**" precedes a letter that is not "**e**" or "**i**." For instance, "**giorno**" *(day)* is pronounced "**jor**-no," i.e., soft "**g**." From the perspective of an English speaker, this explains how to produce the "**j**" sound before an "**e**" or "**i**" in Italian despite the absence of the letter "**j**" from the Italian alphabet.

To summarize:

g	+	"**e**" or "**i**"	soft "**g**"	"**gelato**" pronounced "**j**e-la-to"
gi	+	"**a**," "**o**," or "**u**"	soft "**g**"	"**giorno**" pronounced "**j**or-no"
g	+	any letter other than "**e**," "**i**," "**n**," or "**li**"	hard "**g**"	"**gatto**" *(cat)* pronounced "**gat**-to"
gh	+	"**e**" or "**i**"	hard "**g**"	"**spaghetti**" pronounced "spa-**get**-tee"
gn			"**ny**" sound	"**gnocchi**" pronounced "**ny**ok-kee"
gli			"**ly**" sound	"**figlia**" pronounced "**fee**-<u>ly</u>a"

❖ Similar to the letters "**c**" and "**g**," the compound consonant "**sc**" is used to form the equivalents of the sounds "**sh**" and "**sk**" in English:

---

[1] There are only few exceptions in which "**gli**" is pronounced with hard "**g**" as "**glee**," and not with "ly" sound, e.g., "**anglicismo**" *(anglicism)*, "**geroglifico**" *(hieroglyph)*, "**glicerina**" *(glycerine)*, "**negligere**" *(to neglect)*, "**gliconio**" *(glyconium)*.

1. If "**sc**" is followed by "**e**" or "**i,**" it is pronounced like *"sh"* in *"sheep,"* e.g., "**scelta**" *(choice)* is pronounced "**sh**el-ta."

2. Otherwise, "**sc**" is pronounced like *"sk"* in *"sky,"* e.g., "**scarpe**" *(shoes)* is pronounced "**sk**ar-pe."

The letter "**h**" is used to change the pronunciation of "**sc**" from "**sh**" to "**sk**" if the "**sc**" precedes an "**e**" or "**i**." For example, "**schema**" *(scheme)* is pronounced "**sk**e-ma."

To summarize:

sc	+	"e" or "i"	"sh" sound	"scelta" pronounced "shel-ta"
sc	+	"a," "o," or "u"	"sk" sound	"scarpe" pronounced "skar-pe"
sch	+	"e" or "i"	"sk" sound	"schema" pronounced "ske-ma"

❖ The letter "**s**," when not part of the compound consonant "**sc**," can sound like English "**s**" or "**z.**" In most cases, the following rule applies:

> If "**s**" is between two vowels or before a voiced consonant ("**b**," "**d**," "**g**," "**l**," "**m**," "**n**," or "**v**"), it is often pronounced like English "**z**," e.g., "**rosa**" *(rose)* is pronounced as "**ro**-**z**a." In most other cases, it is pronounced like the English "**s**" in *"start."*

❖ The letter "**z**" is pronounced as "**ts**" (unvoiced) or "**dz**" (voiced). In general, the "**ts**" sound is used when the "**z**" is doubled or in the middle of a word, e.g., "**pizza**" is pronounced "**pee**-**ts**a," and "**azione**" *(action)* is pronounced "a-**tsyo**-ne." On the other hand, the "**dz**" sound is often used at the beginning of a word, e.g., "**zio**" *(uncle)* is pronounced "**dzee**-yo."

❖ The letter "**q**" is always followed by the letter "**u**" to form the sound "**kw**," e.g., "**questo**" *(this)* is pronounced as "**kwes**-to."

❖ Of the 16 consonants in the original Italian alphabet, 14 consonants can be doubled, that is, all consonants except "**q**" and "**h**," e.g., "**caffè**" *(coffee)*, "**mamma**" *(mom)*, "**nonna**" *(grandma)*, etc. These are represented by double letters throughout the book. They sound stressed with a short pause. Think of the *"n"* sound in *"unnavigable,"* or *"one note"* versus *"one oat."*

❖ To stress soft or hard sounds formed by adding an "i" or "h," e.g., "ci," "ch," "gi," "gh," etc., only the first letter is doubled, e.g., **"messaggio"** *(message)*, **"occhiali"** *(glasses)*, etc.

❖ The letters "a," "e," "i," "o," and "u" are treated as vowels, except when the letters "e" and "i" are used to indicate different pronunciation of a preceding "c" or "g," as discussed earlier.

❖ The vowels "a," "e," and "o," are considered *strong* vowels, whereas "i" and "u" are considered *weak* vowels.

❖ The week vowels "i" and "u" form the sounds "y" and "w" when unstressed and preceded or followed by another vowel. Below are some examples:

ai	"ay" sound	"zaino" *(backpack)* pronounced "dzay-no"
ie	"ye" sound	"ieri" *(yesterday)* pronounced "ee-ye-ree"
io	"yo" sound	"fiore" *(flower)* pronounced "fyo-re"
ua	"wa" sound	"guardare" *(to look)* pronounced "gwar-da-re"
uo	"wo" sound	"uomo" *(man)* pronounced "wo-mo"
au	"aw" sound	"audio" *(audio)* pronounced "aw-dyo"
iu	"yoo" sound	"più" *(more)* pronounced "pyoo"

❖ Italian is considered to have five vowel letters and seven vowel sounds. Each of the vowels "e" and "o" has an *open* and *closed* sound. The differences are summarized in the following table:

o	open sound	like "o" in "cop"
	closed sound	like "o" in "go" but without the final "w" sound
e	open sound	like "e" in "bed" but a little more open
	closed sound	like "e" in "they" but without the final "y" sound

In general, the open sound is used when the syllable is stressed; otherwise, the closed sound is often used. Knowing when to use the open or closed sound can sometimes be tricky. The best way to master the difference is oral practice and referring to a good dictionary.

❖ Every vowel is pronounced separately, and each with its alphabetical sound. Thus, there are no diphthongs in the English sense, except for the "**i**" and "**u**" when used as weak vowels to form the sounds "**y**" and "**w**," respectively, as discussed earlier.

❖ Every letter is pronounced. There are no silent letters such as "*b*" in *"lamb"* or "*l*" in *"walk."* The only exception to this rule is the letter "**h**" at the beginning of a word, e.g., "**hanno**" *(they have)* pronounced "**an**-no." Notice that we did not consider letters that modify the pronunciation as silent, such as "**i**" in "**g<u>i</u>orno**" (pronounced "**jor**-no") and "**h**" in "**spag<u>h</u>etti**" (pronounced "spa-**get**-tee").

Syllable Stress in Italian Words

In general, Italian is a phonetic language. If you practice enough, you should eventually be able to pronounce most Italian words without listening to an audio transcription or referring to a dictionary.

Knowing which syllable to stress in a polysyllabic[1] word in Italian is critical to speaking comprehensibly and achieving fluency. The good news is that, unlike in English, where syllable stress seems more arbitrary, there are some rules in Italian that diminish the role for guessing and allow you to be right most of the time. It is important to ensure that you master these rules early on as you build your vocabulary. The main rules are:

1. If the last letter is a vowel with an accent, the stress falls on the last syllable. For example, "**città**" *(city)*: cit-**ta**, "**caffè**" *(coffee)*: caf-**fe**, and "**perché**" *(why)*: per-**ke**, where the stressed syllable in the pronunciation script is in bold.

---

[1] Having more than one syllable

2. Most other words in Italian stress the *second-to-last* syllable, also called the *penultimate* syllable.

3. Some words stress the *third-to-last* syllable. Most of these words end with the following suffixes:

-agine	-aggine	-igine	-iggine	-uggine
-edine	-udine	-abile	-ibile	-atico
-ico	-aceo	-ognolo	-oide	-tesi
-dromo	-fago	-filo	-fobo	-fono
-metro	-nomo	-gono	-grafo	-logo
-crate	-cefalo	-gamo	-geno	-mane
-stato	-ttero	-fero	-fugo	-evole

For example, **"microfono"** *(microphone)*: mee-**cro**-fo-no, **"fotografo"** *(photograph)*: fo-**to**-gra-fo, **"sinonimo"** *(synonym)*: see-**no**-nee-mo, etc.

4. In rare cases, and often in some conjugated verbs, the stress falls on the *fourth-to-last* syllable, e.g., **"telefonano"** *(they call)*: te-**le**-fo-na-no.

2. SIMILARITIES TO ENGLISH & PARTICULARITIES OF THE ITALIAN LANGUAGE

English is considered a Germanic language, whereas Italian is a Romance language. Yet, they share a substantial amount of vocabulary. The main reason is attributed to the Norman Conquest of England in the eleventh century, as a result of which the English language borrowed a lot of French words. French Prime Minister Georges Clemenceau (1841-1929) famously claimed that "English is just badly pronounced French." French, like Italian, is a Romance language and shares Latin roots, and thus a lot of vocabulary, with Italian. You can see the connection here between Italian and English via the French language. This is why the US Foreign Service Institute (FSI), which provides language training to diplomats and government employees, ranks Italian in the easiest language learning category for English speakers.

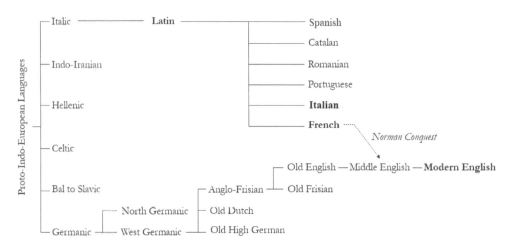

English Cognates in Italian

History aside, we can definitely capitalize on this connection. There are a lot of English cognates in the Italian language. English cognates are words that are directly descended from a common ancestor language, in this case, mostly French. Moreover, since English has become a universal language, some English words have obviously found their way directly into many languages, including Italian.

Although cognates will often have the same meaning in Italian and English, it is important to note that this is not always the case, as languages have evolved separately. For example, the Italian word "**camera**" means *room*, not the device you use to take photos. That would be "**macchina fotografica**." Similarly, the word "**fabbrica**" in Italian means *"factory"* and not *"fabric,"* as you may have guessed. That being said, recognizing English cognates is a powerful tool that can enhance the Italian vocabulary of any English-speaking learner. We will include some English cognates in our vocabulary-building section at the end of each level to help give your Italian vocabulary a jump start.

As we delve into the English cognates, do not feel overwhelmed with the vocabulary. You are not expected to memorize all of the cognates at this basic level. It is only meant to give you an idea about the similarities with English and help provide a sense of the Italian language based on prior knowledge of English.

Take, for example, the Latin verb "claudere," meaning *"to close."* In the development of the Italian language, the "l" preceded by a consonant, e.g., "cl," "pl," "fl," etc., has often changed to "i." Knowing that, you would be more likely to recognize the similarity between the adjectives "**chiuso**" (pronounced "**kyoo**-so") in Italian and *"closed"* in English, both derived from the Latin "claudere." Similar is the case with words such as "**fiamma**" *(flame)*, "**fiore**" *(flower)*, and "**piazza**" *(square or place)*.

Here, we list some parallels between English and Italian words that will make you realize how many Italian words you already know or perhaps are able to guess correctly.

It is also important to note that these are not considered strict rules, but rather useful guidelines to make learning Italian easier for English speakers.

1. Many English words ending in *"-ile"* end in "-ile" in Italian, e.g., "**fragile**" *(fragile)* "**facsimile**" *(facsimile)*, "**ostile**" *(hostile)*.

2. Many English words ending in *"-or"* end in "-ore" in Italian, e.g., "**colore**," "**errore**," "**superiore**."

3. Many English words ending in *"-ble"* end in "-bile" in Italian, e.g., "**possibile**," "**terribile**," "**variabile**."

4. Many English words ending in *"-al"* end in "-ale" in Italian, e.g., "**animale**," "**centrale**," "**personale**."

5. Some English words ending in *"-cal"* break the above *"-al"* ending rule and end in "-co" (masculine) or "-ca" (feminine) in Italian, e.g., "**critico**," "**fisico**," "**politica**."

6. Many English words ending in *"-ic"* end in "-ico" (masculine) or "-ica" (feminine) in Italian, e.g., "**democratico**," "**meccanico**," "**pubblico**."

7. Many English words ending in *"-ant"* or *"-ent"* end in "**-ante**" or "**-ente**" in Italian, respectively, e.g., "**ignor<u>ante</u>**," "**import<u>ante</u>**," "**differ<u>ente</u>**," "**intellig<u>ente</u>**."

8. Many English words ending in *"-ment"* end in "**-mento**" in Italian, e.g., "**docu<u>mento</u>**," "**supple<u>mento</u>**," "**monu<u>mento</u>**."

9. Many English words ending in *"-ist"* end in "**-ista**" in Italian, e.g., "**pian<u>ista</u>**," "**art<u>ista</u>**," "**dent<u>ista</u>**."

10. Many English words ending in *"-am"* or *"-em"* end in "**-amma**" or "**-ema**" in Italian, respectively, e.g., "**progr<u>amma</u>**," "**diagr<u>amma</u>**," "**probl<u>ema</u>**," "**sist<u>ema</u>**."

11. Many English words ending in *"-ous"* end in "**-oso**" (masculine) or "**-osa**" (feminine) in Italian, e.g., "**fam<u>oso</u>**," "**religi<u>oso</u>**," "**curi<u>osa</u>**."

12. Many English words ending in *"-ry"* end in "**-rio**" (masculine) or "**-ria**" (feminine) in Italian, e.g., "**anniversa<u>rio</u>**," "**immagina<u>ria</u>**," "**itinera<u>rio</u>**."

13. Many English words ending in *"-tion"* end in "**-zione**" in Italian, e.g., "**condi<u>zione</u>**," "**educa<u>zione</u>**," "**na<u>zione</u>**," "**situa<u>zione</u>**."

14. Many English words ending in *"-tional"* end in "**-zionale**" in Italian, e.g., "**condi<u>zionale</u>**," "**na<u>zionale</u>**," "**tradi<u>zionale</u>**."

15. Many English words ending in *"-tial"* end in "**-ziale**" in Italian, e.g., "**ini<u>ziale</u>**," "**poten<u>ziale</u>**," "**par<u>ziale</u>**."

16. Many English words ending in *"-ce"* end in "**-za**" in Italian, e.g., "**differen<u>za</u>**," "**importan<u>za</u>**," "**violen<u>za</u>**."

17. Many English words ending in *-cy"* end in "**-zia**" or "**-za**" in Italian, e.g., "**agen<u>zia</u>**," "**democra<u>zia</u>**," "**urgen<u>za</u>**."

18. Many English words ending in *"-ty"* end in "**-tà**" in Italian, e.g., "**elettrici<u>tà</u>**," "**universi<u>tà</u>**," "**possibili<u>tà</u>**."

19. Some English words ending in *"-ly"* end in "**-mente**" in Italian, e.g., "**normal<u>mente</u>**," "**natural<u>mente</u>**," "**total<u>mente</u>**."

20. Many English nouns ending in *"-phy"* end in "-**fia**" in Italian, e.g., "**geografia**," "**fotografia**" *(photography)*, "**filosofia**" *(philosophy)*.

21. Many English words ending in *"-ct"* end in "-**tto**" (masculine) or "-**tta**" (feminine) in Italian, e.g., "**atto**" *(act)*, "**diretto**" *(direct)*, "**corretta**" *(correct)*.

22. Many English words ending in *"-sion"* end in "-**sione**" in Italian, e.g., "**conclusione**," "**conversione**," "**versione**."

23. Many English words ending in *"-ism"* end in "-**ismo**" in Italian, e.g., "**organismo**," "**patriottismo**," "**comunismo**."

24. Many English words ending in *"-id"* end in "-**ido**" (masculine) or "-**ida**" (feminine) in Italian, e.g., "**fluido**," "**liquido**," "**timido**."

25. Many English words ending in *"-ive"* end in "-**ivo**" (masculine) or "-**iva**" (feminine) in Italian, e.g., "**definitivo**," "**nativo**," "**negativo**."

26. Many English verbs ending in *"-fy"* end in "-**ficare**" in Italian, e.g., "**classificare**," "**modificare**," "**verificare**."

27. Many English verbs ending in *"-cate"* end in "-**care**" in Italian, e.g., "**complicare**," "**educare**," "**indicare**."

28. Many English verbs ending in *"-ize"* or *"-yze"* end in "-**izzare**" in Italian, e.g., "**analizzare**," "**minimizzare**," "**organizzare**."

In addition to the above notes, the following minor spelling notes can be useful:

1. Many English words change *"ph"* to "**f**" in Italian, e.g., "**foto**," "**elefante**," "**telefono**."

2. Many English words change *"th"* to "**t**" or "**tt**" in Italian, e.g., "**cattedrale**," "**autore**," "**cattolico**."

3. Many English words change *"ct"* or *"pt"* to "**tt**" in Italian, e.g., "**attore**" *(actor)*, "**effettivo**" *(effective)*, "**ottico**" *(optical)*, "**Egitto**" *(Egypt)*.

4. Many English words change *"x"* to *"s"* or *"ss"* in Italian, e.g., **"esatto"** *(exact)*, **"esperienza"** *(experience)*, **"espressione"** *(expression)*, **"flessibile"** *(flexible)*, **"tossico"** *(toxic)*.

A summary of the above rules is given in the table below:

English	Italian	Examples
-ile	-ile	agile, automobile, facsimile, fragile, ostile
-or	-ore	colore, errore, favore, interiore, inventore, superiore
-ble	-bile	inevitabile, nobile, notabile, possibile, probabile, terribile, variabile
-al	-ale	animale, canale, centrale, criminale, finale, industriale, legale, locale, sociale, musicale, personale
-cal	-co -ca	critico, fisico, logico, magico, meccanico, politico
-ic	-ico -ica	democratico, diabetico, fantastico, plastico, pubblico, romantico
-ant	-ante	elegante, ignorante, importante, tollerante
-ent	-ente	agente, cliente, competente, continente, differente, eccellente, incidente, intelligente, prudente, urgente
-ment	-mento	documento, elemento, monumento, parlamento, supplemento, testamento
-ist	-ista	artista, comunista, dentista, pianista, turista (tourist)
-am	-amma	calligramma, diagramma, programma, telegramma
-em	-ema	emblema, poema, problema, sistema
-ous	-oso -osa	curioso, famoso, furioso, misterioso, nervoso, religioso
-ry	-rio -ria	anniversario, contrario, culinario, dizionario (dictionary), immaginario, itinerario, salario
-tion	-zione	condizione, edizione, nazione, nozione, situazione
-tional	-zionale	addizionale, nazionale, razionale, tradizionale
-tial	-ziale	confidenziale, essenziale, iniziale, parziale, potenziale, presidenziale, residenziale
-ce	-za	differenza, evidenza, violenza, importanza, eleganza
-cy	-za -zia	agenzia, democrazia, aristocrazia, urgenza, clemenza
-ty	-tà	autorità, cavità, dignità, identità, possibilità, unità
-ly	-mente	naturalmente, normalmente, personalmente, probabilmente, totalmente
-phy	-fia	cinematografia, filosofia, fotografia, geografia

-ct	-tto	atto (act), conflitto (conflict), corretto (correct), diretto (direct), effetto (effect), impatto (impact), insetto (insect), perfetto (perfect), prodotto (product)
-sion	-sione	compassione, conclusione, conversione, decisione, discussione, occasione, versione
-ism	-ismo	astigmatismo, comunismo, idealismo, organismo
-id	-ido -ida	avido, splendido, fluido, liquido, lucido, placido, rapido, solido, timido, valido, vivido
-ive	-ivo -iva	attivo, adesivo, additivo, attrattivo, decisivo, definitivo, effettivo, festivo, nativo, negativo
-fy	-ficare	certificare, classificare, glorificare, gratificare, giustificare (justify), modificare, notificare, verificare
-cate	-care	complicare, educare, implicare, indicare
-ize -yze	-izzare	analizzare, autorizzare, civilizzare, minimizzare, organizzare, paralizzare, realizzare, utilizzare
ph	f	elefante, filosofia, fonetico, foto, telefono
th	t tt	autentico (authentic), autore, cattedrale, cattolico
ct pt	tt	attore (actor), conduttore (conductor), dottore (doctor), elettrico (electrical), ottico (optical), ottimale (optimal), trattore (tractor), vittorioso (victorious)
x	s ss	esatto (exact), esperienza (experience), espressione (expression), flessibile (flexible), tossico (toxic)

As mentioned earlier, there are some *false cognates*. It can be useful to be familiar with these false friends to avoid some embarrassing errors. Below is a list of some of the most common ones:

Italian Word	Meaning in English	English Cognate	Meaning of cognate in Italian
annoiare	*to bore*	annoy	infastidire
attuale	*current*	actual	reale
confrontare	*to compare*	confront	affrontare
eventualmente	*possibly*	eventually	infine
fattoria	*farm*	factory	fabbrica
grosso	*big*	gross	schifoso
inviare	*to send*	envy	invidiare
libreria	*bookstore*	library	biblioteca
morbido	*soft*	morbid	morboso
ricordare	*to remind or remember*	record	registrare

Negation in Italian

Luckily, forming the negation in Italian is a simple procedure, without many exceptions. We simply add "**non**" in front of the verb (and before any object pronoun before the verb), e.g., "**Non gioco a calcio**" *(I don't play soccer)*, "**Non lo voglio**" *(I don't want it)*. We can have a double negative in Italian without changing the meaning to affirmative, e.g., "**Non lo faccio mai**" *(I never do it)*.

Uses of the Written Accents in Italian

In Italian, there are two written accents: acute (´) and grave (`). The only letters that can be accented in Italian are: "**a**," "**i**," "**o**," "**u**," and "**e**." The letter "**e**" can take an acute "**é**" or grave "**è**" accent to indicate a closed or open vowel sound, respectively. The other four letters can only take a grave accent, i.e., "**à**," "**ì**," "**ò**," and "**ù**."

We have encountered one common use of the written accent in Italian, that is, to indicate stress on the last syllable of a word, e.g., "**città**" *(city)*, "**caffè**" *(coffee)*, "**perché**" *(why)*, "**ventitré**" *(twenty-three)*, etc. In general, the acute accent is used with causal conjunctions ending in "**-ché**," e.g., "**perché**" *(why)* or compound words ending in "**-tré**," e.g., "**ventitré**" *(twenty-three)*, whereas in most other cases, the grave accent is used.

Another important use of written accents in Italian is to distinguish between the meaning of monosyllabic words that would otherwise be written in the same manner. For example, "**e**" is used as a conjunction meaning *"and,"* whereas "**è**" is the verb *"to be"* in the second-person singular form of the present tense, meaning *"is."* Below are more examples:

Word without accent	Meaning in English	Word without accent	Meaning in English
da	*from*	dà	*gives*
ne	*of it*	nè	*neither*

si	*oneself*	sì	*yes*
se	*if*	sè	*himself/herself*
la	*the*	là	*there*

Another optional use of the written accent, that is optional, is to distinguish between two words different meanings depending on the syllable the stress falls on. For example, "**principi**" means *"princes,"* whereas "**princìpi**" means *"principles."* Similarly, "**ancora**" is an adverb meaning *"still,"* whereas "**àncora**" means *"anchor."* Remember that the use of the accent in these examples is optional, and the context can often determine the meaning without the need for an accent.

Punctuation in Italian

In general, Italian punctuation marks are used the same way as in English. For instance, interrogation and exclamation marks are used in Italian at the end of a question or exclamation, such as "**Come stai?**" *(How are you?)* and "**Che peccato!**" *(What a pity!)*.

Punctuation is also important to distinguish a question from a statement. For instance, the sentence "**Il caffè è caldo**" *(The coffee is hot)* is a statement. Adding a question mark to the end of the sentence "**Il caffè è caldo?**" makes it a question. This is how many questions are formed in Italian. Obviously, the intonation needs to change in the spoken language.

Another way to form a "**sì**" *(yes)* or "**no**" *(no)* question from a statement is to place the subject to the end, e.g., "**È caldo il caffè?**" *(Is the coffee hot?)*.

We do not use any auxiliary to reorder the sentence using the English approach to form a question, that is, saying "**È il caffè caldo?**" is grammatically incorrect.

Finally, some contractions in Italian are mandatory, such as "**l'acqua**" *(the water)*, while others are optional, e.g., "**dove è**" *(where is)* is optionally contracted as "**dov'è**." Unfortunately, there is no universal rule. You will know which contractions are optional as you practice and go through the lessons.

Abbreviations in Italian

The concepts behind the formation of acronyms and abbreviations in Italian are very similar to those in English. One notable exception is the doubling of the letters in the abbreviation of some plural nouns, e.g., "**Poste e Telegrafi**" *(Posts and Telegraphs)* is abbreviated as "**PP. TT.**" For more detail on this rule and a list of common abbreviations in Italian, interested readers can refer to **Appendix D** at the end of this book.

Capitalization in Italian

The words are capitalized in cases almost identical to those in English, with a few notable exceptions that are not capitalized in Italian, mainly:

- ❖ Adjectives of nationalities and languages, e.g., "**italiano**" *(Italian)*, "**canadese**" *(Canadian)*, "**spagnolo**" *(Spanish)*, etc.

- ❖ Days and months, e.g., "**martedì**" *(Tuesday)*, "**gennaio**" *(January)*, "**luglio**" *(July)*, etc.

As we will learn in **Lesson 5** of this level, there are two forms of the *singular* second-person subject personal pronoun *"you"*: one formal, i.e., "**Lei**," and one informal, i.e., "**tu**." The *plural* second-person subject personal pronoun *"you"* also has two forms: one formal, i.e., "**Loro**," and one informal, i.e., "**voi**." The formal *"you"* is always capitalized in both singular and plural forms.

It is also worth noting that all alphabet letters are feminine in Italian. For example, when referring to a letter in Italian, one may say: **la "a" in "padre"** *(the "a" in "father")*, referring to the letter "**a**" using the feminine article "**la**." We will learn more about masculine and feminine nouns and adjectives in **Level II, Lesson 1**.

3. GENDER AND PLURAL

The vast majority of Italian words end in a vowel. This is part of the reason spoken Italian has a melodic recognizable tone.

This rule, however, is not universal. Not all Italian words end with a vowel, e.g., "**il**" *(the)*, "**con**" *(with)*, "**in**" *(in)*. In addition, there are many foreign words that have made inroads into the Italian life and dictionary such as "**sport**" and "**Internet.**"

The vowel at the end of the word often identifies the gender and number of a noun or adjective. Many masculine nouns and adjectives in Italian end with "**-o**" in singular and "**-i**" in plural. On the other hand, many feminine nouns and adjectives end with "**-a**" in singular and "**-e**" in plural.

Furthermore, some Italian words end in "**-e**" in their singular form, and it can be hard to tell if they are masculine or feminine. To form the plural, the final "**e**" is changed to "**i**," regardless of the gender of the word.

	Singular	Plural
Masculine	-o	-i
Masculine or Feminine	-e	
Feminine	-a	-e

Notably, the word "**gente**" *(people)* in Italian, unlike in English, is singular, e.g., "**La gente va e viene**" *(people come and go)*. There are words that are only used in plural form such as "**baffi**[m]" *(mustache)*, "**forbici**[f]" *(scissors)*, "**occhiali**[m]" *(glasses)*, and "**pantaloni**[m]" *(pants)*.

Throughout the book, we use the superscripts [m] and [f] to refer to masculine and feminine genders, respectively.

Adjectives in Italian, unlike in English, come after the noun they describe, for example, "**edificio alto**" *(tall building)*. There are some exceptions to this rule, for example, "**grande**[1] **città**" *(big or great city)*. Many adjectives that come before the noun are *indefinite adjectives*, which will be covered in **Level III, Lesson 4**.

Nouns and adjectives in Italian have only two genders: *masculine* and *feminine*. There is no neuter gender. The gender of an adjective follows the gender of the noun it describes.

For the purpose of brevity throughout the book, we often refer only to the masculine singular form of an adjective. We trust that by learning the following basic rules, you will be able to guess the feminine and plural forms most of the time.

Let us summarize some important rules in the context of examples:

1. Words ending in "**-o**" are generally masculine, and the plural is formed by changing the final "**o**" to "**i**." For example:

libro[m]	*book*	**libri**[m]	*books*
gatto[m]	*cat*	**gatti**[m]	*cats*
telefono[m]	*phone*	**telefoni**[m]	*phones*
zio[m]	*uncle*	**zii**[m]	*uncles*

There are only a few exceptions of words ending in "**-o**" that are feminine, such as: "**mano**" *(hand)*, "**radio**" *(radio)*, "**libido**" *(libido)*, "**foto**" *(photo)*, "**auto**" *(car)*, and "**moto**" *(motorcycle)*.

2. Words ending in "**-a**" are generally feminine, and the plural is formed by changing the final "**a**" to "**e**." For example:

casa[f]	*house*	**case**[f]	*houses*
camicia[f]	*shirt*	**camicie**[f]	*shirts*
sedia[f]	*chair*	**sedie**[f]	*chairs*
zia[f]	*aunt*	**zie**[f]	*aunts*

There are some exceptions such as:

---

[1] If the adjective "**grande**" is placed after the noun, it means *"big"* or *"large,"* e.g., "**una città grande**" *(a big city)*. On the other hand, if it is placed before the noun, it can also mean *"great,"* e.g., "**una grande città**" *(a great city)*, "**una grande amica**" *(a great friend)*, etc.

a. Words that end in "**-ma**" or "**-ta**" and originate from *Greek* These are masculine, and the plural is formed by changing the final "**a**" to "**i**." For example:

problema[m]	*problem*	**problemi**[m]	*problems*
sistema[m]	*system*	**sistemi**[m]	*systems*
clima[m]	*climate*	**climi**[m]	*climates*
tema[m]	*topic*	**temi**[m]	*topics*
diploma[m]	*diploma*	**diplomi**[m]	*diplomas*
dramma[m]	*drama*	**drammi**[m]	*dramas*
dilemma[m]	*dilemma*	**dilemmi**[m]	*dilemmas*
diagramma[m]	*diagram*	**diagrammi**[m]	*diagrams*
pianeta[m]	*planet*	**pianeti**[m]	*planets*
poeta[m]	*poet*	**poeti**[m]	*poets*

This exception does not apply to words that did *not* originate from *Greek*, such as "**forma**[f]" *(form)* and "**piattaforma**[f]" *(platform)*, whose plurals are "**forme**[f]" and "**piattaforme**[f]," respectively.

b. Words that end in "**-ista**" and refer to masculine or feminine people performing a profession, such as:

tassista[m,f]	*taxi driver*	**tassisti**[m] **tassiste**[f]	*taxi drivers*
artista[m,f]	*artist*	**artisti**[m] **artiste**[f]	*artists*
analista[m,f]	*analyst*	**analisti**[m] **analiste**[f]	*analysts*
pianista[m,f]	*pianist*	**pianisti**[m] **pianiste**[f]	*pianists*

The feminine form is used for groups that consist exclusively of feminine-gender members. Even if one masculine-gender member of that group exists, we must use the masculine form.

3. Words ending in "**-e**" can be masculine or feminine, and the plural is formed by changing the final "**e**" to "**i**." For example:

colore[m]	*color*	**colori**[m]	*colors*
madre[f]	*mother*	**madri**[f]	*mothers*

padre^m	*father*	**padri**^m	*fathers*
chiave^f	*key*	**chiavi**^f	*keys*

It can be difficult to determine if a noun ending with "**-e**" is masculine or feminine and a dictionary is often needed. Most nouns ending in "**-ice**" are feminine. They are often the feminine forms of masculine nouns ending in "**-ore**."

attore^m	*actor*	**attori**^m	*actors*
attrice^f	*actress*	**attrici**^f	*actresses*
autore^m	*author*	**autori**^m	*authors*
autrice^f		**autrici**^f	
direttore^m	*director*	**direttori**^m	*directors*
direttrice^f		**direttrici**^f	
imperatore^m	*emperor*	**imperatori**^m	*emperors*
imperatrice^f	*empress*	**imperatrici**^f	*empresses*
pittore^m	*painter*	**pittori**^m	*painters*
pittrice^f		**pittrici**^f	
scrittore^m	*writer*	**scrittori**^m	*writers*
scrittrice^m		**scrittrici**^m	

In general, most nouns ending with "**-ione**" are feminine, and most nouns ending in "**-one**," but not "**-ione**," are masculine. For example:

nazione^f	*nation*	**nazioni**^f	*nations*
televisione^f	*television*	**televisioni**^f	*televisions*
opinione^f	*opinion*	**opinioni**^f	*opinions*
cordone^m	*rope*	**cordoni**^m	*ropes*
mattone^m	*brick*	**mattoni**^m	*bricks*
pallone^m	*ball*	**palloni**^m	*balls*

However, there are few exceptions, such as "**copione**" *(script)* which is masculine.

4. Although the most common gender pattern is a feminine noun with an "**-a**" ending that corresponds to a masculine noun with an "**-o**" ending, this is not the only gender pattern in Italian.

We have encountered masculine nouns ending in "**-ore**" whose feminine forms end in "**-ice**," e.g., "**autore**^m" and "**autrice**^f," meaning *"author."* Another irregular but common feminine form is using the ending **"-essa."** This is common with some masculine nouns ending in **"-ore," "-ante," "-ente," "-eta,"** and **"-one."** For example:

professore[m] professoressa[f]	*professor*	professori[m] professoresse[f]	*professors*
presidente[m] presidentessa[f]	*president*	presidenti[m] presidentesse[f]	*presidents*
poeta[m] poetessa[f]	*poet*	poeti[m] poetesse[f]	*poets*
leone[m] leonessa[f]	*lion* *lioness*	leoni[m] leonesse[f]	*lions* *lionesses*

Some nouns ending in **"-e"** in masculine have an **"-a"** ending in their feminine forms. For example:

cameriere[m] cameriera[f]	*waiter* *waitress*	camerieri[m] cameriere[f]	*waiters* *waitresses*
infermiere[m] infermiera[f]	*nurse*	infermieri[m] infermiere[f]	*nurses*

Some nouns do not change form in masculine or feminine. For example:

cantante[m,f]	*singer*	cantanti[m,f]	*singers*
francese[m,f]	*French*	francesi[m,f]	*French (plural)*
inglese[m,f]	*English*	inglesi[m,f]	*English (plural)*

Finally, there are other nouns that do not follow any pattern. For example, the feminine form of **"dio"** *(god)* is **"dea"** *(goddess)*.

5. Words under the following categories have the same singular and plural forms:

   a. Foreign words used in Italian. Most such words are masculine. For example:

film[m]	*film*	film[m]	*films*
bar[m]	*bar*	bar[m]	*bars*
sport[m]	*sport*	sport[m]	*sports*
taxi[m]	*taxi*	taxi[m]	*taxis*
autobus[m]	*bus*	autobus[m]	*buses*

re^m	*king*	re^m	*kings*
gru^m	*crane*	gru^m	*cranes*
hotel^m	*hotel*	hotel^m	*hotels*

b. Most words ending in an accented vowel. For example:

città^f	*city*	città^f	*cities*
caffè^m	*coffee*	caffè^m	*coffees*
università^f	*university*	università^f	*universities*
tribù^f	*tribe*	tribù^f	*tribes*
virtù^f	*virtue*	virtù^f	*virtues*

c. Words that end in "-si." Most such words are feminine. For example:

crisi^f	*crisis*	crisi^f	*crises*
analisi^f	*analysis*	analisi^f	*analyses*

d. Feminine words that end in "-o," except "mano^f" (*hand*), whose plural is "mani^f." For example:

radio^f	*radio*	radio^f	*radios*
auto^f	*car*	auto^f	*cars*
foto^f	*photo*	foto^f	*photos*
moto^f	*motorcycle*	moto^f	*motorbikes*

Notice that the nouns "auto," "foto," and "moto" are short forms of the feminine nouns "automobile^f," "fotografia^f," and "motocicletta^f," respectively.

6. There are a few words that are masculine in singular form and feminine in plural form. For example:

braccio^m	*arm*	braccia^f	*arms*
dito^m	*finger*	dita^f	*fingers*
ginocchio^m	*knee*	ginocchia^f	*knees*
labbro^m	*lip*	labbra^f	*lips*
uovo^m	*egg*	uova^f	*eggs*

7. Some words undergo spelling changes to form the plural. These often fall under one of these categories:

a. Words with "**-co/-ca**" and "**-go/-ga**" endings often add "**h**" to form plurals with "**-chi/-che**" or "**-ghi/-ghe**" endings, especially if the "**-co/-ca**" or "**-go/-ga**" is not preceded by "**e**" or "**i**." For example:

giocoᵐ	*game*	**giochi**ᵐ	*games*
parcoᵐ	*park*	**parchi**ᵐ	*parks*
albergoᵐ	*hotel*	**alberghi**ᵐ	*hotels*
lagoᵐ	*lake*	**laghi**ᵐ	*lakes*

Notice that the purpose of these changes is to maintain the desired soft or hard pronunciation of the "**c**" or "**g**."

If an "**e**" or "**i**" precedes the "**-co/-ca**" or "**-go/-ga**," the masculine plural form often ends in "**-ci**" or "**-gi**," leading to change in the "**c**" or "**g**" pronunciation from hard to soft sound. For example:

amicoᵐ **amica**ᶠ	*friend*	**amici**ᵐ **amiche**ᶠ	*friends*
grecoᵐ **greca**ᶠ	*Greek*	**greci**ᵐ **greche**ᶠ	*Greeks*
biologoᵐ **biologa**ᶠ	*biologist*	**biologi**ᵐ **biologhe**ᶠ	*biologists*
psicologoᵐ **psicologa**ᶠ	*psychologist*	**psicologi**ᵐ **psicologhe**ᶠ	*psychologists*

Notice that this exception applies only to the masculine form, whereas the feminine form still adds an "**h**" in the plural.

In general, the suffixes "**-logo**" and "**-loga**," referring to a profession in singular, change to "**-logi**" and "**-loghe**," respectively, in plural.

Finally, there are a number of words, mostly masculine, that do not follow the aforementioned rules. For example:

porcoᵐ	*pig*	**porci**ᵐ	*pigs*
ficoᵐ	*fig*	**fichi**ᵐ	*figs*
sindacoᵐ	*mayor*	**sindaci**ᵐ	*mayors*
monacoᵐ	*monk*	**monaci**ᵐ	*monks*

b. Words with "**-cia**" and "**-gia**" endings often remove the "**i**" to form plurals with "**-ce**" and "**-ge**" endings, if the "**-cia**" or "**-gia**" ending is preceded by a consonant. For example:

arancia^f	*orange*	**arance**^f	*oranges*
faccia^f	*face*	**facce**^f	*faces*
spiaggia^f	*beach*	**spiagge**^f	*beaches*

If the "**-cia**" or "**-gia**" ending is preceded by a vowel, the regular plural is formed with "**-cie**" or "**-gie**" ending. For example:

camicia^f	*shirt*	**camicie**^f	*shirts*
ciliegia^f	*cherry*	**ciliegie**^f	*cherries*
valigia^f	*suitcase*	**valigie**^f	*suitcases*

c. Words with the the "**-io**" ending remove the final "**o**" to form plurals with the "**-i**" ending. For example:

figlio^m	*son*	**figli**^m	*sons*
occhio^m	*eye*	**occhi**^m	*eyes*
orologio^m	*clock/watch*	**orologi**^m	*clocks/watches*

If the "**i**" in the final "**-io**" is in the stressed syllable of the word, the plural is formed with the "**-ii**" ending. For example:

invio^m	*dispatch*	**invii**^m	*dispatches*
zio^m	*uncle*	**zii**^m	*uncles*

8. Some words have completely irregular plurals. For example:

uomo^m	*man*	**uomini**^m	*men*
dio^m	*god*	**dèi**^m	*gods*
bue^m	*ox*	**buoi**^m	*oxen*
ala^f	*wing*	**ali**^f	*wings*
arma^f	*weapon*	**armi**^f	*weapons*
tempio^m	*temple*	**templi**^m	*temples*

9. Some words have a different meaning when used as masculine versus when used as feminine. For example:

posto^m	*place*	**posta**^f	*mail*

| modo^m | way | moda^f | fashion |
| capitale^m | capital (money) | capitale^f | capital (city) |

4. CARDINAL NUMBERS

uno, una	1	ventuno	21	duecento	200
due	2	ventidue	22	trecento	300
tre	3	ventitré	23	quattrocento	400
quattro	4	trenta	30	cinquecento	500
cinque	5	trentuno	31	seicento	600
sei	6	trentadue	32	settecento	700
sette	7	trentatré	33	ottocento	800
otto	8	quaranta	40	novecento	900
nove	9	quarantuno	41	mille	1.000
dieci	10	quarantadue	42	duemila	2.000
undici	11	cinquanta	50	tremila	3.000
dodici	12	cinquantuno	51	diecimila	10.000
tredici	13	cinquantadue	52	centomila	100.000
quattordici	14	sessanta	60	centomilauno	100.001
quindici	15	settanta	70	centomiladieci	100.010
sedici	16	ottanta	80	un milione	1.000.000
diciassette	17	novanta	90	due milioni	2.000.000
diciotto	18	cento	100	dieci milioni	10.000.000
diciannove	19	centouno	101	un miliardo	1.000.000.000
venti	20	centodue	102	due miliardi	2.000.000.000

❖ The number "0" in Italian is "**zero**," pronounced as "**dze**-ro."

❖ Before a masculine noun, "**uno**" becomes "**un**," e.g., "**un cane**" *(a dog)*, "**un gatto**" *(a cat)*. You will encounter a similar dropping of the final "o" with a few other words in Italian, such as "**buono**" *(good)* and "**bello**" *(beautiful)*, e.g., "**Questo ristorante è buono**" *(This restaurant is good)*, "**Questo è un buon ristorante**" *(This is a good restaurant)*.

❖ The numbers 21-99 are formed by contracting the combination of the tens (**venti, trenta, quaranta, … etc.**) and the units (**uno, due, tre, … etc.**). The following two changes apply, if necessary:

1. The vowel at the end of the tens is dropped if the unit starts with a vowel ("<u>u</u>no" and "<u>o</u>tto"), e.g., "vent<u>u</u>no" (21), "trent<u>o</u>tto" (38), "quarant<u>u</u>no" (41), "novant<u>o</u>tto" (98), etc.

2. Numbers with *"three"* in their units are written with an acute accent on their endings, e.g., "venti<u>tré</u>" (23), "trenta<u>tré</u>" (33), "ottanta<u>tré</u>" (83), etc.

❖ The multiples of hundred (200-900) are formed by combining (**due, tre, ... etc.**) and "**cento**" to form (**duecento, trecento, ... etc.**).

❖ We use a *comma* to separate *decimals* and a *period* to separate *thousands* in Italian. For instance, the number **2.155,25** in Italian is equivalent to *2,155.25* in English.

❖ Numbers of more than two digits in length can be concatenated or written separately. Unlike in English, the conjunction *"and"* is not used anywhere between units, tens, hundreds, thousands, etc., e.g., "**quattrocentocinquantuno**" (451) can also be written "**quattrocento cinquantuno.**"

❖ The word for *a thousand* in Italian is "**mille.**" To refer to multiples of a thousand, we use "**mila**" instead, e.g., "**tremila**" (3.000), "**cinquemila**" (5.000), etc.

❖ When describing items in millions or billions, one must add "**di**" after "**milione(-i)**" or "**miliardo(-i),**" e.g., "**un milione di studenti**)" *(a million students)*, "**due miliardi di abitanti**" *(two billion inhabitants).*

❖ Notice that, in Italian, we cannot use the English way of expressing years, as in *"nineteen seventy-three"* (1973); that is, saying "**diciannove settantatré**" is incorrect. The correct way is to say "**mille novecento settantatré.**"

❖ The basic arithmetic operations in Italian are as follows:

+	più	*plus*
-	meno	*minus*

×	per	*times*
÷	diviso (per)	*divided by*
=	fa, uguale (a)	*equals*

5. SUBJECT PERSONAL PRONOUNS

Subject personal pronouns in Italian serve the same function as their English counterparts by pointing out who carries out the action described by the verb.

io	*I*	1st person singular
tu	*you (informal)*	2nd person singular
Lei	*you (formal)*	2nd person singular
lui/lei	*he/she*	3rd person singular
noi	*we*	1st person plural
voi	*you (informal)*	2nd person plural
Loro	*you (formal)*	2nd person plural
loro	*they*	3rd person plural

❖ More often than not, the subject personal pronoun is dropped because the verb endings can be sufficient to refer to the subject, as you will learn in **Lesson 6** of this level.

❖ There are two forms of the singular *"you"* in Italian; the first is the informal **"tu"** and is used with familiar people (e.g., child, relative, friend, peer, etc.), and the second is the formal **"Lei,"** which is used with older people and with people we are not familiar with or to show respect.

❖ Similarly, there are two forms of the plural *"you"* in Italian; the first is the informal **"voi"** and is used with familiar, and the second is the formal **"Loro,"** which is used with older people and with people we are not familiar with or to show respect.

❖ Notice that the formal (or polite) forms **"Lei"** *(you - singular)* and **"Loro"** *(you - plural)* are capitalized to distinguish them from the non-capitalized **"lei"** *(she)* and **"loro"** *(they)*, respectively.

❖ Notice that we did not include an equivalent to the English subject pronoun *"it."* Since the subject pronoun is often dropped, as we will see in **Lesson 6** of this level, the pronoun *"it"* is often not used. In formal speech, the pronouns **"esso,"** *(masculine)* and **"essa,"** *(feminine)*, meaning *"it,"* can be used, although they are not so common in daily spoken language. The plural equivalents are: **"essi,"** *(masculine)* and **"esse,"** *(feminine)*, respectively.

❖ There are two more pronouns that can replace **"lui"** *(he)* and **"lei"** *(she)*. The two pronouns are: **"egli"** *(he)* and **"ella"** *(she)*, and are rarely used in ordinary conversation.

6. PRESENT INDICATIVE TENSE I

Verbs in their infinitive form in Italian have one of three endings: "-**are**," "-**ere**," or "-**ire**." When conjugated, these endings are replaced with different conjugation suffixes based on the subject. In English, verb conjugation in the present tense is quite simple. For example, the verb *"to break"* is conjugated as follows: *I/you/we/they break, he/she/it breaks.* Thus, there are only two conjugation forms of the verb *"to break"* in the simple present tense, which are *"break"* and *"breaks."* In Italian, it is a little more complicated. Regular verbs in the present indicative tense follow the conjugation rules shown in the following table, with an example from each verb group: "-**are**," "-**ere**," and "-**ire**." First, the stem is formed by removing the final "-**are**," "-**ere**," or "-**ire**." Then, the conjugation ending is added depending on the personal pronoun.

	-are ending parlare *(to speak)*	-ere ending vendere *(to sell)*	-ire ending (Type I) partire *(to leave)*	-ire ending (Type II) finire *(to finish)*
io	parlo	vendo	parto	finisco
tu	parli	vendi	parti	finisci
lui/lei	parla	vende	parte	finisce
noi	parliamo	vendiamo	partiamo	finiamo
voi	parlate	vendete	partite	finite
loro	parlano	vendono	partono	finiscono

Notice that there are two types of "-**ire**" verbs. Type II requires the addition of "-**isc**-" between the stem and the conjugation suffix normally used with Type I for all forms except "**noi**" and "**voi**." Unfortunately, only practice and a good dictionary can help you determine the type of an "-**ire**" verb.

In Italian, unlike in English, we generally drop the subject pronoun because the conjugation is usually sufficient to indicate the subject. For instance, we could say "**Io parlo italiano**" or "**Parlo italiano**" *(I speak Italian)*. Both are considered perfect speech and grammatically correct. It even sounds more native to drop the subject pronoun in informal speech. Opting to use the subject pronoun can sound less natural in some contexts, because it can indicate an emphasis on the subject rather than the verb.

Not all verbs are regular in the present indicative tense. For example, the verbs "**essere**" *(to be)* and "**avere**" *(to have)* are two important verbs in Italian used to form sentences and as auxiliary verbs. Both are completely irregular and are conjugated as follows:

	essere *(to be)*	**avere** *(to have)*
io	sono	ho
tu	sei	hai
lui/lei	è	ha
noi	siamo	abbiamo
voi	siete	avete
loro	sono	hanno

We will learn more about irregular verbs in the present indicative tense in **Level II, Lesson 2**.

It is important to note that the present tense we have discussed so far is also called the present *indicative* tense to distinguish it from the present *subjunctive* tense. The indicative and the subjunctive are two different moods. You do not have to worry about the difference for now. We will cover the subjunctive mood in more advanced lessons starting in **Level IV, Lesson 7**. As we progress with more advanced tenses in the levels to come, refer to **Appendix B** to use the provided verb conjugation chart as a cheat sheet and gain perspective on the different moods and tenses in Italian.

7. THE ARTICLES

In Italian, both definite and indefinite articles must agree with the noun they describe in gender and number.

Definite Articles

Below are the definite articles in Italian, equivalent to *"the"* in English. We have seven definite articles in Italian because the definite article has to agree with the noun in both gender and number. In addition, some nouns that begin with a vowel or certain consonants require different definite articles.

	Singular	Plural
Before a **masculine** noun that begins with a vowel	l'	
Before a **masculine** noun that begins with "z," "gn," "ps," or "s" + consonant	lo	gli
Before any other **masculine** noun	il	i
Before a **feminine** noun that begins with a vowel	l'	
Before any other **feminine** noun	la	le

❖ If an adjective precedes the noun, the definite article is adjusted according to the beginning of the adjective. For example, **"l'amico"** means *"the friend,"* whereas **"il buon amico"** means *"the good friend."* Notice the change in the definite article from **"l"** to **"il."**

❖ The article **"gli"** is used before any plural masculine noun (or preceding adjective) that begins with a vowel, **"z," "gn," "ps,"** or **"s"** + consonant, e.g., **"gli amici"** *(the friends),* **"gli gnocchi"** *(the dumplings),* **"gli studenti"** *(the students),* etc.

❖ The feminine plural article **"le"** is used before any plural feminine plural noun (or preceding adjective), regardless of whether it begins with a vowel or consonant, e.g., **"le ore"** *(the hours)*, **"le donne"** *(the women)*, **"le zone"** *(the zones)*, etc.

❖ Using the proper article in Italian is more complicated than in English or other Romance languages such as Spanish or French. After determining whether the noun is singular or plural, you need to think of the following three questions:

1. Is the noun masculine or feminine?
2. Does the noun or preceding adjective begin with a vowel?
3. Does the noun or preceding adjective begin with **"z,"** **"gn,"** **"ps,"** or **"s"** + consonant?

If you answer "yes" to any of these questions, you make a decision on which definite article to use. If you answer "no," you proceed to the next question. The order of the question is slightly different if the noun is singular or plural. The steps are depicted in the following chart:

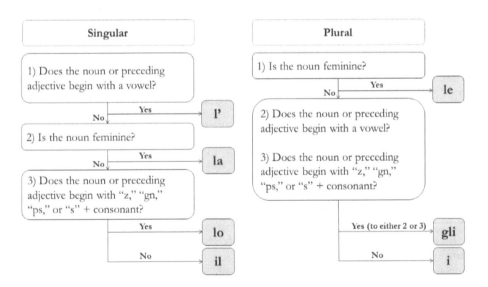

❖ There are two common adjectives in Italian that undergo similar form-changing contractions to the definite articles: **"bello"**

(beautiful) and **"quello"** *(that)*, e.g., **"quell'amico"** *(that friend)*, **"begli uccelli"** *(beautiful birds).*[1]

	l'	lo	il	la	i	gli	le
bello	bell'	bello	bel	bella	bei	begli	belle
quello	quell'	quello	quel	quella	quei	quegli	quelle

The adjective **"bello"** can be placed before or after the noun. Notice that the contraction applies to the adjective **"bello"** only if it precedes the noun. Otherwise, the contractions are not applied, e.g., **"uccelli belli"** *(beautiful birds).*

There will be more detail on **"quello"** and other demonstrative adjectives and pronouns in **Level II, Lesson 4.**

We hope that you will not let the complexity of the definite articles in Italian frustrate you, and that, with little practice using the Anki cards of this lesson, you will master the definite articles.

Indefinite Articles

There are four indefinite articles in Italian; two masculine articles: **"un"** and **"uno,"** and two feminine articles: **"un'"** and **"una."** These are equivalent to *"a"* or *"an"* in English. The table below indicates when to use each of these four indefinite articles:

Before a **masculine** noun that begins with "z," "gn," "ps," or "s" + consonant	**uno**
Before any other **masculine** noun	**un**
Before a **feminine** noun that begins with a vowel	**un'**
Before any other **feminine** noun	**una**

---

[1] Another adjective that changes form, but only in the singular before a proper noun, is "santo" *(saint)*, which has the form:
- "Sant'": before a proper masculine or feminine noun that starts with a vowel, e.g., "Sant'Antonio" *(St. Anthony)*, "Sant'Anna" *(St. Ann).*
- "Santo": before a proper masculine noun that starts with "z," "gn," "ps," or "s" + consonant, e.g., "Santo Stefano" *(St. Stephen).*
- "San": before any other proper masculine noun, e.g., "San Marco" *(St. Mark).*
- "Santa": before any other proper feminine noun, e.g., "Santa Maria" *(St. Mary).*

❖ Similar to the definite articles, if an adjective precedes the noun, the indefinite article is adjusted according to the beginning of the adjective. For example, "**un'amica**" means *"a (female) friend,"* whereas "**una buona amica**" means *"a good (female) friend."* Notice the change in the indefinite article from "**un'**" to "**una.**"

❖ The article "**uno**" is used before any masculine noun (or preceding adjective) that begins with "**z**," "**gn**," "**ps**," or "**s**" + consonant, e.g., "**uno sport**" *(a sport)*, "**uno gnocco**" *(a dumpling)*, "**uno zio**" *(an uncle)*, etc. All other masculine nouns use the indefinite article "**un**," e.g., "**un amico**" *(a friend)*, "**un ragazzo**" *(a boy)*, "**un gatto**" *(a cat)*, etc.

❖ The article "**un'**" is used before any feminine noun (or preceding adjective) that begins with a vowel, e.g., "**un'amica**" *(a friend)*, "**un'ora**" *(an hour)*, "**un'isola**" *(an island)*, etc. All other feminine nouns use the indefinite article "**una**," e.g., "**una casa**" *(a house)*, "**una zia**" *(an aunt)*, "**una porta**" *(a door)*, etc.

Use of the Definite Article in Italian versus English

There are cases in which Italian uses the definite article when in English, it would be omitted, such as:

1. Abstract concepts or speaking in a general sense, e.g., "**La scienza è importante**" *(Science is important)*, "**Gli animali sono intelligenti**" *(Animals are intelligent)*.

2. Languages and nationalities, e.g., "**l'italiano**" *(Italian)*, "**i tedeschi**" *(Germans)*. Exceptionally, we drop the definite article in Italian when the language name is an object of some verbs, e.g., "**Parlo e insegno italiano**" *(I speak and teach Italian)*, or after the preposition "**in**," e.g., "**scritto in italiano**" *(written in Italian)*.

3. Days of the week when referring to a repeated action or habit on the same day of every week, e.g., "**Vado in palestra il giovedì**" *(I go to the gym on Thursdays)*. If we do not refer to a

repeated action, we do not use the definite article, e.g., "**Arrivo lunedì**" (*I arrive on Monday*).

4. Body parts and clothes, e.g., "**Alza la mano**" (*Raise your hand*), "**Mettiti le scarpe**" (*Put on your shoes*).

5. Telling time, e.g., "**Sono le due**" (*It's two o'clock*), "**Ci incontriamo dopo l'una**" (*We meet after one o'clock*).

6. Before a personal title, such as "**signore**" (*Mr.*), "**signora**" (*Mrs.*), "**dottore**" (*doctor*), "**professore**" (*professor*), etc., e.g., "**il professor Kennedy**," "**la signora Anna**," "**il dottor Marco**." An exception is made when addressing the person directly, e.g., "**Signor Flavio, come sta?**" (*Mr. Flavio, how are you?*).
   Notice the dropping of the final "**e**" in "**professore**," "**signore**," and "**dottore**" when followed by a masculine proper name. This is common in Italian with many profession titles.

7. Before each noun in the case of multiple nouns, e.g., "**il padre e la madre**" (*the father and mother*), "**i cani e i gatti**" (*the dogs and cats*). Although you can use one definite article in English to refer to all nouns, the grammatically correct way in Italian is to repeat the definite article for each noun.

Like in English, it is common to omit the definite article before the seasons of the year, e.g., "**in estate**" (*in summer*), "**in inverno**" (*in winter*), "**in autunno**" (*in autumn*), "**in primavera**"" (*in spring*).

8. INTERROGATIVE PRONOUNS & ADJECTIVES

Interrogative pronouns are important tools that we use to form questions. If the interrogative pronoun is followed by a noun, it becomes an interrogative adjective, e.g., "**Quale edificio è più alto?**" (*Which building is taller?*). In this case, the interrogative "quale" is considered an interrogative adjective. If it is not followed by a noun, "quale" becomes an interrogative pronoun, e.g., "Quale è più alto?" *(Which is taller?).*

Interrogative pronoun/adjective	English meaning	Examples
Che? Che cosa? Cosa?	*What?*	**Cosa stai facendo?** *What are you doing?*
Chi?	*Who/Whom?*	**Chi ha fatto questo?** *Who did this?*
Di chi?	*Whose?*	**Di chi è questo libro?** *Whose book is this?*
Come?	*How?*	**Come lo hai fatto?** *How did you do it?*
Quale(i)?	*Which?*	**Quali sono le tue chiavi?** *Which ones are your keys?*
Quanto(-a,-i,-e)?	*How much?* *How many?*	**Quanto costa questo cappotto?** *How much does this coat cost?*
Quando?	*When?*	**Quando vuoi venire?** *When do you want to come?*
Dove?	*Where?*	**Dove sei ora?** *Where are you now?*
Perché?	*Why?*	**Perché non vuoi mangiare?** *Why don't you want to eat?*

❖ The interrogative "**che**" *(what)*, on its own, is often used as an interrogative adjective followed by a noun, e.g., "**Che libro hai letto?**" *(What book did you read?).*

❖ Although we can use "**che**" as an interrogative pronoun, e.g., "**Che hai letto?**" *(What did you read?),* the more accepted forms are "**che cosa**" and "**cosa**," both meaning *"what,"* e.g., "**Che cosa hai letto?**" and "**Cosa hai letto?**" both mean *"What book did you read?"*

❖ The interrogative pronoun "**perché**," meaning *"Why,"* can also be used as a conjunction meaning *"because."*

❖ The interrogative "**quale**" *(which)* has the plural form "**quali**," whereas "**quanto**" *(when)* has a feminine form "**quanta**." The two singular forms "**quanto**" and "**quanta**" have the plural forms "**quanti**" and "**quante**," respectively.

❖ When the interrogatives "**cosa**," "**come**," "**dove**," and "**quale**" are followed by "**è**" *(is)*, the following abbreviations are common but not mandatory in written Italian:

What is …?	**Cos'è …?**	**Cosa è …?**
How is …?	**Com'è …?**	**Come è …?**
Where is …?	**Dov'è …?**	**Dove è …?**
Which is ,…?	**Qual è …?**	**Quale è …?**

Notice that an apostrophe is needed with the interrogatives "**cosa**," "**come**," and "**dove**," but not in the case of "**quale**."

II. Vocabulary Building

This section contains some vocabulary that you will need to get you going at this basic level. As you go over it in the book, we recommend that you use the Anki flashcards to study and memorize the new vocabulary as a more efficient and less boring way of learning and reviewing the material.

1. VERBS I

Below is a list of the most common 40 verbs in Italian. You can start by adding them to your vocabulary to improve your comprehension of Italian speech and writing. Use the Anki flashcards created for this section to help you memorize the meaning of each verb in its proper context. We limit verb conjugation here to the infinitive and the regular present tense which are what we have learned so far.

English	Italian	Examples
arrive	arrivare	Mi aspetto di **arrivare** tardi domani. *I expect to **arrive** late tomorrow.*
believe	credere	**Credo** che i miei genitori oggi non vengano. *I **believe** that my parents won't come today.*
call	chiamare	Mia madre mi **chiama** sempre di notte. *My mom always **calls** me at night.*

can be able to	potere	Ho bisogno delle mie scarpe per **poter** correre. *I need my shoes to **be able to** run.*
change	cambiare	Devi **cambiare** la tua routine quotidiana. *You have to **change** your daily routine.*
close	chiudere	Non mi piace **chiudere** le finestre nel pomeriggio. *I don't like to **close** the windows in the afternoon.*
come	venire	Penso che mio fratello non voglia **venire**. *I think that my brother doesn't want to **come**.*
create	creare	Gli scienziati **creano** sempre nuovi metodi. *Scientists always **create** new methods.*
do **make**	fare	Vogliamo **fare** tutto oggi. *We want to **do** everything today.*
drink	bere	Vuoi **bere** acqua? *Do you want to **drink** water?*
eat	mangiare	Il venerdì **mangiamo** alle quattro. *On Fridays, we **eat** at four o'clock.*
exit **leave** **go out**	uscire	Ci piace **uscire** nel fine settimana. *We like to **go out** on the weekend.*
explain	spiegare	Questo insegnante **spiega** molto bene le lezioni. *This teacher **explains** the lessons very well.*
finish **end**	finire	Mi aspetto di **finire** il romanzo molto presto. *I expect to **finish** the novel very soon.*
give	dare	**Danno** la propria vita per aiutare gli altri. *They **give** their lives to help others.*
go	andare	Non voglio **andare** a scuola domani. *I don't want to **go** to school tomorrow.*
have	avere	Voglio **avere** un buon lavoro. *I want to **have** a good job.*
learn	imparare	Voglio **imparare** la storia della Turchia. *I want to **learn** about the history of Turkey.*
live	vivere	Maria **vive** in un piccolo quartiere. *Maria **lives** in a small neighborhood.*
look **watch**	guardare	Mi piace **guardare** scene belle. *I like to **look at** beautiful scenes.*
love	amare	**Amo** il suono degli uccelli. *I **love** the sound of birds.*
open	aprire	I panifici non **aprono** molto tardi. *Bakeries don't **open** very late.*
put	mettere	Devi **mettere** i vestiti nell'armadio. *You must **put** the clothes in the wardrobe.*
read	leggere	**Leggo** l'italiano, ma non lo parlo bene. *I **read** Italian, but I don't speak it well.*

receive	ricevere	**Riceviamo** sempre ospiti in estate. *We always **receive** guests in the summer.*
say tell	dire	Deve **dire** la verità. *He must **tell** the truth.*
see	vedere	Me piace **vedere** mia madre tutti i giorni. *I like to **see** my mom every day.*
sleep	dormire	È più salutare **dormire** presto. *It is healthier to **sleep** early.*
speak talk	parlare	Lei **parla** fluentemente tre lingue. *She **speaks** three languages fluently.*
start	iniziare cominciare	Possiamo **iniziare** le lezioni alle 8:00. *We can **start** classes at 8 a.m.*
study	studiare	I ragazzi **studiano** con i loro amici. *The boys **study** with their friends.*
take	prendere	Preferirei **prendere** l'autobus la prossima volta. *I'd prefer to **take** the bus next time.*
think	pensare	Non voglio **pensare** al futuro adesso. *I don't want to **think** of the future now.*
travel	viaggiare	Mi piacerebbe **viaggiare** in Cina quest'anno. *I would like to **travel** to China this year.*
understand	capire comprendere	Non riesco a **capire** cosa sta dicendo. *I can't **understand** what he's saying.*
use	usare utilizzare	Non **usiamo** il treno in questa parte del mondo. *We don't **use** the train in this part of the world.*
walk	camminare	**Cammino** sempre dopo aver cenato. *I always **walk** after having dinner.*
want to	volere	Cosa ti spinge a **voler** essere una persona migliore? *What drives you to **want** to be a better person?*
work	lavorare	**Lavoro** come ragioniere. *I **work** as an accountant.*
write	scrivere	Questo autore **scrive** romanzi divertenti. *This author **writes** entertaining novels.*

In addition to the above new verbs, we add 20 English cognates that are easy to memorize.

English	Italian	Examples
accept	accettare	Spiacente! Non posso **accettare** il tuo invito. *Sorry! I can't **accept** your invitation.*
calm	calmare	Mi piace leggere per **calmare** i nervi. *I like to read to **calm** my nerves.*
cancel	cancellare annullare	Forse dovrei **cancellare** i miei piani. *Perhaps I should **cancel** my plans.*

circulate	circolare	L'aria dovrebbe **circolare** attraverso la stanza. *The air should **circulate** through the room.*
compensate	compensare	Devo **compensare** per il ritardo. *I have to **compensate** for arriving late.*
confirm	confermare	Puoi **confermare** il numero? *Can you **confirm** the number?*
continue	continuare proseguire	La strada **prosegue** verso il fiume. *The street **continues** to the river.*
copy	copiare	In passato era difficile **copiare** i libri. *In the past, it was hard to **copy** books.*
decide	decidere	Tu stesso **decidi** quale macchina vuoi comprare. *You yourself **decide** which car you want to buy.*
depend	dipendere	I risultati **dipendono** da molte variabili. *The results **depend** on many variables.*
describe	descrivere	Non so come **descrivere** quella città. *I don't know how to **describe** that city.*
enter	entrare[1] in	Dobbiamo **entrare** presto nell'edificio. *We must **enter** the building early.*
exist	esistere	**Esistono** molte lingue nel mondo. *A lot of languages **exist** in the world.*
form	formare	I quattro paesi **formano** un'alleanza. *The four countries **form** an alliance.*
insult	insultare	Non è educato **insultare** gli altri. *It is not polite to **insult** other people.*
interfere	interferire	Non dovresti **interferire** nella loro relazione. *You shouldn't **interfere** in their relationship.*
observe	osservare	La polizia **osserva** i suoi movimenti. *The police **observe** his movements.*
organize	organizzare	Voglio **organizzare** un viaggio questo mese. *I want to **organize** a trip this month.*
resolve	risolvere	Voglio **risolvere** questo problema di matematica. *I want to **resolve** this math problem.*
rob steal	rubare	Ci sono ladri che **rubano** solo automobili. *There are thieves who only **steal/rob** cars.*

2. ADJECTIVES I

Below is a list of the most common 50 adjectives in Italian. Use the Anki cards created for this section to help you memorize the

---

[1] Whereas the verb *"enter"* is not followed by a preposition in English, the verb "**entrare**" in Italian is followed by "**in**."

meaning of each word in proper contexts. Notice that an adjective must agree with the noun in number and gender.

English	Italian	Examples
bad	cattivo brutto	Il servizio è **cattivo** qui. *The service is **bad** here.*
beautiful	bello	La vista è molto **bella**. *The view is very **beautiful**.*
better	migliore[1]	Spero sempre in un domani **migliore**. *I always hope for a **better** tomorrow.*
big	grande[2]	I nostri vicini hanno una casa **grande**. *Our neighbors have a **large** house.*
boring	noioso	Questa lezione è molto **noiosa**. *This class is very **boring**.*
busy	occupato	Sono molto **occupato** questo fine settimana. *I'm very **busy** this weekend.*
cheap **inexpensive**	a buon mercato economico	Sto cercando un volo **economico**. *I'm looking for a **cheap** flight.*
clean	pulito	Il mio bagno deve essere sempre **pulito**. *My bathroom must always be **clean**.*
closed	chiuso	Il cinema oggi è **chiuso**. *The cinema is **closed** today.*
cold	freddo	Mi piace il caffè **freddo**. *I like **cold** coffee.*
crazy	pazzo folle	Questo ragazzo è **pazzo**. *This boy is **crazy**.*
difficult	difficile	Il calcolo delle tasse può essere **difficile**. *Calculating taxes can be **difficult**.*
dirty	sporco	Questo è il cesto della biancheria **sporca**. *This is the **dirty** laundry basket.*
dry	secco	Questa regione ha un clima **secco**. *This region has a **dry** climate.*
easy	facile	Questo rompicapo è molto **facile**. *This puzzle is very **easy**.*
expensive	caro costoso	Quel vestito è molto **costoso**. *That dress is very **expensive**.*

[1] As an adverb, the word "**meglio**" is used instead, e.g., "**Posso camminare meglio adesso**" *(I can walk better now).*

[2] Before a masculine singular noun beginning with a consonant other than "**z**," "**ps**," "**gn**," or "**s**" + consonant, we can use "**gran**," or "**grande**." Before any singular noun beginning with a vowel, the contraction "**grand'**" can optionally be used, e.g., "**un grand'amico**" *(a great friend).*

fast	veloce rapido	Questa macchina è molto **veloce**. *This car is very fast.*
fun	divertente	Il viaggio di domani sarà **divertente**. *Tomorrow's trip is going to be fun.*
good	buono [1]	Questo è un **buon** libro. *This is a good book.*
happy	felice	Il denaro da solo non ti rende **felice**. *Money alone doesn't make you happy.*
hard (inflexible)	duro	Questo gesso non mi sembra **duro**. *This plaster doesn't seem hard to me.*
high tall	alto	Questo albero è molto **alto**. *This tree is very tall.*
hot	caldo	Il tè è molto **caldo**. *The tea is very hot.*
long	lungo	D'estate le giornate sono **lunghe**. *In the summer, the days are long.*
much	molto tanto	C'è ancora **molto** lavoro da fare. *There is still much work to be done.*
many	molti/-e tanti/-e	Ci sono **molte** case qui. *There are many houses here.*
new	nuovo	Questa è la mia macchina **nuova**. *This is my new car.*
old	vecchio	La casa di mia nonna è molto **vecchia**. *My grandmother's house is very old.*
open	aperto	Il supermercato è già **aperto**. *The supermarket is already open.*
poor	povero	Quest'uomo è **povero**. *This man is poor.*
quiet	tranquillo	Mi piace leggere in un posto **tranquillo**. *I like to read in a quiet place.*
ready	pronto	Sono **pronto** per le vacanze. *I am ready for vacation.*
rich	ricco	Le persone **ricche** hanno molti soldi. *Rich people have a lot of money.*
sad	triste	È un uomo molto **triste**. *He is a very sad man.*
same	stesso	Ho due camicie dello **stesso** colore. *I have two shirts of the same color.*

[1] Before a masculine noun, the final "o" is dropped, e.g., "**Questo ristorante è buono**" (*This restaurant is good*), "**Questo è un buon ristorante**" (*This is a good restaurant*).

short	basso[1] corto[1]	Mio fratello è **basso**. *My brother is **short**.*
sick	malato ammalato	Vado a trovare mio nonno **malato**. *I'm going to visit my **sick** grandfather.*
slow	lento	È più salutare mangiare a un ritmo **lento**. *It's healthier to eat at a **slow** pace.*
small	piccolo	Carlo ha un naso **piccolo**. *Carlo has a **small** nose.*
soft	morbido	Questo pane è molto **morbido**. *This bread is very **soft**.*
strong	forte	Il mio cavallo è molto **forte**. *My horse is very **strong**.*
sure certain	sicuro	Cerco sempre di rispondere se sono **sicuro**. *I always try to answer if I'm **certain**.*
sweet	dolce	Questo rinfresco mi sembra troppo **dolce**. *This refreshment seems too **sweet** to me.*
tired	stanco	Dopo il lavoro torno a casa **stanco**. *After work, I get home **tired**.*
too much	troppo	Non voglio mangiare **troppo** zucchero oggi. *I don't want to eat **too much** sugar today.*
ugly	brutto	Questa è una **brutta** notizia. *This is **ugly** news.*
weak	debole	Ha un corpo **debole** perché mangia a malapena. *He has a **weak** body because he hardly eats.*
wet	bagnato	Non mi piace andare a letto con i capelli **bagnati**. *I don't like going to bed with my hair **wet**.*
worse	peggiore	Nel **peggiore** dei casi, annulli. *In the **worst** case, you cancel.*
young	giovane	Non sarai **giovane** per sempre. *You won't be **young** forever.*

In addition to the above new adjectives, we add 30 more English cognates that are easy to memorize.

English	Italian	Examples
accurate	accurato	L'ora sul mio orologio non è **accurata**. *The time on my watch isn't **accurate**.*

[1] The direct translation of "**basso**" is *"low,"* and the direct translation of "**corto**" is *"short."* However, only when we refer to the height of a person or an object, we use "**basso**" to mean *"short,"* and we do not use "**corto**."

adult	adulto	Questo farmaco è solo per pazienti **adulti**. *This medication is for **adult** patients only.*
aggressive	aggressivo	Il gatto del mio amico è molto **aggressivo**. *My friend's cat is very **aggressive**.*
common	comune	Quel marchio è molto **comune** qui. *That brand is very **common** here.*
complete	completo	Il processo **completo** è molto lungo. *The **complete** process is very long.*
complex	complesso	Questa struttura è molto **complessa**. *This structure is very **complex**.*
convenient	conveniente	È **conveniente** riporre i vestiti qui. *It is **convenient** to store the clothes here.*
correct **right**	corretto	Devi selezionare l'opzione **corretta**. *You must select the **right** option.*
diverse	diverso	Mi piace mangiare cibi **diversi**. *I like to eat **diverse** foods.*
exact	esatto	Non conosco la posizione **esatta**. *I don't know the **exact** location.*
excellent	eccellente ottimo	I suoi voti sono **eccellenti**. *His grades are **excellent**.*
familiar	familiare	Il suo volto mi sembra **familiare**. *His face seems **familiar** to me.*
frank	franco	Cerca di essere **franco** con suo padre. *He tries to be **frank** with his father.*
global	globale	Internet facilita la comunicazione **globale**. *The internet facilitates **global** communication.*
honest	onesto	Ho bisogno della tua **onesta** opinione. *I need your **honest** opinion.*
impatient	impaziente	È una persona **impaziente**. *He is an **impatient** person.*
important	importante	Conservo i file **importanti** qui. *I store **important** files here.*
intelligent	intelligente	Mia madre è molto **intelligente**. *My mom is very **intelligent**.*
interesting	interessante	Questo libro è molto **interessante**. *This book is very **interesting**.*
necessary	necessario	È **necessario** andare periodicamente dal medico. *It's **necessary** to go to the doctor periodically.*
obvious	ovvio	È **ovvio** che la porta è aperta. *It is **obvious** that the door is open.*
patient	paziente	Le madri sono **pazienti** con i loro figli. *Mothers are **patient** with their children.*
personal	personale	Questo è il mio diario **personale**. *This is my **personal** diary.*

practical	pratico	È **pratico** avere le cose organizzate. *It's **practical** to have things organized.*
rare	raro	È molto **raro** trovare pietre preziose lì. *It's very **rare** to find precious stones there.*
real	reale vero	Ovviamente, i mostri non sono **reali**. *Obviously, monsters aren't **real**.*
remote	remoto	Ho un ufficio **remoto**. *I have a **remote** office.*
sincere	sincero	È meglio che tu sia **sincero** con questo. *It is better that you be **sincere** with this.*
special	speciale	Preparerò una ricetta **speciale** per te. *I am going to prepare a **special** recipe for you.*
stupid	stupido	Questi errori mi fanno sentire **stupido**. *These errors make me feel **stupid**.*

3. COUNTRIES & NATIONALITIES I

A *country* in Italian is "**un paese**" and a *nationality* is "**una nazionalità**." The following are some countries and nationalities (or demonyms) in Italian:

Africa	**Africa**[f]	*African*	africano/-a
Argentina	**Argentina**[f]	*Argentinian*	argentino/-a
Asia	**Asia**[f]	*Asian*	asiatico/-a
Australia	**Australia**[f]	*Australian*	australiano/-a
Brazil	**Brasile**[m]	*Brazilian*	brasiliano/-a
Canada	**Canada**[m]	*Canadian*	canadese
China	**Cina**[f]	*Chinese*	cinese
Colombia	**Colombia**[f]	*Colombian*	colombiano/-a
Croatia	**Croazia**[f]	*Croatian*	croato/-a
Cuba	**Cuba**[f]	*Cuban*	cubano/-a
Egypt	**Egitto**[m]	*Egyptian*	egiziano/-a
England	**Inghilterra**[f]	*English*	inglese
Europe	**Europa**[f]	*European*	europeo/-a
France	**Francia**[f]	*French*	francese
Germany	**Germania**[f]	*German*	tedesco/-a
Iran	**Iran**[m]	*Iranian*	iraniano/-a
Iraq	**Iraq**[m]	*Iraqi*	iracheno/-a
Italy	**Italia**[f]	*Italian*	italiano/-a
Japan	**Giappone**[m]	*Japanese*	giapponese
Jordan	**Giordania**[f]	*Jordanian*	giordano/-a
Latin America	**America Latina**[f]	*Latin American*	latinoamericano/-a

Mexico	Messico[m]	Mexican	messicano/-a
Morocco	Marocco[m]	Moroccan	marocchino/-a
Palestine	Palestina[f]	Palestinian	palestinese
Panama	Panama[f]	Panamanian	panamense
Poland	Polonia[f]	Polish	polacco/-a
Russia	Russia[f]	Russian	russo/-a
South America	Sudamerica[m] America[f] del Sud	South American	sudamericano/-a
Spain	Spagna[f]	Spanish	spagnolo/-a
Turkey	Turchia[f]	Turkish	turco/-a
Uruguay	Uruguay[m]	Uruguayan	uruguaiano/-a

4. COLORS I

The word *"color"* in Italian is **"colore"** (pronounced co-**lo**-re). Some of the basic colors in Italian are:

black	nero/-a	orange	arancione[m,f]
blue	blu azzurro/-a	purple	viola[m,f] porpora[m,f]
brown	marrone[m,f] bruno/-a	red	rosso/-a
gray	grigio/-a	white	bianco/-a
green	verde[m,f]	yellow	giallo/-a

5. TIMES & SEASONS

A *day* in Italian is **"un giorno,"** and a *week* is **"una settimana."** The *days of the week* or **"i giorni della settimana"** are:

Monday	lunedì[m]	Friday	venerdì[m]
Tuesday	martedì[m]	Saturday	sabato[m]
Wednesday	mercoledì[m]	Sunday	domenica[f]
Thursday	giovedì[m]	weekend	fine[m] settimana

Today is **"oggi,"** and *tomorrow* is **"domani,"** followed by **"dopodomani"** *(the day after tomorrow)*. *Yesterday* is **"ieri,"** preceded by **"avantieri"** *(the day before yesterday)*.

Tonight is "**stanotte**" or "**questa notte**" (literally *this night*), *last night* is "**ieri notte**" or "**la scorsa notte**," and *tomorrow night* is "**domani notte**" (literally *tomorrow at night*).

The main periods of the day are "**la mattina**" *(morning)*, "**il pomeriggio**" *(afternoon)*, and "**la notte**" *(night)*. We generally use the preposition "**di**" to say "**di mattina/ pomeriggio /notte**" *(in the morning/ afternoon or at night)*.

A *month* in Italian is "**un mese**" and a *year* is "**un anno**." A *decade* is "**un decennio**" or "**una decade**," and a *century* is "**un secolo**."

The *months of the year* or "**i mesi dell'anno**" are:

January	gennaio^m	July	luglio^m
February	**febbraio**^m	*August*	**agosto**^m
March	**marzo**^m	*September*	**settembre**^m
April	**aprile**^m	*October*	**ottobre**^m
May	**maggio**^m	*November*	**novembre**^m
June	**giugno**^m	*December*	**dicembre**^m

Notice from the two tables above that the days and months are not capitalized in Italian, and they are all masculine.

Finally, a *season* in Italian is "**una stagione**." The *seasons of the year* or "**le stagioni dell'anno**" are:

autumn, fall	**autunno**^m	*summer*	**estate**^f
spring	**primavera**^f	*winter*	**inverno**^m

6. DIRECTIONS I

A *direction* in Italian is "**un'indicazione**." A *map* is "**una mappa**," and a *street* is "**una via**."

The four geographical directions of a *compass* or "**una bussola**" are:

east	**est**^m	*south*	**sud**^m
north	**nord**^m	*west*	**ovest**^m

And the four main directions *right*, *left*, *up*, and *down* are:

right	**destra**	*up*	**su**
left	**sinistra**	*down*	**giù**

To describe the location of an object with respect to another, one can use:

above *on top (of)*	**sopra**	*there*	**lì** **là**
here	**qui** **qua**	*to the left of*	**a sinistra di**
inside	**dentro**	*to the right of*	**a destra di**
near	**vicino (a)**	*far (from)*	**lontano (da)**
outside	**fuori (da)**	*toward*	**verso**
straight ahead	**dritto**	*under* *beneath*	**sotto**

There is a subtle difference between **"qui"** and **"qua,"** both translated as *"here,"* and between **"lì"** and **"là,"** both translated as *"there."* The difference is that **"qua"** and **"là"** tend to be less specific about the location. However, this subtle difference is not often respected.

There is also the word **"ecco"** which is used to call the attention to something and is often translated as *"here"* in expressions such as: **"Ecco l'autobus"** *(Here is the bus)*, **"Ecco le mie domande"** *(Here are my questions)*, **"Ecco perché"** *(Here is why)*, **"Eccolo"** *(Here it is)*, **"Eccomi"** *(Here I am)*, etc.

7. FAMILY I

A *family* in Italian is **"una famiglia."** The status of being *single* is **"celibe^m"** or **"nubile^f,"** and *married* is **"sposato^m"** or **"sposata^f."** Some *members of the family,* or **"i membri della famiglia,"** are:

aunt	**zia^f**	*grandmother*	**nonna^f**
couple	**coppia^f**	*grandson*	**nipote^m**
cousin	**cugino/-a**	*husband*	**marito^m**
dad	**papà^m**	*mother*	**madre^f**
daughter	**figlia^f**	*mom*	**mamma^f**

daughter-in-law	**nuora**[f]	*relatives*	**parenti**[m] **famigliari**[m]
father	**padre**[m]	*son*	**figlio**[m]
fiancé *boyfriend*	**fidanzato**[m]	*son-in-law*	**genero**[m]
fiancée *girlfriend*	**fidanzata**[f]	*spouse*	**sposo/-a**
granddaughter	**nipote**[f]	*uncle*	**zio**[m]
grandfather	**nonno**[m]	*wife*	**moglie**[f]

8. ANATOMY I

Body in Italian is "**il corpo**," and some *body parts*, or "**le parti del corpo**," are:

arm	**braccio**[m]	*hand*	**mano**[f]
back	**schiena**[f]	*head*	**testa**[f]
blood	**sangue**[m]	*heart*	**cuore**[m]
brain	**cervello**[m]	*leg*	**gamba**[f]
ear	**orecchio**[m]	*lip*	**labbro**[m]
eye	**occhio**[m]	*mouth*	**bocca**[f]
face	**faccia**[f]	*nose*	**naso**[m]
finger	**dito**[m]	*shoulder*	**spalla**[f]
foot	**piede**[f]	*stomach*	**stomaco**[m]
hair	**capelli**[m]	*toe*	**dito**[m] **del piede**

9. PEOPLE I

The following is some vocabulary that we use to describe *people*, "**la gente**" in Italian. Notice how the word "**gente**" is singular in Italian whereas the word *"people"* is plural in English.

baby *infant*	**bebè**[m] **neonato**[m]	*minor*	**minore**[m,f]
boss	**capo**[m] **padrone**[m]	*neighbor*	**vicino/-a**
boy	**ragazzo**[m] **ragazzino**[m]	*nobody*	**nessuno/-a**
businessman	**uomo d'affari** **imprenditore**[m]	*person*	**persona**[f]

child	bambino/-a	player	giocatore[m] giocatrice[f]
criminal	criminale[m,f]	president	presidente[m] presidentessa[f]
date appointment	appuntamento[m]	queen	regina[f]
everyone everybody	tutti	roommate	coinquilino/-a
friend	amico/-a	some people	alcune persone[f]
girl	ragazza[f] ragazzina[f]	someone	qualcuno
human	umano[m]	student	studente[m]
king	re[m]	thief	ladro/-a
man	uomo[m]	woman	donna[f]

10. ANIMALS I

The word *"animal"* in Italian is **"animale"** (pronounced a-nee-**ma**-le). Below are some animal names in Italian:

bird	uccello[m]	hen	gallina[f]
bull	toro[m]	horse	cavallo[m]
cat	gatto/-a	mouse	topo[m]
chicken	pollo[m]	pet	animale domestico[m]
cow	mucca[f] vacca[f]	pig	maiale[m] porco[m]
dog	cane[m] cagna[f]	rabbit	coniglio[m]
donkey	asino[m]	rat	ratto[m]
duck	anatra[f]	rooster	gallo[m]
fish	pesce[m]	sheep	pecora[f]
fly	mosca[f]	turkey	tacchino[m]

LEVEL II: BEGINNER

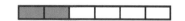

I. Introductory Topics & Grammar

At this level, you will continue to familiarize yourself with some of the fundamental grammar rules and basic topics that will enhance your Italian-language knowledge.

1. PREPOSITIONS

Here are some of the most used prepositions in Italian with the most common meanings in different contexts.

Prep.	Meaning	Examples	
a	to	Vado **a** scuola la mattina.	*I go **to** school in the morning.*
	at	Finirò **a** mezzogiorno.	*I will finish **at** noon.*
	by	Fatto **a** mano.	*Made **by** hand (handmade).*
	in	Vivo **a** Roma.	*I live **in** Rome.*
	on	Tornerò a casa **a** piedi.	*I will come back home **on** foot.*
	per	Costa 20 dollari **a** notte.	*It costs 20 dollars **per** night.*
accanto a	beside / next to	C'è un gatto **accanto** alla sedia.	*There is a cat **beside** the chair.*
attraverso	across / through	È possibile nuotare **attraverso** il fiume.	*It is possible to swim **across** the river.*
con	with	Parla **con** il suo amico.	*He speaks **with** his friend.*
contro	against	Sono **contro** l'ingiustizia.	*I am **against** injustice.*
da	from	Ho viaggiato **da** Londra alla Corea.	*I traveled **from** London to Korea.*
	since	Non fumo **da** aprile.	*I haven't smoked **since** April.*
	for	Non fumo **da** due anni.	*I haven't smoked **for** two years.*
	as (a)	**Da** bambino, ero timido.	***As a** kid, I was shy.*
	by	È stato dipinto **da** Bosch.	*It was painted **by** Bosch.*
davanti a / di fronte a	in front of	Sono **davanti** alla scuola.	*I am **in front of** the school.*
dentro	inside	La palla è **dentro** la scatola.	*The ball is **inside** the box.*
di	of	Il colore **di** quella macchina è blu.	*The color **of** that car is blue.*
	from	Lei è **di** Madrid.	*She is **from** Madrid.*
	about	Parlano **di** lui.	*They talk **about** him.*

dietro	behind	L'albero è **dietro** la casa.	The tree is **behind** the house.
dopo	after	Ho dormito **dopo** pranzo oggi.	I slept **after** lunch today.
durante	during	Possiamo uscire **durante** il giorno.	We can go out **during** the day.
fino a	until	Ho lavorato **fino a** mezzanotte.	I worked **until** midnight.
	as far as	La luce arriva **fino al** parco.	The light reaches **as far as** the park.
fuori di	outside	Il garage è **fuori d**al centro commerciale.	The garage is **outside** the shopping mall.
in	in	Vivo **in** Italia.	I live **in** Italy.
	to	Andrò **in** Italia.	I will go **to** Italy.
lungo	along	Ci sono case **lungo** il lago.	There are houses **along** the lake.
per	for (duration)	Lavorerò lì **per** due anni.	I will work there **for** two years.
	for (destination)	Domani partirò **per** Barcellona.	I will leave **for** Barcelona tomorrow.
	by	Ti ho contattato **per** telefono.	I contacted you **by** phone.
	because of	Soffrivano **per** la mancanza d'acqua.	They suffered **because of** the lack of water.
	in order to	Studiamo **per** imparare.	We study **in order to** learn.
prima di	before	Ti chiamo **prima di** partire.	I will call you **before** leaving.
secondo	according to	**Secondo** la legge, è vietato.	**According to** the law, it is prohibited.
senza	without	Un pesce non può vivere **senza** acqua.	A fish can't live **without** water.
sopra	above over on top of	La mosca è **sopra** il tavolo.	The fly is **above** the table.
sotto	under	Il gatto è **sotto** la sedia.	The cat is **under** the chair.
su	on	La chiave è **su**l tavolo.	The key is **on** the table.
	about	Il dibattito **su** quell'incidente è finito.	The debate **about** that incident is over.
tra fra	between	L'uccello è bloccato **tra** i rami.	The bird is stuck **between** the branches.
	among	Sono il più alto **tra** i miei amici.	I am the tallest **among** my friends.
	in	Partiremo **tra** una settimana.	We will leave **in** a week.
verso	toward	Corse **verso** l'uscita.	She ran **toward** the exit.
vicino a	near	Vivo **vicino** alla città.	I live **near** the city.

❖ The prepositions "**a**," "**da**," "**di**," "**in**," and "**su**" contract when followed by a definite article. Remember that there are seven definite articles in Italian: "**l'**," "**lo**," "**il**," "**la**," "**i**," "**gli**," and "**le**." This results in the following possible combinations:

	l'	lo	il	la	i	gli	le
a	all'	allo	al	alla	ai	agli	alle
da	dall'	dallo	dal	dalla	dai	dagli	dalle
di	dell'	dello	del	della	dei	degli	delle
in	nell'	nello	nel	nella	nei	negli	nelle
su	sull'	sullo	sul	sulla	sui	sugli	sulle

Although optional, you may also use or encounter the following three contractions of the preposition "**con**" *(with)*, especially in spoken Italian:

	il	la	l'
con	col	colla	coll'

Other prepositions do not contract.

Contractions add to the complexity of the prepositions in Italian. Practice is your best approach to learn them. Here are some examples:

a	+ lo	= allo	Verrò con te **allo** stadio.	*I'll go with you **to the** stadium.*
da	+ il	= dal	Voglio imparare **dal** libro.	*I want to learn **from the** book.*
di	+ la	= della	Il colore **della** macchina è blu.	*The color **of the** car is blue.*
in	+ l'	= nell'	La valigia è **nell'**armadio.	*The suitcase is **in the** wardrobe.*
su	+ gli	= sugli	C'è molta polvere **sugli** occhiali.	*There is a lot of dust **on the** glasses.*

The definite article is dropped from some expressions that are commonly used in daily life such as: "**a casa**" *(at home)*, "**in macchina**" *(by car)*, "**in centro**" *(in downtown)*, etc.

❖ The preposition "**a**" is used to mean *"in"* when referring to the proper name of a city (or a smaller area), e.g., "**Vivo a Roma**" *(I live in Rome)*. For larger areas, we use the preposition "**in**," e.g., "**Vivo in California**" *(I live in California)*, "**L'ho visto in Spagna**" *(I saw it in Spain)*.

❖ The preposition "**in**" generally means *"in"* in English. However, when referring to a destination that is larger than a city, the preposition "**in**" can also be translated as *"to,"* e.g., "**Andrò in California**" *(I will go to California)*, "**Ho viaggiato in Spagna**" *(I traveled to Spain)*.

❖ The preposition "**da**" can have several meanings:

1. The basic meaning of *"from"* in English with its versatile use to indicate the starting point of a movement, source or origin, separation, etc. For example:

Ho viaggiato **da** Londra alla Corea.	*I traveled **from** London to Korea.*
Vengo **da** Firenze.	*I come (am) **from** Florence.*
Separa l'acqua **da** questa miscela.	*Separate the water **from** this mixture.*

2. The equivalent of *"since"* or *"for"* in time expressions that typically use the present perfect or present perfect continuous tense in English. For example:

Non fumo **da** aprile.	*I haven't smoked **since** April.*
Non fumo **da** due anni.	*I haven't smoked **for** two years.*

    Notice that, in Italian, the present tense is used before "**da**" to convey the equivalent meaning in English.

    Keep in mind that to describe a defined duration in the future, the preposition "**per**" must be used instead. For example:

Lavoro lì **da** due anni.	*I have worked there **for** two years.*
Lavorerò lì **per** due anni.	*I will work there **for** two years.*

3. The equivalent of *"to"* or *"for"* when used to indicate purpose or reason. For example:

Qualcosa **da** bere	*Something **to** drink*
Una casa **da** vendere	*A house **for** sale*

4. The meaning of being at someone's house or workplace. In this context, "**da**" is often translated as *"at,"* but can also mean *"to"* if preceded by the verb *"go."* For example:

Siamo **da** Marco.	*We are **at** Marco's place.*
Domani vado **dal** dentista.	*I will go **to** the dentist tomorrow.*

5. The meaning of the preposition *"by"* in English, referring to an agent in the passive voice. For example:

Un software sviluppato **da** Microsoft.	*A software developed **by** Microsoft.*
Dipinto **da** un artista anonimo.	*Painted **by** an anonymous artist.*

6. The expression *"as (a) …"* in English. For example:

Te lo dico **da amico**.	*I tell you **as a** friend.*
Da bambini, ci divertivamo molto.	***As** kids, we had a lot of fun.*

❖ To express the meaning of *"about"* (e.g., to talk *about* someone or watch a documentary *about* something), we often use "**su**" or "**circa**." For example:

Ho visto un documentario **su** quella guerra.	*I watched a documentary **about** that war.*
Ho letto un libro **circa** la vita in Giappone.	*I read a book **about** life in Japan.*

In some contexts, we could use "**di**" to mean *"about."* For example:

Parlano **di** lui.	*They talk **about** him.*
Voglio leggere un libro **di** scienze.	*I want to read a book **about** science.*

❖ The preposition "**tra**" or "**fra**" often means *"between."* If used to indicate the future, it can mean *"in,"* as in: "**Ci vediamo tra un mese**" *(See you in a month).*

2. PRESENT INDICATIVE TENSE II

As we discussed in Level I, Lesson 6, regular verbs in the present indicative tense follow the conjugation rules shown in the table:

	-are ending parlare *(to speak)*	-ere ending vendere *(to sell)*	-ire ending (Type I) partire *(to leave)*	-ire ending (Type II) finire *(to finish)*
io	parlo	vendo	parto	finisco
tu	parli	vendi	parti	finisci
lui/lei	parla	vende	parte	finisce
noi	parliamo	vendiamo	partiamo	finiamo
voi	parlate	vendete	partite	finite
loro	parlano	vendono	partono	finiscono

Some verbs deviate from the general conjugation rules in the present indicative tense. Some of these deviations are simple and easy to apply, while others may require some practice. You could also use Anki cards to practice more examples until you master this lesson. In addition, you can use the summary in the cheat sheets in **Appendix B** as a quick reference.

Let us examine five groups of irregular verbs in the present indicative tense.

#1: Completely Irregular Verbs

The *first* group contains 14 verbs that are common, yet completely irregular, that is, they do not follow a particular pattern of conjugation. These verbs should be practiced and memorized.

	io	tu	lui/lei	noi	voi	loro
andare *(to go)*	vado	vai	va	andiamo	andate	vanno
avere *(to have)*	ho	hai	ha	abbiamo	avete	hanno
bere *(to drink)*	bevo	bevi	beve	beviamo	bevete	bevono
essere *(to be)*	sono	sei	è	siamo	siete	sono
dare *(to give)*	do	dai	dà	diamo	date	danno
dire *(to say/tell)*	dico	dici	dice	diciamo	dite	dicono
dovere *(must)*	devo/ debbo	devi	deve	dobbiamo	dovete	devono/ debbono

fare *(to do/make)*	faccio	fai	fa	facciamo	fate	fanno
potere *(can)*	posso	puoi	può	possiamo	potete	possono
sapere *(to know)*	so	sai	sa	sappiamo	sapete	sanno
stare *(to stay)*	sto	stai	sta	stiamo	state	stanno
scegliere *(to choose)*	scelgo	scegli	sceglie	scegliamo	scegliete	scelgono
uscire *(to go out)*	esco	esci	esce	usciamo	uscite	escono
volere *(to want)*	voglio	vuoi	vuole	vogliamo	volete	vogliono

Notice that the verb "**stare**" can also mean *"to be"* in some contexts, e.g., "**Come stai?**" *(How are you?)*, "**Sto bene**" *(I am well)*, etc.

In addition to these 14 verbs, any verb that is derived from or written similar to these verbs uses the same conjugation patterns. For example, the verb "**rifare**" *(to redo or remake)* is conjugated like the verb "**fare**," and the verb "**riuscire**" *(to succeed)* is conjugated like the verb "**uscire**."

#2: Add "g" to the Stem in "io" and "loro" forms

The *second* group adds a "**g**" to the stem of the verb in the "**io**" and "**loro**" forms. There are four common verbs in this group:

	salire *(to go up)*	rimanere *(to remain)*	venire *(to come)*	tenere *(to hold)*
io	sal**g**o	riman**g**o	vengo	tengo
tu	sali	rimani	vieni	tieni
lui/lei	sale	rimane	viene	tiene
noi	saliamo	rimaniamo	veniamo	teniamo
voi	salite	rimanete	venite	tenite
loro	sal**g**ono	rimangono	vengono	tengono

Notice that the verbs "**venire**" and "**tenere**" also change the stem in the "**tu**" and "**lui/lei**" forms from "**ven-**" and "**ten-**" to "**vien-**" and "**tien-**," respectively.

Verbs that derive from the four verbs in this group are conjugated similarly. For example, the verbs "**contenere**" *(to contain)* and "**intervenire**" *(to intervene)* follow the same conjugation patterns of the verbs "**tenere**" and "**venire**," respectively.

#3: Other Minor Stem Changes

The *third* group includes verbs with relatively minor stem changes. For example, the verb "**apparire**" *(to appear)* changes the stem from "**appar-**" to "**appai-**" when conjugated in the "**io**" and "**loro**" forms, whereas the verb "**udire**" *(to hear)* changes the stem from "**ud-**" to "**od-**" in all forms except "**noi**" and "**voi.**" In general, the "**noi**" and "**voi**" forms remain unchanged in this group of verbs. Here are four common verbs in this group:

	apparire *(to appear)*	morire *(to die)*	sedere *(to sit)*	udire *(to hear)*
io	appaio	muoio	siedo[1]	odo
tu	appari	muori	siedi	odi
lui/lei	appare	muore	siede	ode
noi	appariamo	moriamo	sediamo	udiamo
voi	apparite	morite	sedete	udite
loro	appaiono	muoiono	siedono[2]	odono

In addition to these four verbs, similar verbs follow the same conjugation patterns. For example, the verbs "**comparire**" *(to appear or become visible)*, "**riapparire**" *(to reappear)*, "**scomparire**" *(to disappear)*, "**sparire**" *(to disappear or vanish)*, and "**trasparire**" *(to transpire)* follow the same conjugation patterns of the verb "**apparirie**," and the verb "**possedere**" *(to possess)* follows the same conjugation patterns of the verb "**sedere.**"

#4: Orthographic Changes

The *fourth* group includes verbs that are regular in essence but change spelling to maintain proper pronunciation. These are the verbs ending in "**-care**," "**-gare**," "**-ciare**," "**-giare**," and "**-gliare**."

1. Verbs ending in "**-care**" and "**-gare**" add an "**h**" to the stem in the "**tu**" and "**noi**" forms before the "**-i**" and "**-iamo**" endings, respectively, e.g., "**cercare**" *(to search)*, "**pagare**" *(to pay)*,

---

[1] Another accepted irregular conjugation of the "**io**" form is "**seggo.**"
[2] Another accepted irregular conjugation of the "**loro**" form is "**seggono.**"

"**giocare**" *(to play)*, "**praticare**" *(to practice)*, "**negare**" *(to deny or refuse)*, "**caricare**" *(to load)*, "**pregare**" *(to pray or beg)*, "**sporcare**" *(to make dirty)*, and "**litigare**" *(to argue)*.

2. Verbs in "**-ciare**," "**-giare**," and "**-gliare**" drop the "**i**" from the stem in the "**tu**" and "**noi**" forms before the "**-i**" and "**-iamo**" endings, respectively, to avoid the double "**i**," e.g., "**cominciare**" *(to start or begin)*, "**mangiare**" *(to eat)*, "**baciare**" *(to kiss)*, "**lasciare**" *(to leave)*, "**strisciare**" *(to crawl)*, "**arrangiare**" *(to arrange)*, "**viaggiare**" *(to travel)*, "**tagliare**" *(to cut)*, and "**sbagliare**" *(to make a mistake)*.

3. Most other verbs that end in "**-iare**," that is, excluding "**-ciare**," "**-giare**," and "**-gliare**," follow the same pattern and drop the "**i**" from the stem in the "**tu**" and "**noi**" forms before the "**-i**" and "**-iamo**" endings, respectively, to avoid the double "**i**," e.g., "**abbreviare**" *(to abbreviate)*, "**cambiare**" *(to change)*, "**copiare**" *(to copy)*, "**iniziare**" *(to begin)*, "**studiare**" *(to study)*, and "**variare**" *(to vary)*.

   However, the exception to the rule is that some verbs drop the "**i**" from the stem only in the "**noi**" form and maintain the double "**i**" in the "**tu**" form, e.g., "**avviare**" *(to start)*, "**fuorviare**" *(to mislead)*, "**inviare**" *(to send)*, "**obliare**" *(to forget)*, "**rinviare**" *(to postpone)*, "**sciare**" *(to ski)*, and "**spiare**" *(to spy)*.

Finally, keep in mind that verbs ending in "**-cere**" and "**-gere**" do not undergo any spelling change, but instead change the pronunciation to the hard sounds "**k**" (as in *"kit"*) and "**g**" (as in *"get"*) in the "**io**" and "**loro**" forms before the "**-o**" and "**-ono**" endings, respectively, e.g., "**conoscere**" *(to know)*, "**piangere**" *(to cry)*, and "**vincere**" *(to win)*.

Here is a summary in the context of some examples:

	io	tu	lui/lei	noi	voi	loro
cer**care**	cerco	cerchi	cerca	cerchiamo	cercate	cercano
pa**gare**	pago	paghi	paga	paghiamo	pagate	pagano

baciare	bacio	baci	bacia	baciamo	baciate	baciano
mangiare	mangio	mangi	mangia	mangiamo	mangiate	mangiano
tagliare	taglio	tagli	taglia	tagliamo	tagliate	tagliano
studiare	studio	studi	studia	studiamo	studiate	studiano
inviare	invio	invii	invia	inviamo	inviate	inviano
vincere	vinco	vinci	vince	vinciamo	vincete	vincono
piangere	piango	piangi	piange	piangiamo	piangete	piangono

#5: Contracted Infinitive Verbs with "-rre" Endings

Finally, the *fifth* group includes some special, but not so common, verbs that end in "-**arre**," "-**orre**," and "-**urre**." These verbs did not initially appear under the three main verb types in Italian with "-**are**," "-**ere**," and "-**ire**" endings. These verbs belong to a group of verbs called *contracted infinitive* verbs. In these verbs, the stem of the infinitive is shorter than that of the conjugated verb. For instance, the verb "**tradurre**" *(to translate)* is conjugated in the "**io**" form as "**traduco**." Notice that the stem of the infinitive is "**trad-**," whereas the stem of the conjugated verb is "**traduc-**." The reason for that often goes back to the Latin origin of the verb, which is "traducere." This explains the irregular conjugation of many Italian verbs, some of which even belong to the three main verb types, for example, "**dire**" *(to say,* Latin: "dicere"), "**fare**" *(to do or make,* Latin: "facere"), and "**porre**" *(to put,* Latin: "ponere"). In general, verbs in this group are considered "-**ere**" verbs because they lost an internal "-**e-**" when derived from their Latin origin.

Let us examine some conjugation examples of contracted infinitive verbs that end with "-**arre**," "-**orre**," and "-**urre**."

	-arre ending trarre *(to pull)*	-orre ending porre *(to put)*	-urre ending tradurre *(to translate)*
io	tra**gg**o	pon**g**o	traduco
tu	trai	poni	traduci
lui/lei	trae	pone	traduce
noi	traiamo	poniamo	traduciamo
voi	traete	ponete	traducete
loro	tra**gg**ono	pon**g**ono	traducono

Other examples include:

-arre ending	-orre ending	-urre ending
"contrarre" *(to contract)*	"comporre" *(to compose)*	"condurre" *(to lead or conduct)*
"distrarre" *(to distract)*	"esporre" *(to exhibit)*	"dedurre" *(to deduce)*
"sottrarre" *(to subtract)*	"imporre" *(to impose)*	"produrre" *(to produce)*

3. POSSESSIVE ADJECTIVES & PRONOUNS

Possessive adjectives *(my, your, his/her, our, their)* come before a noun, e.g., *"This is my house,"* while possessive pronouns *(mine, yours, his/hers, ours, theirs)* are used to replace a noun and its possessive adjective, e.g., *"This house is mine."*

In Italian, possessive adjectives and pronouns must agree in gender and number with the noun they describe, except for the possessive **"loro"** *(their)*, which is invariable.

Moreover, the definite article must precede the possessive as an essential part that agrees with it in gender and number. This may sound a little unfamiliar and less natural to English speakers.

	Sing. Masc.	Sing. Fem.	Plural Masc.	Plural Fem.
my (mine)	il mio	la mia	i miei	le mie
your(s) (informal singular)	il tuo	la tua	i tuoi	le tue
his/her(s)/your(s) (form. sing.)	il suo	la sua	i suoi	le sue
our(s)	il nostro	la nostra	i nostri	le nostre
your(s) (informal plural)	il vostro	la vostra	i vostri	le vostre
their(s)/your(s) (formal plural)	il loro	la loro	i loro	le loro

❖ The formal possessive *"your(s)"* should be capitalized in plural **"il/la/i/le Loro,"** and singular: **"il Suo," "la Sua," "i Suoi,"** and **"le Sue."**

❖ Note that, unlike in English, the possessive adjective agrees in number and gender with the noun it describes and not the subject, e.g., **"i miei fratelli"** *(my brothers)*. Note that we use **"i miei"** because the *noun* we describe is *masculine* and *plural*, although the subject is singular. Similarly, in the example "**le nostre madri**" (*our mothers*), the possessive adjective "**le nostre**" agrees in gender and number with the noun it describes, "**madri**."

❖ The possessive adjective can come after the noun if the emphasis is placed on the possessor and the noun is preceded by an indefinite article or a verb, e.g., "**un amico mio**" (*a friend of mine*), "**un problema tuo**" (*your problem*), "**Sono affari tuoi**" (*That's your business*), etc.

❖ One can also insert the adjective "**proprio/-a**" (*own*) between the possessive pronoun and the noun for emphasis, e.g., "**il suo proprio telefono**" (*his own phone*), "**la tua propria casa**" (*your own house*), etc. The plural forms of "**proprio**" and "**propria**" are "**propri**" and "**proprie**," respectively, e.g., "**con le proprie mani**" (*with one's own hands*).

❖ The definite article is *optional* and can be dropped after the verb "**essere**," e.g., "**Non è tuo, è mio**," (*It is not yours, it's mine*), "**Quella casa, è nostra**" (*That house is ours*).

❖ The definite article is not used to precede the possessive adjective with the following singular unmodified kinship nouns, except for "**loro**":

padre *(father)*	marito *(husband)*	suocero *(father-in-law)*
madre *(mother)*	moglie *(wife)*	suocera *(mother-in-law)*
figlio *(son)*	zio *(uncle)*	cognato *(brother-in-law)*
figlia *(daughter)*	zia *(aunt)*	cognata *(sister-in-law)*
fratello *(brother)*	genero *(son-in-law)*	cugino *(male cousin)*
sorella *(sister)*	nuora *(daughter-in-law)*	cugina *(female cousin)*

For example:

mio padre	*my father*
tua madre	*your mother*
sua zia	*his/her aunt*
le sue zie	*his/her aunts*
la sua zia vecchia	*his/her old aunt*
il loro figlio	*their brother*

Notice that, in the last three examples, the kinship name is either not singular, modified, or preceded by "**loro**." Thus, the definite article is needed before the possessive adjective.

The definite article is still needed, if a possessive pronoun is used, e.g., "**Mio padre sta bene, e il tuo,?**" *(My father is well, and yours?).*

The definite article with the following kinship nouns is optional, when singular and unmodified, except for "**loro**":

papà *(dad)*	e.g., mio papà	(or)	il mio papà
mamma *(mom)*	e.g., tua mamma	(or)	la tua mamma
nonno *(grandfather)*	e.g., suo nonno	(or)	il suo nonno
nonna *(grandmother)*	e.g., sua nonna	(or)	la sua nonna

4. DEMONSTRATIVE PRONOUNS & ADJECTIVES

Demonstrative adjectives *(this, that, these, those)* come before a noun, e.g., "*I want this book,*" while possessive pronouns (same as demonstrative adjectives: *this, that, these, those*) are used to replace a noun and its possessive adjective, e.g., "*I want this.*"

Demonstrative pronouns and adjectives must agree in gender and number with the noun being described.

Demonstrative Pronouns

Let us start with the demonstrative pronouns:

	Masc. Singular	Feminine Singular	Masc. Plural	Feminine Plural
this (one)/these (ones)	questo	questa	questi	queste
that (one)/those (ones)	quello	quella	quelli	quelle

In general, "**questo**," "**questa**," "**questi**," and "**queste**" are used to refer to nouns close to the speaker. On the other hand, "**quello**," "**quella**," "**quelli**," and "**quelle**" are used to refer to nouns far away from the speaker.

Let us take some examples:

A: Which chair do you want? B: *That one.*	A: Quale sedia^f vuoi? B: **Quella.**
A: Which language do you prefer? B: *This one.*	A: Quale lingua^f preferisci? B: **Questa.**
A: Which books did you read? B: *These ones.*	A: Quali libri^m hai letto? B: **Questi.**
A: Which cell phone do you use? B: *This one.*	A: Quale cellulare^m utilizzi? B: **Questo.**
A: Which schools are the best? B: *Those ones.*	A: Quali scuole^f sono le migliori? B: **Quelle.**

The demonstrative pronouns **"questo"** and **"quello"** can also be used to refer to a whole sentence or concept, e.g., "**Questo non è accettabile**" (*This is not acceptable*), or to point at something without mentioning it, e.g., "**Deve essere quello**" (*It has to be that*).

Demonstrative Adjectives

Let us now examine the demonstrative adjectives.

In the case of the demonstrative adjectives of nearness, i.e., *"this"* and *"these,"* the demonstrative adjectives are identical to the demonstrative pronouns, that is, **"questo," "questa," "questi,"** and **"queste."** For example, **"questo ragazzo"** (*this boy*), **"questa macchina"** (*this car*).

Notice that it is optional to use the form **"quest'"** instead of **"questo"** or **"questa"** before a noun that begins with a vowel, e.g., **"quest'amica"** (*this friend*) is short for **"questa amica."**

In the case of the demonstrative adjectives of farness, i.e., *"that"* and *"those,"* recall from **Level I, Lesson 7** that **"quello"** is one of two common adjectives that change form like the definite articles, depending on the number and gender of the following noun and whether the noun begins with a vowel or certain consonants.

	l'	lo	il	la	i	gli	le
quello	quell'	quello	quel	quella	quei	quegli	quelle

To summarize, the following are the demonstrative adjectives in Italian:

	Masc. Singular	Feminine Singular	Masc. Plural	Feminine Plural
this/these	questo	questa	questi	queste
that/those	quell'[V] quello[Z] quel	quell'[V] quella	quegli[V][Z] quei	quelle

[V] before a noun (or preceding adjective) that begins with a **vowel**

[Z] before a noun (or preceding adjective) that begins with "**z**," "**gn**," "**ps**," or "**s**" + consonant

Let us take some examples:

A: Which chair do you want? B: *That chair.*	A: Quale sedia[f] vuoi? B: **Quella** sedia.
A: Which language do you prefer? B: *This language.*	A: Quale lingua[f] preferisci? B: **Questa** lingua.
A: Which books did you read? B: *These books.*	A: Quali libri[m] hai letto? B: **Questi** libri.
A: Which cell phone do you use? B: *This cell phone.*	A: Quale cellulare[m] utilizzi? B: **Questo** cellulare.
A: Which schools are the best? B: *Those schools.*	A: Quali scuole[f] sono le migliori? B: **Quelle** scuole.
A: Which of your uncles lives here? B: *That uncle.*	A: Quale dei tuoi zii[m] abita qui? B: **Quello** zio.
A: Which lawyers have you contacted? B: *Those lawyers.*	A: Quali avvocati[m] hai contattato? B: **Quegli** avvocati.
A: Which pants should I wear? B: *Those pants.*	A: Quali pantaloni[m] dovrei indossare? B: **Quei** pantaloni.
A: Which of your friends works here? B: *That friend.*	A: Quale dei tuoi amici[m] lavora qui? B: **Quell'** amico.

5. OBJECT PERSONAL PRONOUNS

Object pronouns can be divided into three classes: *prepositional, direct,* and *indirect* object pronouns.

Prepositional Object Pronouns

Prepositional object pronouns come after a preposition, such as "**di**" *(of, from,* or *about),* "**con**" *(with),* "**in**" *(in),* "**senza**" *(without),* etc.

Prepositional object pronouns are the same as subject pronouns except in the first- and second-person singular cases.

Personal Subject Pronoun	Prepositional Object Pronoun	Examples
io	me	Parlano di **me**. *They talk about **me**.*
tu	te	Questo regalo è per **te**. *This gift is for **you**.*
lui/lei	lui/lei	Esco con **lui**. *I go out with **him**.*
noi	noi	Non è contro di **noi**. *He is not against **us**.*
voi	voi	Mi fido di **voi**. *I trust in **you**.*
loro	loro	Non vado senza di **loro**. *I won't go without **them**.*

The reflexive prepositional pronouns are a special case of the prepositional object pronouns, such as *"myself," "yourself," "himself,"* etc. This is used when the subject and the object pronoun refer to the same person.

Subject Pronoun	Reflexive Prepositional Object Pronoun	Examples
io	me	Non parlo di **me**. *I don't talk about **myself**.*
tu	te	Hai comprato un regalo per **te**. *You bought a gift for **yourself**.*
lui/lei	se	Lei loda **se** stessa. *She praises **herself**.*
noi	noi	Lo facciamo per **noi**. *We do it for **ourselves**.*
voi	voi	Pensate solo a **voi**. *You only think of **yourselves**.*
loro	se	Parlano di **se** stessi. *They talk about **themselves**.*

❖ More often than not, the reflexive prepositional object pronoun is followed by the adjective **"stesso," "stessa," "stessi,"** or **"stesse,"** meaning *"same"* for emphasis. For example, in the expression **"Parlo di me stesso,"** meaning *"I speak about myself,"* the adjective **"stesso"** is added to emphasize that one is speaking about himself. The expression **"Parlo di me"** has the same meaning but without the emphasis.

❖ Note that **"se"** can mean *"himself,"* *"herself,"* *"itself,"* *"yourself"* (formal singular), *"themselves,"* or *"yourselves"* (formal plural), depending on the subject that it refers to.

Direct and Indirect Object Pronouns

The second and third classes of object pronouns are direct and indirect object pronouns. This tends to be one of the most challenging grammar lessons for English-speaking students. Nevertheless, the use of direct and indirect objects is so ubiquitous that we feel obliged to cover it at this beginner level. Feel free to return to this lesson at times of confusion if you do not fully grasp all the details.

Before we delve into the details, let us first define the difference between the two classes, since the distinction in English is not always clear. The direct object is the noun directly acted upon, whereas the indirect object is usually the noun (or person) receiving the direct object. For example, in the expressions *"He gives it to us"* and *"I give it to you,"* the *"it"* is the direct object acted upon in both examples, whereas *"us"* is the indirect object in the first example and *"you"* in the second. In English, we use *"me," "you," "him," "her," "us,"* and *"them,"* regardless of whether we are referring to a direct or indirect object. In Italian, there are some differences.

❖ The direct and indirect object pronouns generally come before the verb, e.g., **"ce lo dà"** (*He gives it to us*). Attachment to the end of the verb will be discussed as an exception.

❖ The indirect object always comes before the direct object when they are both in the same sentence.

❖ Unlike in English, we do not add the equivalent of *"to"* before the indirect object, e.g., *"I give it to you"* becomes *"**te lo do**"* where *"**te**"* means *"to you"* in this context.

Now, let us learn the direct and indirect object pronouns and their equivalents in English.

Direct Object Pronoun	Indirect Object Pronoun	English Equivalent
mi	mi	me
ti	ti	you (informal singular)
lo/la	gli/le	him/her/it/you (formal singular)
ci	ci	us
vi	vi	you (informal plural)
li/le	gli/gli	them/you (formal plural)

Notice that the direct and the indirect object pronouns are only different in the third-person singular and plural forms. The direct and indirect objects for the formal *"you,"* in singular and plural forms, should be capitalized.

Let us take some examples:

He knows me.	**Mi** conosce.	"**mi**" is a direct object
He knows us.	**Ci** conosce.	"**ci**" is a direct object
That book! I want it. *That pen! I want it.*	Quel libro! **Lo** voglio. Quella penna! **La** voglio.	Depending on the gender, "**lo**" or "**la**" is used as the direct object *"it"*
I know him. *I will give him something.*	**Lo** conosco. **Gli** darò qualcosa.	"**lo**" is a direct object "**gli**" is an indirect object
I know her. *I will give her something.*	**La** conosco. **Le** darò qualcosa.	"**la**" is a direct object "**le**" is an indirect object
Those guys! I know them. *I will give them something.*	Quei ragazzi! **Li** conosco. **Gli** darò qualcosa.	"**li**" is a direct object "**gli**" is an indirect object
Those girls! I know them. *I will give them something.*	Quelle ragazze! **Le** conosco. **Gli** darò qualcosa.	"**le**" is a direct object "**gli**" is an indirect object

Notice that "**gli**" is the indirect object used both for third-person masculine singular *"him,"* and for third-person masculine and feminine plural *"them."*

Attaching Object Pronouns to Verb Ends

Now, let us look at the three cases in which the direct or indirect object pronoun attaches to the end of the verb. Object pronouns attach to the infinitive, gerund (ending with "-**ando**" or "-**endo**," equivalent to "-*ing*" in English), or affirmative imperative. Note that the final "-**e**" of the verb is dropped when the pronoun is attached to the infinitive or gerund.

Voglio **farlo**.	*I want to do it.*	obj. pron. + infinitive
Sto **guardandolo**.	*I am watching it.*	direct obj. pron. + gerund
Aprilo.	*Open it.*	dir. obj. pron. + imperative
Chiedigli dei soldi.	*Ask him for money.*	ind. obj. pron. + imperative

Keep in mind that attachment is optional in some of the cases above. The sentences in the first and the second columns of the following examples are equivalent.

Voglio **farlo**.	**Lo** voglio **fare**.	*I want to do it.*
Sto **guardandolo**.	**Lo** sto **guardando**.	*I am watching it.*

Combining Direct and Indirect Object Pronouns

We will examine how to combine direct and indirect objects in the same sentence through the following two examples:

❖ Let us take the example: *"She sells me the house."* This translates to:

Lei mi vende la casa.

In the above example, we recognize that "**la casa**" *(the house)* is the direct object being acted upon, i.e., being sold, whereas "**mi**" *(me)* is the indirect object that receives the direct object, i.e., the house is being sold *to me.*

Let us first focus on the direct object in "**Lei vende la casa**" *(She sells the house)*. If we remove the direct object, "**la casa**" *(the house)*, to say *"She sells it,"* we must use "**lo**" or "**la**" to refer to the

direct object pronoun *"it."* Since **"la casa"** is feminine, we must use **"la"**:

Lei <u>la</u> vende.

Next, we add the indirect object **"mi"** *before* the direct object **"la"** to say *"She sells <u>it to me</u>"*:

Lei <u>mi</u> <u>la</u> vende. (This would be wrong)

When the indirect object **"mi"** is followed by the direct object **"la,"** the indirect object is changed to **"me."** Thus, we instead say:

Lei <u>me</u> <u>la</u> vende. *(She sells <u>it to me</u>.)*

❖ Let us take another example: *"I send <u>him</u> a gift."* This translates to:

Io <u>gli</u> mando un regalo.

Here, **"un regalo"** *(a gift)* is the direct object, whereas **"gli"** *(him)* is the indirect object.

Let us first focus on the direct object in **"Io mando un regalo …"** *(I send a gift …)*. If we remove the direct object **"un regalo"** *(a gift)* to say *"I send <u>it</u> …,"* we must use **"lo"** or **"la"** to refer to the direct object pronoun *"it."* Since **"un regalo"** is masculine, we must use **"lo"**:

Io <u>lo</u> mando …

Now, we add the indirect object **"gli"** *before* the direct object **"lo"** to say *"I send <u>it to him</u>"*:

Io <u>gli</u> <u>lo</u> mando. (This would be wrong)

When the indirect object **"gli"** is followed by the direct object **"lo,"** they form one word **"glielo."** Thus, we instead say:

Io glielo mando.

In general:

1. When the indirect object **"mi,"** **"ti,"** **"ci,"** or **"vi"** is followed by the direct object **"lo,"** **"la,"** **"li,"** or **"le,"** the indirect object is changed to **"me,"** **"te,"** **"ce,"** or **"ve,"** respectively.

mi/ti/ci/vi +	lo	=	me/te/ce/ve lo
	la	=	me/te/ce/ve la
	li	=	me/te/ce/ve li
	le	=	me/te/ce/ve le

2. When the indirect object **"gli"** or **"le"** is followed by the direct object **"lo,"** **"la,"** **"li,"** or **"le,"** they form one word:

gli/le +	lo	=	glielo
	la	=	gliela
	li	=	glieli
	le	=	gliele

Here are a few more examples:

I send ***them to her.***	Io **glieli** mando.	*le + li = glieli*
I send ***it to them.***	Io **glielo** mando.	*gli + lo = glielo*
I send ***her to them.***	Io **gliela** mando.	*gli + la = gliela*

6. RELATIVE PRONOUNS

Most interrogative pronouns can be used as relative pronouns, e.g., **"Qui è <u>dove</u> voglio essere"** *(Here is <u>where</u> I want to be)*, **"Te lo dirò <u>quando</u> mi ricorderò"** *(I will tell you <u>when</u> I remember)*, etc. The most common relative pronouns used in Italian are **"chi"** *(who)*, **"che"** *(that/who)*, and **"cui"** *(which/whom)*. Here is a summary of some relative pronouns in Italian:

Relative pronoun	English meaning	Examples
che	*that*	Il tè **che** ti piace è qui.
	who	*The tea **that** you like is here.*
cui	*which*	Questa è la persona a **cui** hanno chiesto.
	whom	*This is the person **whom** they asked?*

chi	*those who* *whoever*	**Chi** vince prende tutto. ***Whoever** wins takes it all.*
il quale (sing. m.) **la quale** (sing. f.) **i quali** (pl. m.) **le quali** (pl. f.)	*which*	Discutono di un argomento importante, **il quale** ti riguarda. *They are discussing an important topic **which** affects you.*
il cui (sing. m.) **la cui** (sing. f.) **i cui** (pl. m.) **le cui** (pl. f.)	*whose*	È l'uomo **i cui** due figli sono dottori. *This is the man **whose** two sons are doctors.*
del quale (sing. m.) **della quale** (sing. f.) **dei quali** (pl. m.) **delle quali** (pl. f.)	*whose*	È l'uomo **del quale** due figli sono dottori. *This is the man **whose** two sons are doctors.*

❖ The relative pronoun "**che**," meaning *"that"* or *"who,"* is the most generic and can refer to a thing, a place, or a person. As long as it is not preceded by a preposition such as "**a**," "**di**," "**con**," "**tra**," etc., the use of "**che**" is often appropriate in most contexts.

❖ The pronoun "**cui**" is often used to convey more complex meanings when preceded by a preposition, such as "**di cui**" *(about which/whom)*, "**a cui**" *(whom or at whom)*, "**con cui**" *(with whom)*, e.g., "**Questa è la persona <u>a cui</u> hanno chiesto**" *(This is the person <u>whom</u> they asked)*, "**Questo è il libro <u>su cui</u> discutono**" *(This is the book <u>about which</u> they debate)*, etc.

❖ The relative pronoun "**chi**" can only refer to a person or persons, and cannot refer to a thing or a place. It is always singular even if it refers to multiple persons, and is often used in proverbs and general statements meaning *"those who"* or *"whoever,"* e.g., "**<u>Chi</u> vince, detta le regole**" *(<u>Whoever</u> wins sets the rules)*, "**Non mi piace <u>chi</u> giura**" *(I don't like <u>those who</u> swear)*, etc. As a general rule, if you refer to a person and follow that by a simple relative pronoun such as *"who"* or *"that,"* "**che**" is often used instead, e.g., "**Il mio amico, <u>che</u> è ingegnere, me lo ha detto**" *(My friend, <u>who</u> is an engineer, told me this)*.

❖ Since "**che**," "**chi**," and "**cui**" all can refer to a person, it is important to emphasize when to use each. The following is a summary in the context of some examples:

"che," "chi," & "cui"?	Explanation
Questo è il ristorante **che** ha aperto la scorsa settimana. *This is the restaurant **that** opened last week.*	Referring to a place using the simple relative pronoun *"that"* right after the noun. Thus, use "**che**."
Questo è l'insegnante **che** mi ha insegnato al liceo. *This is the teacher **who** taught me in high school.*	Referring to a person using the simple relative pronoun *"who"* right after the noun. Thus, use "**che**."
Questo è il film **di cui** vi ho parlato. *This is the movie **about which** I told you.*	Referring to a thing using the relative pronoun *"which"* preceded by a preposition. Thus, use "**cui**."
Sono i giocatori **con cui** giocavo. *They are the players **with whom** I used to play.*	Referring to a person using the relative pronoun *"whom"* preceded by a preposition. Thus, use "**cui**."
Chi è interessato cercherà una risposta. ***Those who** are interested will look for an answer.*	Referring to a group of people using *"those who"* in general. Thus, use "**chi**."

❖ The relative pronoun "**il quale**" (and its gender and number variants) can replace "**che**" or "**cui**" in formal writing, but are not commonly used in spoken Italian, e.g., "**Leggerò il libro, il quale era nel garage**" (*I will read the book, the one that was in the garage*), "**Pulirò la sedia dietro la quale il gatto gioca**" (*I will clean the chair behind which the cat plays*), etc.

❖ The relative pronoun "**cui**," preceded by a definite article, has a similar use to the English *"whose"* e.g., "**Questo è l'uomo il cui figlio è dottore**" (*This is the man whose son is a doctor*).

❖ The relative pronouns "**del quale**," "**della quale**," "**dei quali**," and "**delle quali**" can also be used in a similar way to "**il cui**," "**la cui**," "**i cui**," and "**le cui**," respectively, e.g., "**Questo è** l'uomo <u>del quale</u> il figlio è dottore" *(This is the man <u>whose</u> son is a doctor).*

7. ORDINAL NUMBERS I

Ordinal numbers describe the order of a noun. Thus, it is considered an adjective and must agree in gender and number with the noun. Here are the ordinal numbers in Italian from 1 to 10. Notice the four possible different endings (and the superscript variants) for each ordinal number depending on the gender and number of the noun.

uno, una, un'	1	primo/-a/-i/-e	$1.^o$ / $1.^a$ / $1.^i$ / $1.^e$
due	2	secondo/-a/-i/-e	$2.^o$ / $2.^a$ / $2.^i$ / $2.^e$
tre	3	terzo/-a/-i/-e	$3.^o$ / $3.^a$ / $3.^i$ / $3.^e$
quattro	4	quarto/-a/-i/-e	$4.^o$ / $4.^a$ / $4.^i$ / $4.^e$
cinque	5	quinto/-a/-i/-e	$5.^o$ / $5.^a$ / $5.^i$ / $5.^e$
sei	6	sesto/-a/-i/-e	$6.^o$ / $6.^a$ / $6.^i$ / $6.^e$
sette	7	settimo/-a/-i/-e	$7.^o$ / $7.^a$ / $7.^i$ / $7.^e$
otto	8	ottavo/-a/-i/-e	$8.^o$ / $8.^a$ / $8.^i$ / $8.^e$
nove	9	nono/-a/-i/-e	$9.^o$ / $9.^a$ / $9.^i$ / $9.^e$
dieci	10	decimo/-a/-i/-e	$10.^o$ / $10.^a$ / $10.^i$ / $10.^e$

❖ The ordinal numbers are abbreviated as follows:

1. Masculine/Singular: cardinal number + " . " + " ^{o} ," e.g., "**primo**" ($1.^o$), "**quarto**" ($4.^o$), "**nono**" ($9.^o$).

2. Feminine/Singular: cardinal number + " . " + " ^{a} ," e.g., "**prima**" ($1.^a$), "**quarta**" ($4.^a$), "**nona**" ($9.^a$).

3. Masculine/Plural: cardinal number + " . " + " ^{i} ," e.g., "**primi**" ($1.^i$), "**quarti**" ($4.^i$), "**noni**" ($9.^i$).

4. Feminine/Plural: cardinal number + " . " + " ^{e} ," e.g., "**prime**" ($1.^e$), "**quarte**" ($4.^e$), "**none**" ($9.^e$).

❖ Unlike in English, where dates are described using ordinal numbers, e.g., *"the 24th of October,"* in Italian, dates are expressed using cardinal numbers, e.g., "**il 24 (di) ottobre.**" A notable exception is the first day of the month, in which case the ordinal number is used, e.g., **"il primo (di) novembre."**

Fractional Numbers

❖ Fractional numbers from *third* to *tenth* are the same as the ordinal number, e.g., **"un quarto dei giocatori"** (*a fourth of the players*), **"un quinto delle risorse"** (*a fifth of the resources*), etc.

❖ To describe the fractional number 1/2 *(half)*, we use the adjective **"mezzo"** (masculine) or **"mezza"** (feminine), both of which can be abbreviated as **"mezz'"** before a vowel, e.g., **"mezzo chilo"** *(half a kilo)*, **"mezz'ora"** *(half an hour)*, **"mezza dozzina"** *(half a dozen)*, etc.

❖ We also use the feminine noun **"metà"** to describe half the quantity of something, and it is often followed by **"di,"** e.g., **"metà del terreno"** *(half of the land)*.

❖ The main difference that you need to remember to distinguish between **"mezzo/-a"** and **"metà"** is that the former is often an adjective, whereas the latter is a noun, e.g., **"metà della classe"** *(half of the class)*, and in a few cases, can be an adverb, e.g., **"a metà"** *(halfway or half-finished)*.

❖ In numbers formed by an integer and a fraction, the **"un"** can be dropped only before 1/2, if preceded by an integer, e.g., 1 ½ **(uno e mezzo)**, 3 ¼ **(tre e un quarto)**, 5 ⅛ **(cinque e un ottavo)**.

We will cover higher ordinal numbers and fractions in **Level VI, Lesson 1.**

8. Basic Phrases

Learning greetings and short conversations is essential for taking the first steps to communicate in any language. Take some time to practice the following formal and informal basic phrases.

Ciao	*Hi (informal)* *Bye (informal)*
Buongiorno.	*Good morning.*
Buon pomeriggio.	*Good afternoon.*
Buona sera.	*Good evening.*
Buona notte.	*Good night.*
Come sta?	*How are you? (formal, singular)*
Come stai?	*How are you? (informal, singular)*
Cosa c'è? Cosa succede?	*What's up?*
Sto bene.	*I am fine.*
Molto bene.	*Very good.*
Non molto bene.	*Not so good.*
Così così.	*So-so.*
Arrivederci.	*Goodbye. (formal)*
Buona giornata.	*Have a nice day.*
Grazie.	*Thank you.*
Prego.	*You're welcome. It's nothing.*
Per favore.	*Please.*
Non tanto.	*Nothing much.*
Mi dispiace.	*Sorry.*
Scusi. Mi scusi.	*Excuse me. (formal)*
Scusa. Scusami.	*Excuse me. (informal)*
Piacere.	*Nice to meet you.*
A dopo.	*See you later.*
A presto.	*See you soon.*
A domani.	*See you tomorrow.*
Benvenuto. (addressing a male) Benvenuta. (addressing a female)	*Welcome.*
Come ti chiami?	*What is your name? (informal, singular)*
Come si chiama?	*What is your name? (formal, singular)*
Mi chiamo…	*My name is …*
Sono …	*I am …*
Quanti anni hai?	*How old are you? (informal, singular)*
Quanti anni ha?	*How old are you? (formal, singular)*
Ho 20 anni.	*I am 20 years old.*
Di dove sei?	*Where are you from? (informal, singular)*
Di dove è?	*Where are you from? (formal, singular)*
Da che parte?	*From which part?*

Vengo da ...	*I am from ... (I come from ...)*
Dove sei stato?	*Where have you been?*
Non capisco.	*I don't understand.*
Parli inglese?	*Do you speak English? (informal, singular)*
Parla inglese?	*Do you speak English? (formal, singular)*
Dove vivi?	*Where do you live? (informal, singular)*
Dove vive?	*Where do you live? (formal, singular)*
Quanto costa questo?	*How much does this cost?*
Il conto, per favore.	*The bill, please.*
Mi puoi aiutare?	*Can you help me? (informal)*
Puoi parlare più lentamente?	*Can you speak more slowly? (informal)*
Come posso arrivare?	*How can I get there?*

II. Vocabulary Building

Here, we cover basic verbs and adjectives in the first two sections, then we go over nouns from different categories.

1. VERBS II

Below is a list of the next most common 60 verbs in Italian:

English	Italian	Examples
allow	permettere	Mia madre non mi **permette** di mangiare caramelle. *My mom doesn't **allow** me to eat candy.*
answer	rispondere	Non sarò in grado di **rispondere** al telefono. *I won't be able to **answer** the phone.*
ask (question)	fare una domanda [1]	Voglio **fare una domanda** importante. *I want to **ask** an important question.*
ask (request)	chiedere [1]	Non devi aspettare per **chiedere** aiuto. *You don't need to wait to **ask** for help.*
bother annoy	infastidire	I profumi forti mi **infastidiscono**. *Strong scents **bother** me.*
build	costruire	Voglio **costruire** una recinzione qui. *I want to **build** a fence here.*
buy	comprare	Carlo **compra** il pane tutti i giorni. *Carlo **buys** bread every day.*

---

[1] We use "**fare una domanda**" (*to ask a question*) when we refer to asking questions. On the other hand, we use "**chiedere**" (*to ask for*) when we refer to requesting something or ordering from a restaurant.

choose	scegliere	**Scelgo** spesso gusti alla frutta. *I often **choose** fruit flavors.*
clean	pulire	Devo **pulire** il bagno al più presto. *I must **clean** the bathroom later.*
cook	cucinare	Mio fratello **cucina** tutti i giorni. *My brother **cooks** every day.*
cover	coprire	Dovrei **coprire** l'impasto con un canovaccio. *I should **cover** the dough with a cloth.*
cry	piangere	Non mi piace vedere le persone **piangere**. *I don't like to see people **cry**.*
dance	ballare danzare	Non **ballo** molto bene. *I don't **dance** very well.*
die	morire	Vuole fare testamento prima di **morire**. *He wants to write a will before **dying**.*
dine	cenare	Andremo a **cenare** al ristorante italiano. *We'll go **dine** at the Italian restaurant.*
disappear	scomparire	Le zanzare **scompaiono** in inverno. *Mosquitoes **disappear** in winter.*
discover	scoprire	Voglio **scoprire** un caffè vicino a casa. *I want to **discover** a café close to home.*
draw	disegnare	Voglio **disegnare** questo paesaggio. *I want to **draw** this landscape.*
drive	guidare	Voglio imparare a **guidare**. *I want to learn how to **drive**.*
express	esprimere	Fa bene **esprimere** le emozioni. *It's good to **express** emotions.*
find	trovare	Devo **trovare** le mie chiavi. *I must **find** my keys.*
forget	dimenticare	**Dimentico** sempre la mia password. *I always **forget** my password.*
get obtain	ottenere	Dove posso **ottenere** del cibo? *Where can I **get** food?*
go shopping	andare a fare shopping	Possiamo **andare a fare shopping** questo sabato. *We can **go shopping** this Saturday.*
grow	crescere	Questo albero **cresce** molto velocemente. *This tree **grows** very fast.*
hear	sentire udire	**Sento** una voce provenire da lontano. *I **hear** a voice coming from afar.*
help	aiutare	Mio figlio **aiuta** sempre in giardino. *My son always **helps** in the garden.*
joke	scherzare	**Scherzo** molto con i miei cugini. *I **joke** a lot with my cousins.*
kiss	baciare	**Bacio** il mio gatto sul naso ogni giorno. *I **kiss** my cat on its nose every day.*

laugh	ridere	È bello **ridere** di tanto in tanto. *It's good to **laugh** from time to time.*
lie	mentire	Mio figlio **mente** sulla sua età. *My son **lies** about his age.*
listen to **hear**	ascoltare	Devi **ascoltare** altre opinioni. *You must **listen to** other opinions.*
lose	perdere	**Perdo** sempre le monete più piccole. *I always **lose** the smaller coins.*
mean	significare volere dire	Cosa **vuoi dire?** *What do you **mean?***
need	avere bisogno di	**Ho bisogno di** prendermi cura dei miei bambini. *I **need** to take care of my children.*
pay	pagare	**Pago** tutte le bollette all'inizio del mese. *I **pay** all my bills at the start of the month.*
plan	pianificare	**Pianifico** sempre cosa mangerò. *I always **plan** what I'll eat.*
play **(sports)**	giocare	Mio cugino **gioca** a calcio il sabato. *My cousin **plays** football on Saturdays.*
rain	piovere	Potrebbe **piovere** questo mercoledì. *It may **rain** this Wednesday.*
relax	rilassare	È bello **rilassare** le gambe. *It's good to **relax** your legs.*
repair	riparare	Devi **riparare** quella macchina. *You have to **repair** that car.*
reply **respond**	rispondere	Non **risponde** mai ai miei messaggi. *He never **responds** to my messages.*
rest	riposare	Mi piace **riposare** in piscina. *I like to **rest** by the pool.*
run	correre	È pericoloso **correre** veloci per strada. *It is dangerous to **run** fast in the street.*
search for **look for**	cercare	Vuole **cercare** le chiavi per uscire. *She wants to **search for** the keys to go out.*
sell	vendere	Questo negozio **vende** solo dolci. *This store only **sells** desserts.*
send	inviare mandare	Dovrei **mandar**gli un messaggio. *I should **send** him a message.*
share	condividere	Devi **condividere** con tuo fratello. *You have to **share** with your brother.*
show	mostrare	Voglio **mostrar**ti la cucina. *I want to **show** you the kitchen.*
sing	cantare	Quel giovane **canta** magnificamente. *That young man **sings** beautifully.*
smile	sorridere	**Sorrido** sempre per le foto. *I always **smile** for photos.*

smoke	fumare	Qui non è consentito **fumare**. *Smoking is not allowed here.*
snow	nevicare	**Nevica** molto in inverno. *It snows a lot in winter.*
swim	nuotare	Vado a **nuotare** nel fiume. *I go swimming in the river.*
teach	insegnare	Voglio **insegnar**ti come si fa. *I want to teach you how it's done.*
translate	tradurre	Puoi **tradurre** questo file? *Can you translate this file?*
try	provare cercare di	**Cerco** sempre **di** arrivare in anticipo. *I always try to arrive early.*
wait (for)	aspettare	Deve **aspettare** l'autobus. *He has to wait for the bus.*
wash	lavare	Devi **lavare** i piatti dopo cena. *You must wash the dishes after dinner.*
win	vincere	Posso **vincere** la gara. *I can win the race.*

In addition to the above new verbs, let us take advantage of English cognates to memorize the following verbs.

English	Italian	Examples
abandon	abbandonare	Alcune persone **abbandonano** i loro hobby. *Some people abandon their hobbies.*
accuse	accusare	Non va bene **accusare** senza fondamento. *It's not okay to accuse without grounds.*
appear	apparire	Una celebrità potrebbe **apparire** oggi nello show. *A celebrity may appear today on the show.*
appreciate	apprezzare	**Apprezzo** molto quello che fanno i miei genitori. *I really appreciate what my parents do.*
comprehend	comprendere	Non riesco a **comprendere** queste istruzioni. *I can't comprehend these instructions.*
confess	confessare	**Confesso** di aver mangiato tutti i biscotti. *I confess I ate all the cookies.*
consider	considerare	Devi **considerare** come si sentono gli altri. *You must consider how others feel.*
consist	consistere	Il complesso **consiste** di tre castelli. *The complex consists of three castles.*
consult	consultare	Ho bisogno di **consultare** un professionista. *I need to consult a professional.*
count	contare	Mio figlio piccolo sa **contare** fino a dieci. *My little son knows how to count to ten.*

differentiate	differenziare	Non sono in grado di **differenziare** i gatti. *I am unable to **differentiate** between the cats.*
distribute	distribuire	Il postino **distribuisce** la posta al mattino. *The postman **distributes** the mail in the morning.*
divide	dividere	Questa strada **divide** le due città. *This street **divides** the two cities.*
estimate	stimare	**Stimo** che sarà fatto in 30 minuti. *I **estimate** it'll be done in 30 minutes.*
explore	esplorare	Adoro **esplorare** le città che non conosco. *I love **exploring** cities I don't know.*
extend	estendere	Vogliamo **estendere** il nostro soggiorno qui. *We want to **extend** our stay here.*
force	forzare	Non dovresti **forzare** la serratura. *You shouldn't **force** the lock.*
ignore	ignorare	Non è facile **ignorare** i rumori forti. *It's not easy to **ignore** loud noises.*
imitate	imitare	Il mio fratellino mi **imita** sempre. *My little brother always **imitates** me.*
inform	informare	Devi **informar**mi se hai intenzione di uscire. *You have to **inform** me if you plan on going out.*
limit	limitare	**Limito** le mie caramelle a una a settimana. *I **limit** my candies to one per week.*
manipulate	manipolare	Non è bello **manipolare** le persone. *It's not nice to **manipulate** people.*
mention	menzionare	Questo libro non **menziona** tutti i dettagli. *This book doesn't **mention** all the details.*
minimize	minimizzare	Non dovremmo **minimizzare** la situazione. *We shouldn't **minimize** the situation.*
modify **edit**	modificare	Devo **modificare** alcuni dati nel documento. *I must **modify** some data in the document.*
pass	passare [1]	Potrei **passare** da casa tua più tardi. *I could **pass** by your house later.*
prefer	preferire	**Preferisco** le verdure al pane. *I **prefer** vegetables to bread.*
pronounce	pronunciare	Non è facile **pronunciare** il mio nome in inglese. *It's not easy to **pronounce** my name in English.*
prosper	prosperare	Le imprese **prosperano** in estate. *Businesses **prosper** in the summer.*
regulate	regolare	Il governo vuole **regolare** il mercato. *The government wants to **regulate** the market.*

---

[1] The verb **"passare"** can also mean *"to spend (time),"* e.g., **Mi piace passare il tempo nel parco"** *(I like spending time in the park).*

reside	risiedere	**Risiede** vicino alla capitale. *She* **resides** *near the capital.*
select	selezionare	Devi **selezionare** la risposta giusta. *You must* **select** *the right answer.*
suffer	soffrire	A nessuno piace **soffrire** di malattie. *No one likes to* **suffer** *from illnesses.*
verify check	verificare	I medici **verificano** i risultati dopo il test. *The doctors* **verify** *the results after the test.*

2. ADJECTIVES II

Below is a list of adjectives that we need at this level. Notice that an adjective must agree with the noun in number and gender.

English	Italian	Examples
additional	aggiuntivo	Ho bisogno di una busta **aggiuntiva**. *I need an* **additional** *envelope.*
any	qualsiasi	Mi piace il gelato di **qualsiasi** gusto. *I like ice cream of* **any** *flavor.*
available	disponibile	Il sedile del passeggero è **disponibile**. *The passenger's seat is* **available**.
awake	sveglio	Cerco di rimanere **sveglio** in classe. *I try to remain* **awake** *in class.*
basic	di base	Dovresti conoscere le regole **di base**. *You should know the* **basic** *rules.*
blond	biondo	I capelli del mio vicino sono **biondi**. *My neighbor's hair is* **blond**.
both	entrambi	**Entrambi** i genitori sono invitati. **Both** *parents are invited.*
comfortable	comodo confortevole	Questa poltrona è molto **comoda**. *This armchair is very* **comfortable**.
each	ogni	**Ogni** persona è differente. **Each** *person is different.*
empty	vuoto	Il posto è **vuoto**. *The seat is* **empty**.
equal	uguale pari	Entrambe le pareti sono **uguali**. *Both walls are* **equals**.
fair just	giusto	Cerco sempre di essere **giusto** con i miei figli. *I always try to be* **fair** *with my children.*
faraway distant	lontano	I miei nonni vivono in un paese **lontano**. *My grandparents live in a* **faraway** *country.*
favorite	preferito favorito	Qual è il tuo film **preferito**? *What is your* **favorite** *movie?*

fresh	fresco	L'acqua con il cetriolo ha un sapore **fresco**. *Water with cucumber has a **fresh** taste.*
friendly	amichevole	Il mio gatto è molto **amichevole**. *My cat is very **friendly**.*
full	pieno	Voglio che il serbatoio sia **pieno**. *I want the tank to be **full**.*
funny	divertente buffo	Quest'uomo è molto **divertente**. *This man is very **funny**.*
healthy	sano salutare	Mangiare verdura tutti i giorni è **sano**. *Eating vegetables every day is **healthy**.*
light (weight)	leggero	Quando viaggio, preparo una valigia **leggera**. *When I travel, I pack a **light** suitcase.*
lonely	solitario	Il mio gatto è un animale **solitario**. *My cat is a **lonely** animal.*
loud noisy	rumoroso	Mio figlio è molto **rumoroso**. *My son is very **loud**.*
lucky	fortunato	Sei molto **fortunato** se vinci oggi. *You are very **lucky** if you win today.*
nearby close	vicino	L'università si trova in un quartiere **vicino**. *The university is in a **nearby** neighborhood.*
nice cute (object)	carino	Mi comprerò un vestito molto **carino**. *I'll buy myself a very **nice** dress.*
pleasant nice (person)	piacevole simpatico	Mio zio è una persona **piacevole**. *My uncle is a **pleasant** person.*
polite	educato cortese	Mio nipote è un bambino molto **educato**. *My nephew is a very **polite** child.*
reasonable	ragionevole	Il mio capo è molto **ragionevole**. *My boss is very **reasonable**.*
salty	salato	Mi piacciono i popcorn **salati**. *I like **salty** popcorn.*
shy	timido	Mi dispiace, è molto **timido**. *I'm sorry, he's very **shy**.*
silly	sciocco	È **sciocco** preoccuparsi senza motivo. *It's **silly** to worry without a reason.*
simple	semplice	L'esame è molto **semplice**. *The exam is very **simple**.*
strict	severo	Il mio vicino è **severo** con i suoi figli. *My neighbor is **strict** with his children.*
true	vero	Un **vero** amico non ti mente. *A **true** friend doesn't lie to you.*

unfair	ingiusto sleale	Quell'arbitro è molto **ingiusto**. *That referee is very **unfair**.*
unlucky	sfortunato	Mio cugino è una persona **sfortunata**. *My cousin is an **unlucky** person.*
useful	utile	Le forbici sono uno strumento **utile**. *Scissors are a **useful** tool.*
useless	inutile	Senza gas, il mio accendino è **inutile**. *Without gas, my lighter is **useless**.*
weird **strange**	strano	So che sembra **strano**. *I know this looks **strange**.*
worried	preoccupato	Sono molto **preoccupato** per te! *I am very **worried** about you!*
wrong	sbagliato	Non voglio prendere la strada **sbagliata**. *I don't want to take the **wrong** road.*

In addition to the above new adjectives, we add a few more English cognates that are easy to memorize.

English	Italian	Examples
brilliant	brillante	La figlia di mio cugino è **brillante**. *My cousin's daughter is **brilliant**.*
complicated	complicato	Fare la tua propria pasta è **complicato**. *Making your own pasta is **complicated**.*
delicious	delizioso	Questa torta nuziale è **deliziosa**. *This wedding cake is **delicious**.*
dishonest	disonesto	Non mi fido di lui perché è **disonesto**. *I don't trust him because he's **dishonest**.*
educational	educativo	Guardare video **educativi** è utile. *Watching **educational** videos is helpful.*
false **fake**	falso	Quella pianta è **falsa**. *That plant is **fake**.*
famous	famoso	Mio cugino è uno scrittore **famoso**. *My cousin is a **famous** writer.*
feminine **female**	femminile	Il suo stile è piuttosto **femminile**. *Her style is pretty **feminine**.*
festive	festivo	L'estate è un momento **festivo**. *Summer is a **festive** time.*
firm **steady**	fermo	Questo tavolo mi sembra **fermo**. *This table seems **steady** to me.*
generous	generoso	Vogliono fare una **generosa** donazione all'ospedale. *They want to make a **generous** donation to the hospital.*
mental	mentale	La salute **mentale** è estremamente importante. ***Mental** health is extremely important.*

nervous	nervoso	Sono **nervoso** per l'esame. *I'm **nervous** about the exam.*
physical	fisico	Devo fare un esame **fisico**. *I have to get a **physical** exam done.*
political	politico	Non consiglio di parlare di questioni **politiche**. *I don't recommend talking about **political** matters.*
popular	popolare	Mia sorella è **popolare** a scuola. *My sister is **popular** at school.*
precious	prezioso	Un diamante è una pietra **preziosa**. *A diamond is a **precious** stone.*
recent	recente	La notizia è molto **recente**. *The news is very **recent**.*
resident	residente	Infine, otterrò lo status di **residente**. *Finally, I will obtain **resident** status.*
responsible	responsabile	Cerco di essere molto **responsabile** sul lavoro. *I try to be very **responsible** at work.*
serious	serio	Mio nonno è una persona molto **seria**. *My grandfather is a very **serious** person.*
significant	significativo	Il tempo per me è molto **significativo**. *Time is very **significant** to me.*
terrible	terribile	Ho un **terribile** raffreddore. *I have a **terrible** cold.*
typical	tipico	Mi piace il cibo **tipico** della mia città. *I like my town's **typical** food.*
violent	violento	Questo uragano è molto **violento**. *This hurricane is very **violent**.*

3. TRANSPORTATION I

Transportation in Italian is "**il trasporto**." Below are some means of transportation and vocabulary related to transportation and traffic:

airplane	**aereo**^{m}	*penalty*	**pena**^{f} **penalità**^{f}
airport	**aeroporto**^{m}	*pick-up truck*	**camioncino**^{m}
bicycle	**bicicletta**^{f}	*police officer*	**poliziotto**^{m} **agente**^{m} di polizia **ufficiale**^{m} di polizia
boat	**barca**^{f}	*ship*	**nave**^{m}
brakes	**freni**^{m}	*sign*	**segnale**^{m} **cartello**^{m}
bus	**autobus**^{m}	*speed*	**velocità**^{f}

car	**automobile**[f] **macchina**[f] **autovettura**[f]	*subway*	**metropolitana**[f]
driver	**conducente**[m,f] **autista**[m,f]	*ticket (air, train)*	**biglietto**[m]
driver's license	**patente**[f] **di guida**	*ticket (fine)*	**multa**[f]
engine	**motore**[m]	*tire*	**pneumatico**[m]
envelope	**libretto**[m]	*traffic*	**traffico**[m]
flight	**volo**[m]	*train*	**treno**[m]
gasoline	**benzina**[f]	*train station*	**stazione ferroviaria**[f]
package	**pacchetto**[m]	*truck*	**camion**[m]

4. NATURE I

Some vocabulary related to *nature*, or "**la natura**," are:

air	**aria**[f]	*ocean*	**oceano**[m]
beach	**spiaggia**[f]	*park*	**parco**[m]
camp	**campeggio**[m]	*planet*	**pianeta**[m]
canteen	**mensa**[f]	*plant*	**pianta**[f]
cloud	**nuvola**[f]	*river*	**fiume**[m]
coast	**costa**[f]	*root*	**radice**[f]
countryside	**campagna**[f]	*sand*	**sabbia**[f]
desert	**deserto**[m]	*sea*	**mare**[m]
earth	**terra**[f]	*sky*	**cielo**[m]
fire	**fuoco**[m]	*snow*	**neve**[f]
flower	**fiore**[m]	*space*	**spazio**[m]
grass	**erba**[f] **prato**[m]	*star*	**stella**[f]
ground	**terra**[f] **terreno**[m]	*sun*	**sole**[m]
ice	**ghiaccio**[m]	*tree*	**albero**[m]
island	**isola**[f]	*universe*	**universo**[m]
lake	**lago**[m]	*weather*	**tempo**[m]
moon	**luna**[f]	*wind*	**vento**[m]
mountain	**montagna**[f]	*world*	**mondo**[m]

5. PLACES

A *place* in Italian is "**un posto**." This is a list of the most common places we encounter in our daily life:

apartment	**appartamento**^{m}	*hospital*	**ospedale**^{m}
area	**area**^{f}	*hotel*	**hotel**^{m} **albergo**^{m}
bakery	**forno**^{m} **panificio**^{m}	*location*	**posizione**^{f}
bank	**banca**^{f}	*market*	**mercato**^{m}
bar	**bar**^{m}	*office*	**ufficio**^{m}
bookstore	**libreria**^{f}	*parking*	**parcheggio**^{m}
bridge	**ponte**^{m}	*port* *harbor*	**porto**^{m}
building	**edificio**^{m}	*restaurant*	**ristorante**^{m}
center	**centro**^{m}	*school*	**scuola**^{f}
city	**città**^{f}	*shop*	**negozio**^{m}
club (sports)	**club**^{m}	*suburb*	**periferia**^{f}
court (law)	**tribunale**^{m} **corte**^{f}	*theater*	**teatro**^{m}
district	**distretto**^{m}	*university*	**università**^{f}
factory	**fabbrica**^{f}	*village*	**villaggio**^{m} **paese**^{m}
farm	**fattoria**^{f}	*work*	**lavoro**^{m}

6. FOOD I

An important subject in Italian is *food*, or "**il cibo.**" Here is some useful food vocabulary:

apple	**mela**^{f}	*lemon*	**limone**^{m}
apricot	**albicocca**^{f}	*lettuce*	**lattuga**^{f}
banana	**banana**^{f}	*mango*	**mango**^{m}
beef	**manzo**^{m}	*meat*	**carne**^{f}
beer	**birra**^{f}	*milk*	**latte**^{m}
bread	**pane**^{m}	*oil*	**olio**^{m}
broccoli	**broccoli**^{m}	*olive*	**oliva**^{f}
carrot	**carota**^{f}	*orange*	**arancia**^{f}
cheese	**formaggio**^{m}	*pork*	**maiale**^{m}
chicken	**pollo**^{m}	*refreshment*	**rinfresco**^{m}
coffee	**caffè**^{m}	*rice*	**riso**^{m}
egg	**uovo**^{m}	*salad*	**insalata**^{f}
eggplant	**melanzana**^{f}	*salt*	**sale**^{m}
fruit	**frutta**^{f}	*sugar*	**zucchero**^{m}
grape	**uva**^{f}	*tea*	**tè**^{m}
grapefruit	**pompelmo**^{m}	*tomato*	**pomodoro**^{m}

ice cream	**gelato**^m	*vegetable*	**verdura**^f
juice	**succo**^m	*water*	**acqua**^f
lamb	**agnello**^m	*wine*	**vino**^m

7. CLOTHES I

The word *clothes* in Italian is "**i vestiti**." Here you can learn some vocabulary related to clothing:

appearance	**aspetto**^m **apparenza**^f	*pants*	**pantaloni**^m
band	**fascia**^f	*pocket*	**tasca**^f
belt	**cinta**^f **cintura**^f	*purse*	**borsa**^f
bra	**reggiseno**^m	*ring*	**anello**^m
coat	**cappotto**^m	*shirt*	**camicia**^f
glasses	**occhiali**^m	*sunglasses*	**occhiali**^m **da sole**
glove	**guanto**^m	*skirt*	**gonna**^f
hat	**cappello**^m	*t-shirt*	**maglietta**^f
jacket	**giacca**^f	*underwear*	**intimo**^m **biancheria intima**^f
makeup	**trucco**^m	*wallet*	**portafogli**^m

8. EDUCATION

The following are vocabulary related to *education* or "**l'educazione**":

absence	**assenza**^f	*graduate*	**diplomato**^m
academy	**accademia**^f	*history* *story*¹	**storia**^f
arithmetic	**aritmetica**^f	*homework*	**compiti**^m
astronomy	**astronomia**^f	*list*	**lista**^f **elenco**^m
bachelor's degree	**laurea**^f	*master's degree*	**master**^m
backpack	**zaino**^m	*meaning*	**significato**^m
biology	**biologia**^f	*method*	**metodo**^m
board	**pannello**^m	*microscope*	**microscopio**^m

---

[1] A factual account is often referred to as "**storia**^f," whereas a fictional tale is referred to as "**racconto**^m."

break (pause)	**pausa**^{f}	notebook	**quaderno**^{m}
career	**carriera**^{f}	physics	**fisica**^{f}
chalkboard	**lavagna**^{f}	requirement	**requisito**^{m}
chemistry	**chimica**^{f}	response / answer	**risposta**^{f}
clarification	**chiarimento**^{m} **precisazione**^{f}	ruler	**righello**^{m}
class	**lezione**$^{f\,1}$	schedule	**orario**^{m}
course	**corso**^{m}	scholarship	**borsa**^{f} **di studio**
course material	**materiale**^{m} **del corso**	sheet (paper)	**foglio**^{m} **scheda**^{f}
degree	**titolo**^{m} **di studio**	summary	**riassunto**^{m}
doctorate	**dottorato**^{m}	system	**sistema**^{m}
eraser	**gomma**^{f}	technique	**tecnica**^{f}
faculty	**facoltà**^{f}	theory	**teoria**^{f}
good grades	**buoni voti**^{m}	way	**maniera**^{f}

[1] The word **"lezione"** (lesson) is used to refer to the time period we generally call a "class" in English, e.g., **"Prendo lezioni"** (I take classes). There is also the word **"classe"** in Italian which often refers to the participants in a class, e.g., **"Nessuno si è presentato in classe"** (No one showed up in class). To refer to a classroom, we use the word **"aula."**

9. SHOPPING

To go shopping in Italian is **"fare spese,"** whereas **"fare la spesa"** (in singular) means to go grocery shopping. Here you learn some vocabulary related to shopping:

bill	**conto**^{m}	money	**denaro**^{m} **soldi**^{m}
brand	**marca**^{f}	opening time	**orari**^{m} **di apertura**
card	**carta**^{f}	order	**ordine**^{m}
cash	**contanti**^{m}	payment	**pagamento**^{m}
chain	**catena**^{f}	penny	**centesimo**^{m}
complaint	**lamentela**^{f} **reclamo**^{m}	price	**prezzo**^{m}
cost	**costo**^{m}	purchase	**acquisto**^{m}
delivery	**consegna**^{f}	receipt	**ricevuta**^{f}
discount	**sconto**^{m}	register	**cassa**^{f}
fee	**tassa**^{f}	row (line)	**fila**^{f}
invoice	**fattura**^{f}	sale	**vendita**^{f}

kiosk	chiosco^m	shopping mall	centro commerciale^m
label tag	etichetta^f	spree binge	spese folli^f
line queue	coda^f fila^f	surprise	sorpresa^f
market	mercato^m	type	tipo^m
merchant	commerciante^m	value	valore^{m 1}

[1] The word "**valore^m**" can also mean *"courage"* or *"bravery."*

10. MATERIALS

Vocabulary related to *materials*, or "**i materiali**," can be useful to be familiar with. Here is a list of some common vocabulary:

cement	cemento^m	metal	metallo^m
copper	rame^m	petroleum	petrolio^m
cotton	cotone^m	plastic	plastica^f
diamond	diamante^m	silk	seta^f
dust powder	polvere^f	silver	argento^m
fiber	fibra^f	steel	acciaio^m
glass	vetro^m	substance	sostanza^f
gold	oro^m	synthesis	sintesi^f
iron	ferro^m	texture	struttura^f consistenza^f
lead	piombo^m	thread	filo^m
leather	cuoio^m	wood	legno^m
magnet	magnete^m	wool	lana^f

LEVEL III: ELEMENTARY

I. Introductory Topics & Grammar

Start by reading the introductory topics of this level. You will notice that some concepts are unique to the Italian language. You could also use Anki cards to practice with reviews and exercises.

1. VERBS LIKE "PIACERE"

Some expressions use a different sentence structure in Italian compared to that used in English to express the same meaning. One of the most common examples is the use of verbs like **"piacere"** *(to please)*. Let us examine this sentence in Italian:

Mi piace la macchina.

This is often translated as: *"I like the car."*

A more accurate and literal translation would be:

"The car is pleasing to me."

Note that the verb conjugation is in the third-person singular form, **"piace,"** because **"la macchina"** is the subject that does the act of pleasing, and **"mi"** is the object. Thus, the conjugation of the verb **"piacere"** must agree with the subject **"la macchina."**

Let us take another example. If you want to say that someone is interested in ancient cultures, the best way to say that is:

Gli interessano le culture antiche.

Here, we use the verb **"interessare"** *(to interest)*, and the sentence is translated as:

"Ancient cultures interest him."

Note that the verb is conjugated as **"interessano"** because **"le culture antiche"** is the subject, and **"gli"** is the object. Thus, the conjugation of the verb **"interessare"** must agree with the subject **"le culture antiche."**

As you can see, we use the indirect object **"gli"** to express the meaning *"to him,"* that is, that the ancient cultures interest him. However, remember that **"gli"** can also mean *"to him"* or *"to them."* To remove ambiguity and sometimes to show emphasis, we can use the prepositional **"a"** followed by the object or the prepositional object pronoun:

"A Marco interessano le culture antiche," or **"A lui interessano le culture antiche."**

This is translated as:

"Ancient cultures interest Marco," or *"Ancient cultures interest him."*

Below are more examples of expressions with the verb **"piacere"** using the prepositional **"a"** and prepositional object pronoun:

English Example	Indirect Object Pronoun	Prep. Object Pronoun	Italian Equivalent
I like reading.	mi	me	A **me** piace leggere.
You like reading. (singular, informal)	ti	te	A **te** piace leggere.
He likes reading.	lui	lui	A **lui** piace leggere.
She likes reading.	lei	lei	A **lei** piace leggere.
You like reading. (singular, formal)	Lei	Lei	A **Lei** piace leggere.
We like reading.	noi	noi	A **noi** piace leggere.
You like reading. (plural, informal)	voi	voi	A **voi** piace leggere.
They like reading.	loro	loro	A **loro** piace leggere.
You like reading. (plural, formal)	Loro	Loro	A **Loro** piace leggere.

Note again how the verb "**piacere**" does not change conjugation in the examples above because "**leggere**" *(reading)* is singular; thus, it takes the second-person conjugation "**piace**."

Here is a list of verbs like "**piacere**" that are common in Italian:

Verb	Meaning	Example	
annoiare	*to bore*	Mi **annoiano** i videogiochi.	*Video games* **are boring** *to me.*
bastare	*to be enough*	Il cibo gli **basta**.	*The food* **is enough** *for him.*
disgustare	*to disgust*	Mi **disgusta** il tuo comportamento.	*Your behavior* **disgusts** *me.*
fare male	*to be painful*	Le **fa male** la schiena.	*She* **has** *back* **pain**.
importare	*to be important*	Non ci **importa**.	*We don't care.*
interessare	*to interest*	Non mi **interessa** l'argomento.	*I* **am** *not* **interested** *in the topic.*
mancare	*to miss*	Mi **manca** mia sorella.	*I* **miss** *my sister.*
occorrere	*to be necessary to take*	Mi **occorrono** tre giorni per finire.	*It* **takes** *me three days to finish.*
parere	*to seem*	L'idea mi **pare** ragionevole.	*The idea* **seems** *reasonable to me.*
restare	*to be left*	Ci **resta** tempo prima del viaggio?	*Do we have time* **left** *before the trip?*
rimanere	*to remain or be left with*	Gli **rimane** solo un'opzione.	*He* **is left with** *only one option.*
sembrare	*to seem*	Questo ragazzo mi **sembra** strano.	*This guy* **seems** *strange to me.*
servire	*to need or be of use*	Mi **serve** un altro libro.	*I* **need** *one more book.*

2. PRESENT PERFECT TENSE

The present perfect tense in Italian is used to describe events that happened and were completed in the past or happened in the past and continue in the present. In Italian, this tense covers both the present perfect and the simple past tenses in English, that is, *"I spoke"* and *"I have spoken"* are both translated to the same tense in Italian.

Using the Conjugation Auxiliary "Avere" vs. "Essere"

The present perfect is a compound tense, meaning it requires an auxiliary verb. In English, we use the verb *"to have"* in the present tense as an auxiliary, e.g., *"I have done my homework."*

In Italian, some verbs use the auxiliary **"avere"** *(to have)*, while others use the auxiliary **"essere"** *(to be)* in the present tense, followed by the past participle.

The past participle of regular verbs using the auxiliary **"avere"** *(to have)* is formed by adding the appropriate suffix for "-**are**," "-**ere**," and "-**ire**" verbs.

"-**are**" verbs		"verb stem" + "-**ato**"
"-**ere**" verbs	"avere" in the present tense	"verb stem" + "-**uto**"
"-**ire**" verbs		"verb stem" + "-**ito**"

The past participle of regular verbs using the auxiliary **"essere"** *(to be)* is formed in a similar way. One additional requirement here is that the suffix of the past participle must agree with the subject in gender and number, that is, the past participle essentially requires the treatment of an adjective.

"-**are**" verbs		"verb stem" + "-**ato**"/ "-**ata**"/ "-**ati**"/ "-**ate**"
"-**ere**" verbs	"essere" in the present tense	"verb stem" + "-**uto**"/ "-**uta**"/ "-**uti**"/ "-**ute**"
"-**ire**" verbs		"verb stem" + "-**ito**"/ "-**ita**"/ "-**iti**"/ "-**ite**"

Let us look at some examples of verbs conjugated using the auxiliary **"avere"**:

		-are ending e.g., parlare	-ere ending e.g., vendere	-ire ending e.g., finire
io	ho			
tu	hai			
lui/lei	ha	parlato	venduto	finito
noi	abbiamo			
voi	avete			
loro	hanno			

Here are some more examples:

		Examples	
io	ho	Io **ho visitato** l'Egitto l'anno scorso.	*I **visited** Egypt last year.*
tu	hai	Tu **hai finito** il tuo lavoro.	*You **have finished** your work.*
lui/lei	ha	Lui **ha parlato** con sua madre.	*He **spoke** with his mother.*
noi	abbiamo	Noi **abbiamo mangiato** tutto il cibo.	*We **have eaten** all the food.*
voi	avete	Sono sicuro che mi **avete sentito** ieri sera.	*I am sure you **heard** me last night.*
loro	hanno	Loro **hanno lavorato** qui per due anni.	*They **worked** here for two years.*

Notice that in some of these examples, the present perfect tense in Italian corresponds to the present perfect, whereas in others it corresponds to the simple past tense depending on the context.

Now, let us look at some examples of verbs conjugated using the auxiliary "**essere**":

		-are ending e.g., andare	-ere ending e.g., cadere	-ire ending e.g., partire
io	sono	andato/-a	caduto/-a	partito/-a
tu	sei	andato/-a	caduto/-a	partito/-a
lui	è	andato	caduto	partito
lei	è	andata	caduta	partita
noi	siamo	andati/-e	caduti/-e	partiti/-e
voi	siete	andati/-e	caduti/-e	partiti/-e
loro	sono	andati/-e	caduti/-e	partiti/-e

Here are some more examples:

		Examples	
io	sono	**Sono andato** in palestra la scorsa settimana.	*I **went** to the gym last week.*
tu	sei	**Sei partito** presto ieri sera.	*You **left** early last night.*
lui/lei	è	Lui **è caduto** dalle scale.	*He **fell down** the stairs.*
noi	siamo	**Siamo entrati** nella stanza.	*We **have entered** the room.*
voi	siete	Voi **siete arrivati** tardi la scorsa notte.	*You **arrived** late last night.*
loro	sono	Ieri loro **sono usciti** insieme.	*They **went out** together yesterday.*

Finally, you are perhaps wondering when to use the auxiliary "**avere**" and when to use the auxiliary "**essere**" to form the past participle. The vast majority of Italian verbs, including all transitive[1] verbs, are conjugated using the auxiliary "**avere**." Thus, it is easier to memorize the verbs that use "**essere**." First, all transitive non-reflexive verbs use "**avere**." If you can rule that out, the following categories, although not comprehensive, contain most verbs that use "**essere**":

1. A group of intransitive verbs related to *motion* (e.g., to go, to come, to return, to enter, to leave, to fall, to enter, etc.).

andare	*to go*	scappare	*to escape*
arrivare	*to arrive*	scendere	*to go down or descend*
cadere	*to fall*	tornare	*to return*
entrare	*to enter*	uscire	*to go out*
partire	*to leave*	venire	*to come*
salire	*to go up*		

Remember that all the verbs above that use "**essere**" are motion-related. However, not all motion-related verbs use "**essere**." This should serve as a guideline to help you memorize the verbs in this category.

2. A group of intransitive verbs related to *change or transformation* (e.g., to become, to be born, to die, to appear, to disappear, to lose weight, etc.).

apparire	*to appear*	ingrandire	*to get bigger*
cambiare	*to change*	migliorare	*to get better*
crescere	*to grow*	morire	*to die*
dimagrire	*to lose weight*	nascere	*to be born*
diminuire	*to diminish*	peggiorare	*to get worse*
dipendere da	*to depend on or cause*	sparire	*to disappear*
diventare	*to become*	svanire	*to vanish*
guarire	*to heal*	volare	*to fly*

---

[1] A verb is transitive if it requires an object. For example, the *"to bring"* can only be transitive, because the meaning is not complete without an object, e.g., *"I bring."*

Notice that the above verbs use "**essere**" only when they are in transitive form, that is when there is a direct object acted upon. If the verb is transitive, "**avere**" must be used. For example:

Verb	Example	
cambiare *to change*	**È cambiato** molto di recente.	*He **has changed** a lot recently.*
	Ha cambiato il mondo.	*He **has changed** the world.*
crescere *to raise or grow*	**È cresciuta** in città.	*She **grew up** in the city.*
	Ha cresciuto tre figli.	*She **raised** three children.*
guarire *to heal*	La mia pelle **è guarita**.	*My skin **has healed**.*
	La crema **ha guarito** la mia pelle.	*The cream **healed** my skin.*

3. Verbs that are always in the third-person, e.g., "**costare**" *(to cost)*, "**durare**" *(to last)*, "**occorrere**" *(to take or to be necessary)*, "**succedere**" *(to happen)*, etc. Here are some examples:

Verb	Meaning	Example	
costare	*to cost*	Mi **è costato** molto.	*It **has cost** me a lot.*
durare	*to last*	Il volo **è durato** un'ora.	*The flight **lasted** one hour.*
occorrere	*to be necessary or to take*	**Sono** occorsi tre giorni per dipingere la casa.	*It **took** three days to paint the house.*
succedere	*to happen*	Per favore, dimmi cosa **è successo**.	*Please, tell me what **happened**.*

4. Many, but not all, verbs like "**piacere**." Refer to **Lesson 1** of this level. Here are some examples:

Verb	Meaning	Example	
bastare	*to be enough*	Il cibo gli **è bastato**.	*The food **was enough** for him.*
importare	*to be important*	Non ci **è importato**.	*We didn't care.*
mancare	*to miss*	Mi **è mancata** mia sorella.	*I **missed** my sister.*
parere	*to seem*	L'idea mi **è parsa** ragionevole.	*The idea **seemed** reasonable to me.*
sembrare	*to seem*	Questo ragazzo mi **è sembrato** strano.	*This guy **seemed** strange to me.*
servire	*to need or be of use*	Mi **è servito** un altro libro.	*I **needed** one more book.*

5. All reflexive verbs, which will be covered in detail in **Level IV, Lesson 3**, e.g., **"chiamarsi"** *(to call oneself)*, **"lavarsi"** *(to wash oneself)*, etc.

Irregular Past Participles

There are some verbs with irregular past participles that need to be memorized.

Verb	Past Participle	Meaning	Examples	
accendere	acceso	*to switch on*	All'arrivo, ha **acceso** la luce.	*Upon arrival, he* **turned on** *the light.*
aprire	aperto	*to open*	Ho **aperto** la porta.	*I have* **opened** *the door.*
bere	bevuto	*to drink*	Quanto hai **bevuto**?	*How much did you* **drink**?
chiedere	chiesto	*to ask*	Mi ha **chiesto** di aiutarlo.	*He* **asked** *me to help him.*
chiudere	chiuso	*to close*	Oggi il negozio ha **chiuso** tardi.	*The shop* **closed** *late today.*
coprire	coperto	*to cover*	Ho **coperto** il pavimento.	*I have* **covered** *the floor.*
correre	corso	*to run*	Oggi ho **corso** di mattina.	*Today I* **ran** *in the morning.*
cuocere	cotto	*to cook*	Ha **cotto** una bella bistecca.	*He* **cooked** *a nice steak.*
decidere	deciso	*to decide*	Abbiamo **deciso** di partire.	*We* **decided** *to leave.*
dire	detto	*to say*	Te l'ho **detto** dall'inizio.	*I* **told** *you from the beginning.*
discutere	discusso	*to discuss*	Hanno **discusso** l'argomento.	*They* **discussed** *the topic.*
dividere	diviso	*to divide*	Ho **diviso** la torta a fette.	*I* **divided** *the cake into slices.*
fare	fatto	*to do*	Ho **fatto** tutto il lavoro.	*I have* **done** *all the work.*
friggere	fritto	*to fry*	Hai **fritto** la patata?	*Have you* **fried** *the potato?*

leggere	letto	to read	Hai **letto** questo articolo?	*Have you* **read** *this article?*
mettere	messo	to put	Ho **messo** la roba nel furgone.	*I* **put** *the stuff in the van.*
morire	morto	to die	È **morto** l'anno scorso.	*He* **died** *last year.*
nascere	nato	to be born	È **nato** e cresciuto qui.	*He* **was born** *and raised here.*
offendere	offeso	to offend	Mi dispiace se ti ho **offeso**.	*I'm sorry if I* **offended** *you.*
perdere	perso	to lose	Ho **perso** le chiavi.	*I* **lost** *my keys.*
piangere	pianto	to cry	Ha **pianto** per la sua perdita.	*He* **cried** *over his loss.*
porre	posto	to put	Abbiamo **posto** fine a questo.	*We have* **put** *an end to this.*
ridere	riso	to laugh	Ho **riso** quando me l'hanno detto.	*I* **laughed** *when they told me.*
rimanere	rimasto	to remain	Sono **rimasti** con noi per due notti.	*They* **stayed** *with us for two nights.*
risolvere	risolto	to resolve	Lei ha **risolto** il problema.	*She has* **resolved** *the problem.*
rompere	rotto	to break	Lei ha **rotto** la finestra.	*She has* **broken** *the window.*
soddisfare	soddisfatto	to satisfy	Il mio lavoro mi ha **soddisfatto**.	*My work has* **satisfied** *me.*
scegliere	scelto	to choose	Ho **scelto** questo prodotto.	*I* **chose** *this product.*
scendere	sceso	to descend or go down	Lui ha **sceso** le scale.	*He* **went down** *the stairs.*
scrivere	scritto	to write	Ha **scritto** una lettera.	*She has* **written** *a letter.*
soffrire	sofferto	to suffer	Ha **sofferto** molto nella vita.	*He has* **suffered** *a lot in life.*
spegnere	spento	to switch off	Ha **spento** la luce ed è uscito.	*He* **turned off** *the light and went out.*
tradurre	tradotto	to translate	Ho **tradotto** il documento.	*I have* **translated** *the document.*
vedere	visto	to see	Non l'ho **visto**.	*I haven't* **seen** *him.*
venire	venuto	to come	Non è ancora **venuta**.	*She hasn't* **come** *yet.*

| vincere | vinto | *to win* | Ha **vinto** molto facilmente. | *He **won** very easily.* |
| **vivere** | vissuto | *to live* | Hanno **vissuto** qui per anni. | *They have **lived** here for years.* |

❖ Some verbs have both regular and irregular past participle forms:

Verb	Meaning	Regular Past Part.	Irregular Past Part.
vedere	*to see*	veduto	visto
perdere	*to lose*	perduto	perso
succedere	*to happen*	succeduto	successo
seppellire	*to bury*	seppellito	sepolto
cedere	*to search*	ceduto	cesso

Although both regular and irregular forms are considered grammatically correct, note the following:

1. Except for the verb "**cedere**," the use of irregular forms is more common in daily spoken language.

2. The use of "**veduto**," "**perduto**," and "**succeduto**" is often found in literary domain and may sound archaic.

3. The regular form "**perduto**" is often used in the context of morality or soul-searching, e.g., "**anima perduta**" *(lost soul)*. In the context of losing one's way or going astray, the irregular form is often used, e.g., "**Ho perso la mia strada**" *(I have lost my way)*.

4. The regular form "**succeduto**" is often only used when "**succedere**" means *"to succeed,"* as in: "**Il re è succeduto a suo padre**" *(The king succeeded his father)*.

5. The irregular form "**cesso**" of the verb "**cedere**" is used in colloquial language as a noun meaning *"toilet."*

❖ The verbs above can be used with prefixes that change the meaning, but the irregular form remains the same. For example, the verb "**rivedere**," derived from "**vedere**," has two past participle forms: "**riveduto**" and "**rivisto**." Similarly, the past participle of the verb "**assolvere**" *(to absolve)* is "**assolto**," similar to "**risolto**," the past participle of "**risolvere**" *(to resolve)*.

Using the Past Participle as an Adjective

Many adjectives in Italian are the same as the past participle, especially when active meaning is conveyed.

		Examples	
aperto	*open*	La porta è **aperta**.	*The door is **open**.*
benedetto	*blessed*	Si sente **benedetto**.	*He feels **blessed**.*
chiuso	*closed*	La finestra è **chiusa**.	*The window is **closed**.*
confuso	*confused*	Sono **confuso** ora.	*I am **confused** now.*
corrotto	*corrupt*	Questo politico è **corrotto**.	*This politician is **corrupt**.*

In some cases, the past participle and the adjective are different. For example:

Io mi sono **svegliato**.	*I have **woken up**.*	"svegliato" is the past participle
Io sono **sveglio**.	*I am **awake**.*	"sveglio" is an adjective

3. THE VERB "TO KNOW": "SAPERE" VS. "CONOSCERE"

There are two verbs in Italian that mean *"to know"* in English. The two verbs are **"sapere"** and **"conoscere."** Knowing when to use **"sapere"** and when to use **"conoscere"** should not be difficult if you understand the subtle difference between the two concepts of *"knowing."*

In short, the verb **"sapere"** is used to describe knowledge of facts, concepts, skills, abilities, etc. On the other hand, the verb **"conoscere"** is used to describe recognition or familiarity with a person, a place, or an object, including a movie, a site, a brand, etc.

When referring to a language, one could use either **"sapere"** or **"conoscere."** The difference is that **"Conosco l'italiano"** indicates that you know some Italian or that you are familiar with the language, whereas **"So l'italiano"** or **"So parlare l'italiano"** indicates that you know Italian well enough to speak it.

Below is a reminder of the present tense conjugation of both verbs.

	sapere	conoscere
io	so	conosco
tu	sai	conosci
lui/lei	sa	conosce
noi	sappiamo	conosciamo
voi	sapete	conoscete
loro	sanno	conoscono

Here are some examples that use the verbs "**sapere**" and "**conoscere**" and highlight the difference:

"sapere" and "conoscere" Examples	Explanation
Sai se c'è qualcuno dentro? *Do you **know** if there is someone inside?*	When referring to a fact (whether someone is inside or not), use "**sapere**."
Lei non **sa** nuotare. *She doesn't **know** how to swim.*	When referring to a skill, use "**sapere**."
Non **so** dove ci sia una scuola. *I don't **know** where there is a school.*	When referring to a fact (whether a school exists nearby), use "**sapere**."
Non **conosco** molto bene la città. *I don't **know** the city very well.*	When referring to recognizing a place, use "**conoscere**."
Non **conoscono** i miei genitori. *They don't **know** my parents.*	When referring to recognizing a person, use "**conoscere**."
Conosci quel film? *Do you **know** that movie?*	When referring to recognizing a movie, use "**conoscere**."
Conosci l'inglese? (or) **Sai** l'inglese? *Do you **know** English?*	When referring to a language, use "**conoscere**" or "**sapere**."

Expressions that use "Sapere"

The verb "**sapere**" is used in many expressions in Italian, for example:

lo so	*I know*	**chissà?**	*who knows?*
solo per sapere	*just to know*	**per quanto ne so**	*as far as I know*
senza saperlo	*without my knowledge*	**cosa ne so!**	*how should I know?!*

To know each other using "Conoscere"

The verb "**conoscere**" is used to refer to the reciprocal act of knowing each other, for example:

| Ci conosciamo[1] molto bene. | *We **know each other** very well.* |
| Non **si conoscono**[1]. | *They don't **know each other**.* |

[1] More on the use of reflexive verbs will be covered in detail in **Level IV, Lesson 4**.

Use of "Conoscere" Referring to the Past

The verb "**conoscere**" can also mean *"to meet"* when referring to the past, e.g., "**Ho conosciuto mia moglie all'università**" *(I met my wife at university)*.

4. INDEFINITE ADJECTIVES & PRONOUNS

Indefinite adjectives describe a noun in a vague or non-specific way, e.g., "**altra** gente" (*other* people), "**ogni** persona" (*each* person), "**parecchie** cose" (*several* things), "**Tutte** le scuole" (*all* schools). On the other hand, an indefinite pronoun replaces the noun in a vague and non-specific way, e.g., "**Ti dico qualcosa**" (I tell you *something*), "**Parlo con qualcuno**" (I speak to *someone*), "**Va tutto bene**" (*All is well*). Many indefinite pronouns are identical to their indefinite adjective counterpart, e.g., "**tutto**" (*all*), "**altro**" (*other*), "**molto**" (*much* or *many*).

Unlike most adjectives in Italian, indefinite adjectives precede the noun they describe. Some also change form to agree with the noun in gender and number. Indefinite adjectives and pronouns are used abundantly in Italian. Thus, it is very useful to learn the most common ones.

Here is a list of the most common indefinite adjectives and pronouns:

	Meaning		Examples	
abbastanza	*enough*	indef. adj. & pron.	Ho **abbastanza** soldi.	*I have **enough** money.*

troppo, -a, -i, -e	too much, too many	indef. adj. & pron.	Qui c'è **troppa** gente.	*There are **too many** people here.*
l'uno l'altro l'una l'altra	*each other*	indef. adj. & pron.	Devono aiutarsi **l'un l'altro**.	*They must help **each other**.*
l'uno o l'altro l'una o l'altra	*one or the other*	indef. adj. & pron.	Devi scegliere **l'una o l'altra** di queste case.	*You must choose **one or the other** of these houses.*
entrambi, -e	*both*	indef. adj. & pron.	**Entrambe** le opzioni sono disponibili.	***Both** options are available.*
gli altri le altre	*the others*	indef. adj. & pron.	**Gli altri** non sono disponibili.	***The others** are not available.*
il resto	*the rest*	indef. adj. & pron.	**Il resto** del mondo sta soffrendo.	***The rest** of the world is suffering.*
stesso, -a, -i, -e	*same, self*	indef. adj. & pron.	È la **stessa** persona che abbiamo visto ieri sera.	*It is the **same** person we saw last night.*
certo, -a, -i, -e	*certain*	indef. adj. & pron.	Solo **certe** persone possono farlo.	*Only **certain** people can do that.*
altro, -a, -i, -e	*other, another*	indef. adj. & pron.	Vorrei un **altro** bicchiere d'acqua, per favore.	*I'd like **another** glass of water, please.*
tutto, -a	*all, every*	indef. adj. & pron.	Piove **tutto** l'anno nel paese.	***All** year round, it rains in the country.*
tutti, -e	*all, everybody*	indef. adj. & pron.	**Tutti** noi veniamo dall'Australia.	***All** of us are from Australia.*
poco, -a	*little, not much*	indef. adj. & pron.	Abbiamo bisogno di **poco** tempo per arrivare.	*We need **little** time to arrive.*
pochi, -e	*few*	indef. adj. & pron.	Ha **pochi** amici a scuola.	*He has **few** friends at school.*
molto, -a, -i, -e	*much, many*	indef. adj. & pron.	Ci sono **molte** opzioni per i giovani.	*There are **many** options for young people.*
vari(e)	*various*	indef. adj. & pron.	**Vari** campi sono aperti a tutti.	***Various** fields are open to everyone.*
parecchi(e) diversi, -e	*several*	indef. adj. & pron.	Puoi leggere **diversi** libri su questo argomento.	*You can read **several** books on this topic.*
qualsiasi	*any, whichever*	indef. adj. & pron.	Portami **qualsiasi** libro trovi.	*Bring me **any** book you find.*
alcuni, -a qualche	*some, few*	indef. adj. & pron.	Ho solo una casa e **alcuni** libri.	*I only have a house and **some** books.*
ogni ciascuno	*each, every*	indef. adj.	Giochiamo a calcio **ogni** sabato.	We play soccer **every** Saturday.

qualcosa	*something*	indef. pron.	Voglio dire **qualcosa** di molto importante.	I want to say **something** very important.
qualcuno	*someone*	indef. pron.	Ho parlato con **qualcuno** di molto interessante.	I talked with **someone** very interesting.
niente	*nothing*	indef. pron.	Oggi non farò **niente** tutto il giorno.	I am going to do **nothing** all day today.
nessuno	*nobody* *not any*	indef. pron.	Non c'è **nessuno** in ufficio oggi.	**Nobody** is in the office today.
chiunque	*whoever*	indef. pron.	**Chiunque** sia, non è importante.	**Whoever** it is, it is not important.

Note that "**ogni**" and "**ciascuno/-a**" *(each)* can only be used as indefinite adjectives because they are always followed by a noun, e.g., "**ogni libro**" *(each book)*, "**ciascun libro**" *(each book)*, "**ciascun numero**" *(each number)*, "**ciascuno studente**" *(each student)*, etc. On the other hand, "**qualcosa**" *(something)*, "**qualcuno**" *(somebody)*, "**niente**" *(nothing)*, and "**nessuno**" *(nobody)* can only be used as indefinite pronouns because they cannot be followed by a noun, e.g., "**Non è successo niente**" *(Nothing happened)*.

5. CONJUNCTIONS

Conjunctions are important components of any language as they allow the speaker to join sentences and convey useful meanings.

The most common conjunctions in Italian are:

Conjunction	Meaning	Example
e	*and*	Mi piacciono la primavera **e** l'estate. *I like spring **and** summer.*
o	*or*	Prenderò un caffè **o** un tè. *I will drink tea **or** coffee.*
se	*if*	**Se** sono stanco, non esco. *If I am tired, I won't go out.*
ma però	*but*	Voglio dormire **ma** non posso. *I want to sleep, **but** I can't.* Lavoro, **però** non ho soldi. *I work, **but** I have no money.*
bensì	*but rather*	Non vado il sabato **bensì** la domenica. *I won't go on Saturday, **but rather** on Sunday.*

allora	*so*	**Allora**, cosa dobbiamo fare? *So, what should we do?*
secondo	*according to*	**Secondo** i medici, il caffè non fa male. *According to the doctors, coffee is not bad.*
tranne eccetto	*except*	Vado in palestra tutti i giorni **tranne** il venerdì. *I go to the gym every day **except** Friday.*
poi	*then*	Era lì. **Poi** se n'è andato. *He was there. **Then**, he left.*
comunque tuttavia	*however*	Sono stanco. **Comunque**, posso uscire con te. *I am tired. **However**, I can go out with you.*
in modo che	*so that* *in order to*	Riassumerò il libro **in modo che** tu possa capirlo. *I will summarize the book **so that** you can understand it.*
perché	*because*	Studio spagnolo **perché** voglio vivere in Messico. *I study Spanish **because** I want to live in Mexico.*
a causa di	*because of*	Non possiamo uscire **a causa della** neve. *We can't go out **because of the** snow.*
invece di	*instead of*	**Invece di** uscire oggi, vedremo un film. *Instead of going out tonight, we'll watch a movie.*
dato che	*given that*	Vado al bar **dato che** ho abbastanza tempo libero. *I'll go to the coffee shop **given that** I have enough free time.*
quindi pertanto dunque	*therefore*	Era tardi; **quindi**, non siamo usciti ieri sera. *It was late; **therefore**, we didn't go out last night.*
altrimenti	*otherwise*	Spero che non piova; **altrimenti**, non usciamo. *I hope it doesn't rain; **otherwise**, we don't go out.*
anche se benché	*although*	Capisco il problema, **anche se** non riesco a spiegarlo. *I understand the problem, **although** I can't explain it.*
nonostante	*in spite of* *despite*	**Nonostante** sia basso, è un ottimo giocatore. *Despite being short, he is a very good player.*
cioè ovvero	*that is*	Parlo inglese e spagnolo, **cioè** sono bilingue. *I speak English and Spanish, **that is**, I'm bilingual.*
in altre parole	*in other words*	**In altre parole**, dobbiamo lavorare di più. *In other words, we must work harder.*
mentre	*while*	Compriamo qualcosa **mentre** siamo qui. *Let's buy something **while** we are here.*
finché	*as long as*	**Finché** sei preparato, non devi preoccuparti. *As long as you are prepared, you don't need to worry.*
o ... o ...	*either...* *or...*	Bene, **o** partiamo ora **o** più tardi. *Okay, we **either** leave now **or** later.*
né ... né ...	*neither ...* *nor ...*	Il mio italiano non è **né** buono **né** cattivo. *My Italian is **neither** good **nor** bad.*
oltre a	*besides*	**Oltre al** cibo, ordinerò anche da bere. *Besides food, I will order drinks too.*
a parte	*apart from*	**A parte** il clima, non mi piace questo posto. *Apart from the weather, I don't like this place.*

a differenza di	*unlike*	**A differenza di** te, io non conosco il tedesco. *Unlike* you, I don't know German.

❖ If the word following "**e**" *(and)* starts with an "**e**," the "**e**" is replaced with "**ed**" to avoid the double "**e**" sound. This is called euphonic "**d**," e.g., "**corretto ed esatto**" *(correct and exact)*, "**alberi ed erba**" *(trees and grass)*, etc.

Historically, the euphonic "**d**" was used after "**e**" or "**a**" when followed by *any* vowel. Today, it is generally more accepted to use it only when the "**e**" or "**a**" is followed by the *same* vowel, e.g., "**Manderò un messaggio ad Andrea**" *(I will send a message to Andrea)*.

❖ Both "**ma**" and "**però**" mean *"but."* If "**però**" is used at the end of a sentence, it can mean *"though,"* e.g., "**Costa troppo però**" *(It is expensive though)*. Finally, the conjunction "**bensì**" is used to mean *"but"* or *"but rather"* when the first part of the sentence is negative, e.g., "**Non è inverno bensì estate**" *(It is not winter but summer)*.

6. SIMPLE FUTURE TENSE

The simple future tense is used to express events in the future. To form the stem of the verb needed for regular verb conjugation, we drop the final "**e**" of the verb and change the final "**-ar**" to "**-er**" in the case of "**-are**" verbs. The endings are the same for the three types of verbs.

	-are ending parlare *(to speak)*	-ere ending vendere *(to sell)*	-ire ending partire *(to leave)*
io	parlerò	venderò	partirò
tu	parlerai	venderai	partirai
lui/lei	parlerà	venderà	partirà
noi	parleremo	venderemo	partiremo
voi	parlerete	venderete	partirete
loro	parleranno	venderanno	partiranno

❖ In addition to expressing events in the future, the simple future tense can also be used to express conjecture or possibility, e.g.,

"**La ragazza <u>avrà</u> 15 anni**" *(The girl might be 15 years old)*, "**Dove <u>sarà</u> il mio cellulare?**" *(Where could my cell phone be?)*, etc.

Irregular Verbs

There are some verbs that are irregular in the simple future tense, which we attempt to summarize here.

1. Some verbs, in addition to dropping the final "**e**," drop the vowel before the final "**r**" from the infinitive to form the stem. For example, the stem from the verb "**andare**" *(to go)* becomes "**andr-**" instead of "**andar-**." Other examples from this group are: "**avere**" *(to have)*, "**cadere**" *(to fall)*, "**dovere**" *(must)*, "**potere**" *(can)*, "**sapere**" *(to know)*, "**vedere**" *(to see)*, and "**vivere**" *(to live)*.

	andare **andr-**	**avere** **avr-**	**cadere** **cadr-**	**dovere** **dovr-**	**potere** **potr-**
io	and**r**ò	av**r**ò	cad**r**ò	dov**r**ò	pot**r**ò
tu	and**r**ai	av**r**ai	cad**r**ai	dov**r**ai	pot**r**ai
lui/lei	and**r**à	av**r**à	cad**r**à	dov**r**à	pot**r**à
noi	and**r**emo	av**r**emo	cad**r**emo	dov**r**emo	pot**r**emo
voi	and**r**ete	av**r**ete	cad**r**ete	dov**r**ete	pot**r**ete
loro	and**r**anno	av**r**anno	cad**r**anno	dov**r**anno	pot**r**anno

2. Some short verbs with the "**-are**" ending do not change the "**-ar**" to "**-er**" after dropping the final "**e**" to form the stem. The most common verbs in this group are: "**dare**" *(to give)*, "**fare**" *(to do or to make)*, and "**stare**" *(to stay or to be)*.

	dare **dar-**	**fare** **far-**	**stare** **star-**
io	da**r**ò	fa**r**ò	sta**r**ò
tu	da**r**ai	fa**r**ai	sta**r**ai
lui/lei	da**r**à	fa**r**à	sta**r**à
noi	da**r**emo	fa**r**emo	sta**r**emo
voi	da**r**ete	fa**r**ete	sta**r**ete
loro	da**r**anno	fa**r**anno	sta**r**anno

3. Some verbs, in addition to dropping the final "**e**," replace both the consonant and the vowel preceding the final "**r**" of the infinitive with an extra "**r**" to form the stem. For example, the stem from "**tenere**" *(to hold)* is "**terr-**" instead of "**tener-**." The most common verbs in this group are: "**tenere**" *(to hold)*, "**volere**" *(to want)*, and "**venire**" *(to come)*.

	tenere **terr-**	**volere** **vorr-**	**venire** **verr-**
io	terrò	vorrò	verrò
tu	terrai	vorrai	verrai
lui/lei	terrà	vorrà	verrà
noi	terremo	vorremo	verremo
voi	terrete	vorrete	verrete
loro	terranno	vorranno	verranno

4. Some verbs are completely irregular, such as "**essere**" *(to be)* and "**bere**" *(to drink)*, whose stems are "**sar-**" and "**berr-**," respectively.

	essere **sar-**	**bere** **berr-**
io	sarò	berrò
tu	sarai	berrai
lui/lei	sarà	berrà
noi	saremo	berremo
voi	sarete	berrete
loro	saranno	berranno

5. Finally, the same orthographic changes applied to verbs ending in "**-care**," "**-gare**," "**-ciare**," "**-giare**," and "**-gliare**" in the present indicative tense are applied here to maintain the proper pronunciation.

Examples

Here are some examples that use the simple future tense:

L'anno prossimo **andrò** in Italia.	I **will go** to Italy *next year.*
Oggi **non andrò** in palestra.	I **won't go** to the gym *today.*

Comprerà una casa a Roma.	*She **will buy** a house in Rome.*
Studierai duramente solo questo fine settimana.	*You **will study** hard only this weekend.*
Vivranno in una piccola città.	*They **will live** in a small city.*
Dormiremo tutto il giorno domani.	*We **will sleep** all day tomorrow.*

7. TELLING TIME & DESCRIBING THE WEATHER

Telling time and describing the weather are fundamental language skills for any language learner.

Expressing Time in Hours

In Italian, the verb "**essere**" (*to be*) is used in the third-person forms to describe time.

The singular form "**è**" is used for *"one o'clock,"* while other hours (from two to twelve o'clock) use the plural form "**sono**."

È l'una.	*It's one o'clock.*
Sono le tre	*It's three o'clock.*
Sono le undici.	*It's eleven o'clock.*

To ask what time it is, use the expression: "**Che ora è?**" or "**Che ore sono?**" meaning *"What time is it?"* in English, or more literally: *"What hour is it?"* or *"What hours are they?"*, respectively.

To ask *"At what time …?"*, we use "**A che ora …?**"

Expressing Minutes

To express time in hours and minutes, we use the conjunction "**e**" *(and)*.

È l'una **e** trenta.	*It's one-thirty.*
Sono le cinque **e** ventiquattro.	*It's five twenty-four.*

If you want to say: it is minutes to a certain hour, e.g., *"It's five to ten,"* use "**meno**" *(minus)*.

È l'una **meno** dieci.	*It's ten to one.*
Sono le dieci **meno** cinque.	*It's five to ten.*

The *"15 minutes"* and *"30 minutes"* can sometimes be replaced with **"quarto"** *(quarter)* and **"mezzo"** or **"mezza"** *(half)*, respectively.

È l'una meno un **quarto**.	*It's a quarter to one.*
Sono le quattro e **mezza**.	*It's four-thirty.*

Remember that Italians officially use the 24-hour clock format. For example, "1 p.m." is **"le tredici"** *(13:00)* in Italian, whereas midnight is **"le ventiquattro"** *(24:00)*.

Another minor note is that in Italian a period is used instead of the colon used to describe time in English, e.g., **"13.00"** *(1:00 p.m.)*.

Other Time Expressions

The expressions **"a.m."** and **"p.m."** are not commonly used in Italian, but you will hear Italians who tell the time using the twelve-hour clock format adding **"di mattina"** *(in the morning)*, **"del pomeriggio"** *(in the afternoon)*, **"di sera** *(in the evening)*, or **"di notte"** *(at night)*.

Here are some expressions that are used to express time with examples:

di mattina	*in the morning*	*It's 9 a.m.*	Sono le nove **di mattina**.
del pomeriggio	*in the afternoon*	*It's 1 p.m.*	È l'una **del pomeriggio**.
di sera	*in the evening*	*It's 7 p.m.*	Sono le sette **di sera**.
di notte	*at night*	*It's 11 p.m.*	Sono le undici **di notte**.
mezzogiorno	*noon*	*It's noon.*	È **mezzogiorno**.
mezzanotte	*midnight*	*It's midnight.*	È **mezzanotte**.
all'alba	*at dawn*	*We'll meet at dawn.*	Ci vedremo **all'alba**.
in punto	*sharp*	*It's two o'clock sharp.*	Sono le due **in punto**.
precisa, -e	*exactly*	*It's **exactly** five o'clock.*	Sono le cinque **precise**.
circa	*about*	*It's about three o'clock.*	Sono **circa** le tre.

Weather Expressions

Describing the weather in Italian often involves the use of some idiomatic expressions that make little sense if translated into English literally. For example, the expression **"Fa molto caldo"** translates literally to *"It makes much heat."* However, it just means that it is too hot. Similarly, the expression **"C'è il sole,"** which means that the sun is shining, makes little sense when translated literally as *"There is the sun."*

Here, we list a few common ways of describing the weather using some of these idiomatic expressions as well as other simple expressions.

Weather Expressions using the verb "fare"

Che tempo fa?	*What's the weather like?*
Fa bel tempo.	*The weather is good.*
Fa brutto tempo.	*The weather is bad.*
Fa cattivo tempo.	*The weather is awful.*
Fa (molto) freddo.	*It's (too) cold.*
Fa caldo.	*It's hot.*
Fa fresco.	*It's cool.*

Weather Expressions using the "c'è" and "ci sono"

The expression **"c'è"** means *"there is,"* and **"ci sono"** means *"there are."* Both expressions are used in many weather expressions, such as:

C'è il sole.	*The sun is shining.*
C'è la luna.	*The moon is out.*
Ci sono nuvole.	*It's cloudy.*
C'è vento.	*It's windy.*
C'è nebbia.	*It's foggy.*
C'è foschia.	*It's misty.*
C'è umidità.	*It's humid.*
Ci sono tuoni.	*There is lightning.*
C'è una tempesta.	*There is a windstorm.*

Weather Expressions using the verb "essere"

We can also use the verb "**essere**" in the third-person singular form followed by an adjective to describe the weather.

Com'è il tempo?	How's the weather?
È caldo.	It's hot.
È freddo.	It's cold.
È soleggiato.	It's sunny.
È nuvoloso.	It's cloudy.
È sereno.	It is clear.
È piovoso.	It's rainy.
È ventoso.	It's windy.
È scuro.	It's dark.

Weather Expressions using a simple verb

One can also use a simple verb expression in the third-person singular form, such as "**piove**," which is the third-person singular form of the present tense of the verb "**piovere**" (*to rain*). Other examples include:

Piove.	It's raining.
Nevica.	It's snowing.
Pioviggina.	It's sprinkling.
Grandina.	It's hailing.
Tuona.	It's thundering.

8. ADVERBS

An adverb is a word that modifies a verb, an adjective, or another adverb. They usually answer questions such as how, how often, how long, when, where, etc.

A lot of Italian adverbs have the ending "-**mente**," e.g., "**rapidamente**" (*quickly*), "**fortemente**" (*strongly*), etc. This is, more or less, similar to the ending "-*ly*" in English. Nevertheless, there are many other adverbs and adverbial phrases that do not follow this simple rule. We will attempt to classify the most common adverbs into some categories for easier memorization.

Forming an Adverb

Many adverbs in Italian can be formed by simply adding "**-mente**" to the *feminine* singular adjective. If the adjective ends with "**-le**" or "**-re**" preceded by a vowel, we simply drop the final "**-e**." Here are some examples:

Adverb in English	Masculine singular adjective	Feminine singular adjective	Adverb in Italian
slowly	lento	lenta	lentamente
quickly	rapido	rapida	rapidamente
quietly	tranquillo	tranquilla	tranquillamente
exactly	esatto	esatta	esattamente
relatively	relativo	relativa	relativamente
recently	recente	recente	recentemente
strongly	forte	forte	fortemente
easily	facile	facile	facilmente
normally	normale	normale	normalmente
generally	generale	generale	generalmente
literally	letterale	letterale	letteralmente
popularly	popolare	popolare	popolarmente
regularly	regolare	regolare	regolarmente
particularly	particolare	particolare	particolarmente

Some adverbs ending with "**-mente**" slightly deviate from the above rules. For example:

benevolent	benevolo	*benevolently*	benevolmente
light	leggero	*lightly*	leggermente
original	originale	*originally*	originariamente
violent	violento	*violently*	violentemente

Not all adverbs in Italian are formed by adding the "**-mente**" ending, similar to the fact that not all English adverbs are formed by adding "**-ly**" to the corresponding adjective. Some adverbs do not follow any particular rules. For example, the adverb of "**buono**" (*good*) is "**bene**" (*well*), and the adverb of "**cattivo**" (*bad*) is "**male**" (*badly*).

The Adverb "Così"

Another common adverb in Italian is "**così**," which, depending on the context, can be translated as *"such," "so," or "like this."* For example:

È un gatto **così** carino!	*He is **such** a pretty cat.*
Questo gatto è **così** carino!	*This cat is **so** pretty.*
Non ho mai visto un gatto **così**.	*I've never seen a cat **like this**.*

The Adverbs "Anche," "Neanche," and "Nemmeno"

The adverb "**anche**" is used to express agreement with an *affirmative* statement, whereas the adverb "**neanche**" or "**nemmeno**" is used to express agreement with a *negative* statement. For example:

A: Io parlo italiano. B: **Anche** io.	*A: I speak Italian.* *B: Me **too**.*
A: Io non parlo italiano. B: **Neanche** io.	*A: I don't speak Italian.* *B: Me **neither**.*

To show disagreement with affirmative and negative statements, we simply use "**no**" *(no)* and "**sì**" *(yes)*, respectively, for example:

A: Io parlo italiano. B: Io **no**.	*A: I speak Italian.* *B: I **don't**.*
A: Io non parlo italiano. B: Io **sì**.	*A: I don't speak Italian.* *B: I **do**.*

If a verb like "**piacere**" is used, the subject pronoun is replaced with a prepositional "**a**" followed by the prepositional object pronoun. For example:

A: Mi piace il tè. B: **Anche** <u>a me</u>.	*A: I like tea.* *B: Me **too**.*
A: Non mi piace il tè. B: **Nemmeno** <u>a me</u>.	*A: I don't like tea.* *B: Me **neither**.*

We apply the same concept in the case of disagreement, for example:

A: Mi piace il tè.	A: *I like tea.*
B: <u>A me</u> **no**.	B: *I* **don't**.
A: Non mi piace il tè.	A: *I don't like tea.*
B: <u>A me</u> **sì**.	B: *I* **do**.

The Adverbs "Ancora" and "Già"

When followed by a verb in the present tense, "**ancora**" generally means *"still"* in affirmative and negative expressions. However, "**ancora**" can also mean *"yet"* in a negative expression when followed by a verb in the present perfect tense, for example:

Vivo **ancora** in Italia.	I **still** *live in Italy.*
Non parlo **ancora** bene l'inglese.	I **still** *don't speak English well.*
Non sono **ancora** tornato a casa.	I *have* **not** *returned home* **yet**.

One can think of "**già**," meaning *"already,"* as the opposite response to "**non ancora**." Below are some examples in both the present tense and the present perfect tense:

a) Present Tense

Non parlo **ancora** bene l'inglese.	I **still** *don't speak English well.*
Parlo **già** bene l'inglese.	I **already** *speak English well.*

b) Present Perfect Tense

Non sono **ancora** tornato a casa.	I *haven't returned home* **yet**.
Sono **già** tornato a casa.	I *have* **already** *returned home.*

In the present tense, the opposite of "**ancora**" *(still)* is "**non più**" *(no longer)*. For example:

Vivo **ancora** in Italia.	I **still** *live in Italy.*
Non vivo **più** in Italia.	I **no longer** *live in Italy.*

The Adverb "Fa"

The adverb of time "**fa**" means *"ago"* when describing something that happened and ended in the past. Here are some examples:

Ho parlato con mia sorella tre mesi **fa.**	I *spoke to my sister three months* **ago**.
Mi sono svegliato 15 minuti **fa.**	I *woke up 15 minutes* **ago**.

Adverbial Phrases with "Volta" and "Volte"

The feminine noun "**volta**" and its plural "**volte**" are used to describe the frequency of occurrence. The English equivalents are often *"time,"* and its plural *"times,"* e.g., *"how many times did you win?"* Here is a list of some adverbial phrases that use "**volta**":

questa volta	*this time*	**ogni volta meno**	*less and less*
la prossima volta	*next time*	**l'ultima volta**	*last time*
ogni volta	*each time* *every time*	**una volta**	*one time* *once*
per la prima volta	*for the first time*	**per l'ultima volta**	*for the last time*
qualche volta	*at times* *some time*	**di volta in volta**	*from time to time*

Examples of adverbial verbs that use the plural noun "**volte**" include:

a volte	*sometimes*	**tre volte**	*three times*
molte volte **più volte**	*many times*	**parecchie volte**	*several times*
tante volte	*many times*	**Quante volte?**	*How many times?*

Other Adverbs

Given that an adverb can be created easily from a corresponding adjective, it is difficult to cover a vast number of adverbs in the limited space of this book.

Moreover, there are often multiple adverbs that convey a similar meaning. Here are some examples:

1. To say *"certainly"* or *"surely,"* you could use one of the following options: "**certamente**," "**sicuramente**," "**certo**," or even "**senza dubbio**" *(undoubtedly)*.

2. To say *"perhaps"* or *"maybe,"* you could use: "**forse**," "**magari**," or "**può essere**."

3. To say *"really,"* *"truly,"* or *"actually,"* you could use: "**realmente**," "**veramente**," "**davvero**," or "**in realtà**."

Remember that "**attualmente**," in Italian, means *"currently,"* not *"actually."*

4. To say *"finally,"* you could use: "**finalmente**," "**alla fine**," "**infine**," or "**per ultimo**."[1]

In this section, we list some of the most common adverbs and adverbial phrases. You will learn more adverbs as you practice Italian by reading, listening, and understanding the general rules explained in this lesson.

Adverbs of Place

vicino	*near*	**lontano**	*far*
davanti	*in front ahead*	**indietro**	*behind*
dentro	*inside*	**fuori**	*outside*
avanti	*in front ahead*	**ovunque dappertutto**	*everywhere*
da nessuna parte	*nowhere*	**a bordo**	*on board*
in giro	*around*	**in casa**	*at home*

Adverbs of Time

presto	*soon early*	**dopo più tardi**	*later*
in tempo	*on time*	**tardi**	*late*
prima	*before*	**dopo**	*after*
sempre	*always*	**mai**	*never*
spesso sovente	*often*	**all'improvviso improvvisamente**	*suddenly*
solitamente	*usually*	**poi**	*then*
brevemente	*briefly*	**frequentemente**	*frequently*
all'inizio	*in the beginning*	**alla fine**	*in the end*
tutti i giorni	*every day*	**a giorni alterni**	*every other day*

---

[1] There are some differences between these expressions, all meaning *"finally"*:
- "**per ultimo**" means *"lastly"* (in a list or order).
- "**infine**" mean *"at last"'* or *"in the end"* (often regarding something that is hoped for).
- "**finalmente**" and "**alla fine**'" (the former is more formal) can mean *"lastly"''* (in a list or order) or *"in the end"* (not necessarily regarding something that is hoped for).

a breve termine	*in the short term*	**a lungo termine**	*in the long term*
allora	*then* *at that time*	**subito**	*right away* *immediately*
avantieri **l'altro ieri**	*the day before* *yesterday*	**l'altro ieri sera**	*the night before last*
nel frattempo **intanto**	*meanwhile*	**quotidianamente** **giornalmente**	*daily*
settimanalmente	*weekly*	**mensilmente**	*monthly*
ormai	*by now*	**immediatamente**	*immediately*

Adverbs of Quantity

molto	*very* *much*	**solo** [1]	*only* *just*
troppo	*too*	**un po'**	*a little*
di più	*more*	**meno**	*less*
tanto	*so much*	**abbastanza**	*enough*
quasi	*almost*	**affatto**	*not at all*

---

[1] The word **"solo'"** can also be used as an adjective meaning *"alone,"* e.g., **"Si sente solo"** *(He feels alone).*

Adverbs of Manner

come	*as* *like*	**così**	*like this*
insieme	*together*	**separatamente**	*separately*
poco a poco	*little by little*	**passo per passo**	*step by step*
a voce alta	*loudly*	**di fretta**	*in a hurry*
seriamente **sul serio**	*seriously*	**appena**	*just* *barely*
inoltre **peraltro**	*moreover*	**faccia a faccia**	*face to face*
fortunatamente **per fortuna**	*fortunately*	**sfortunatamente** **purtroppo**	*unfortunately*

Adverbial Expressions

volentieri	*willingly*	**a malincuore**	*unwillingly*
consapevolmente	*knowingly*	**alla moda**	*fashionably*
a memoria	*by heart*	**a piedi**	*on foot*
sulla strada	*on the way*	**all'estero**	*overseas* *abroad*

II. Vocabulary Building

Go over the vocabulary in this section. You could Anki cards to help you memorize the meaning of each verb in proper contexts.

1. VERBS III

Below is a list of some important verbs needed for this level:

English	Italian	Examples
access	accedere	Scendendo quelle scale **accedo** al seminterrato. *Down those stairs I **access** the basement.*
advance	avanzare	Per **avanzare** all'università, devi studiare. *To **advance** in university, you have to study.*
arrange (order)	ordinare arrangiare	**Ordinerò** i miei file alfabeticamente. *I **will arrange** my files alphabetically.*
arrange (organize)	organizzare arrangiare	**Organizzerò** un incontro alle 14. *I **will arrange** a meeting at 2 o'clock.*
break (object)	rompere	Devi **rompere** tre uova per la ricetta. *You have to **break** three eggs for the recipe.*
breathe	respirare	Devi **respirare** profondamente prima di tuffarti. *You have to **breathe** deeply before diving in.*
bring	portare [1]	Mi puoi **portare** quel bicchiere? *Can you **bring** me that glass?*
carry	portare [1]	**Porterò** queste borse a casa. *I will **carry** these bags to the house.*
continue	continuare proseguire	**Continuo** a guardare quella serie. *I **continue** to watch that series.*
correct	correggere	**Correggerò** gli esami domani. *I **will correct** the exams tomorrow.*
cross	attraversare	Devi **attraversare** il ponte per arrivare. *You must **cross** the bridge to arrive.*
destroy	distruggere	La guerra può **distruggere** una grande città. *War can **destroy** a large city.*
detect	rilevare	Può **rilevare** se aumenti la tua velocità. *It can **detect** if you increase your speed.*
direct	dirigere	**Dirige** molto bene l'orchestra. *He **directs** the orchestra very well.*

---

[1] Depending on the context, the verb "**portare**" can mean *"to bring," "to carry," "to lead,"* and *"to wear,"* e.g., "**Tu porti il cibo**" *(You bring the food),* "**Questo può portare ad altri problemi**" *(This can lead to other problems),* "**Mi piace portare gli occhiali da sole**" *(I like wearing sunglasses).*

discuss	discutere	Non **discuterò** di questo con te. *I **will** not **discuss** that with you.*
dream	sognare	**Sogno** sempre di andare in Australia. *I always **dream** of going to Australia.*
earn gain	guadagnare	Lui **guadagna** più dei suoi fratelli. *He **earns** more than his brothers.*
employ	impiegare	La mia azienda **impiega** molti lavoratori. *My company **employs** many workers.*
fail	fallire	Non è facile **fallire**. *It isn't easy to **fail**.*
fill	riempire	**Riempio** sempre la vaschetta del ghiaccio. *I always **fill** the ice tray.*
finish	finire terminare	Se **finisco** questo, andremo. *If I **finish** this, we'll go.*
fix (attach)	fissare	Dammi il cacciavite per **fissare** il telaio al muro. *Give me the screwdriver to **fix** the frame to the wall.*
fix (repair)	aggiustare riparare	Dovrei **aggiustare** presto il rubinetto. *I should **fix** the faucet soon.*
fly	volare	**Volerò** a San Francisco. *I **will fly** to San Francisco.*
follow	seguire	Puoi **seguirmi** sui social. *You can **follow** me on social media.*
guess	indovinare	**Indovino** sempre il mio regalo di compleanno. *I always **guess** my birthday gift.*
happen	succedere accadere	Era sincero su quello che poteva **succedere**. *He was frank about what could **happen**.*
hate	odiare detestare	**Odio** quando le zanzare mi pungono. *I **hate** it when mosquitoes bite me.*
have lunch	pranzare	Non posso; voglio **pranzare**. *I can't; I want to **have lunch**.*
hope	sperare	**Spero** di vederti presto. *I **hope** to see you soon.*
keep hold maintain	tenere	**Tengo** sempre un registro delle presenze. *I always **keep** a record of attendance.*
keep save preserve	conservare	**Conservo** sempre gli avanzi. *I always **save** the leftovers.*
kill	uccidere ammazzare	Quel veleno **uccide** le pulci. *That poison **kills** fleas.*
lack	mancare	Questo stufato **manca** di sapore. *This stew **lacks** flavor.*

last	durare	Quei generi alimentari devono **durare** un mese. *Those groceries must **last** for a month.*
let	lasciare	Non voglio **lasciare** che questo mi rallenti. *I don't want to **let** this slow me down.*
mix **blend**	mescolare	Devi prima **mescolare** gli ingredienti secchi. *You must **mix** the dry ingredients first.*
must	dovere[1]	**Devi** visitare tua nonna. *You **must** visit your grandmother.*
notify	avvisare notificare	Puoi **avvisarmi** quando arriva? *Can you **notify** me when it arrives?*
offer	offrire	Il mercato **offre** molti prodotti. *The market **offers** a lot of products.*
perform **fulfill**	eseguire	Gli scienziati **eseguiranno** un esperimento. *The scientists **will perform** an experiment.*
possess	possedere	**Possiede** un'abilità sorprendente. *He **possesses** a surprising skill.*
pull	tirare	Devi **tirare** quella corda per farla cadere. *You have to **pull** on that rope for it to fall.*
push	spingere	Devo **spingerti** avanti? *Should I **push** you forward?*
recommend	consigliare raccomandare	**Raccomando** questo marchio di più. *I **recommend** this brand more.*
remind	ricordare[2]	Puoi **ricordarmi** la data, per favore? *Can you **remind** me of the date, please?*
rent	affittare noleggiare	**Affitto** un appartamento in questo edificio. *I **rent** an apartment in this building.*
require	richiedere	Questo lavoro **richiede** un certificato speciale. *This job **requires** a special certificate.*
ride[3] **(a horse)**	cavalcare	È una bella giornata di sole per **cavalcare**. *It's a nice sunny day for **riding**.*
seem	sembrare	**Sembra** che sia così. *It **seems** it's that way.*
sign	firmare	All'attore piace **firmare** autografi. *The actor likes to **sign** autographs.*
smell	annusare odorare	Devi **annusare** questa cannella. *You must **smell** this cinnamon.*

---

[1] The verb "**dovere**" can also mean *"to owe,"* e.g., "**Ti devo 100 euro**" *(I owe you 100 euros).*

[2] The verb "**ricordare**" can also mean *"to remember."*

[3] The verb "**andare**" *(to go)* can also be used to mean *"to ride,"* e.g., "**andare a cavallo**" *(to go horseback riding)*, "**andare in bici**" *(to ride a bike)*. In addition, the verb "**fare**" *(to do)* can also mean *"to ride"* in some contexts, e.g., "**fare un giro**" *(to go for a ride)*, "**fare il passeggero**" *(to ride as a passenger)*.

sound	suonare	Il campanello **suona** troppo forte. *The doorbell **sounds** too loud.*
split **break**	spaccare dividere	Questa strada **spacca** la città in due. *This street **splits** the city in two.*
switch on **turn on**	accendere aprire	Devo **accendere** la luce per vedere. *I have to **turn on** the light to see.*
taste	assaggiare degustare	Mi piace **assaggiare** tutto il cibo che c'è. *I like to **taste** all the food there is.*
test	testare provare	Devi **testare** il modello prima dell'implementazione. *You must **test** the model before implementation.*
thank	ringraziare	**Ringrazio** i miei amici per avermi aiutato. *I **thank** my friends for helping me.*
train	allenare(-si)	Devo **allenarmi** per la gara. *I have to **train** for the race.*
trust	fidare(-si) confidare	**Confido** nel tuo giudizio. *I **trust** your judgment.*
warn	avvertire	Ti **avverto** che non ti piacerà. *I **warn** you that you won't like it.*
wish	desiderare	I giovani **desiderano** essere più indipendenti. *Young people **wish** to be more independent.*

In addition to the above new verbs, we add a few more English cognates that are easy to memorize.

English	Italian	Examples
abuse	abusare	Non è bene **abusare** della fiducia. *It's not good to **abuse** trust.*
accelerate	accelerare	Cerco di non **accelerare** troppo quando guido. *I try to not **accelerate** too much when I drive.*
accompany	accompagnare	Puoi **accompagnar**mi alla porta? *Can you **accompany** me to the door?*
assist	assistere[1]	Dovete **assistere** le persone quando potete. *You must **assist** people when you can.*
cease	cessare	Quel marchio **cesserà** di esistere. *That brand **will cease** to exist.*
celebrate	celebrare	**Celebrerò** il mio compleanno in crociera. *I **will celebrate** my birthday on a cruise.*

---

[1] The verb "**assistere**" also means *"to attend,"* e.g., "**assistere ad una lezione**" *(to attend a class)*, which is the more common use of the verb "**assistere**." The verb "aiutare" is often used to describe the act of giving help or assistance. The verb "attendere," on the other hand, is often used to mean *"to await"* or *"to wait for."*

combat	combattere	È difficile **combattere** le zanzare. *It's hard to combat the mosquitoes.*
compete	competere	Ama **competere** con suo fratello. *She loves to compete with her brother.*
condemn convict	condannare	Non dovresti **condannare** senza prove. *You shouldn't condemn without proof.*
confine	confinare	L'esercito **ha confinato** i ribelli. *The army has confined the rebels.*
consent	consentire	Ho letto i termini prima di **consentire**. *I read the terms before I consent.*
contemplate	contemplare	Mi piace **contemplare** l'arte di strada. *I like to contemplate street art.*
contrast	contrastare	Quel colore della porta **contrasta** con il muro. *That door color contrasts with the wall.*
contribute	contribuire	Penso di poter **contribuire** a questo progetto. *I think I can contribute to this project.*
convert	convertire	**Convertirò** l'immagine in un altro formato. *I will convert the image to another format.*
convince	convincere	Non sono facile da **convincere**. *I'm not easy to convince.*
criticize	criticare	Mia nonna **critica** sempre tutto. *My grandmother always criticizes everything.*
demonstrate	dimostrare	**Dimostrerò** come è fatto. *I will demonstrate how it's done.*
devastate	devastare	La casa è **devastata**. *The house is devastated.*
examine	esaminare	Puoi **esaminare** questo neo? *Can you examine this mole?*
foment	fomentare	Cerco di **fomentare** la lettura in classe. *I try to foment reading in the class.*
implement	implementare	Vorrei **implementare** sane abitudini. *I would like to implement healthy habits.*
indicate	indicare	Mi puoi **indicare** dov'è il bagno? *Can you indicate to me where the bathroom is?*
influence affect	influire su influenzare	Avere sonno **influisce su**lle mie reazioni. *Being sleepy affects my reactions.*
intensify	intensificare	Il sale **intensifica** i sapori. *Salt intensifies flavors.*
multiply	moltiplicare	Non mi piace **moltiplicare** i numeri. *I don't like to multiply numbers.*
optimize	ottimizzare	Devi **ottimizzare** la velocità di Internet. *You have to optimize your internet speed.*
serve	servire	È generoso **servire** gli altri quando è possibile. *It is generous to serve others when possible.*

supervise oversee	supervisionare	Il mio capo **supervisiona** 30 persone. *My boss **supervises** 30 people.*
torture	torturare	Non è umano **torturare** i prigionieri. *It's not humane to **torture** prisoners.*
vandalize	vandalizzare	**Hanno vandalizzato** il muro. *They **have vandalized** the wall.*
vibrate	vibrare	Il mio cellulare **vibra** quando ricevo un messaggio. *My cell phone **vibrates** when I receive a message.*

2. ADJECTIVES III

Below is a list of some common adjectives in Italian that we need at this level. Notice that an adjective must agree with the noun in number and gender.

English	Italian	Examples
alone	da solo[1]	Mi piace riposare **da solo**. *I like to rest **alone**.*
ancient	antico	Le piramidi d'Egitto sono **antiche**. *Egypt's pyramids are **ancient**.*
attracted	attratto	Le falene sono **attratte** dalla luce. *Moths are **attracted** to light.*
aware conscious	consapevole	Sono **consapevole** di tutte le sfide. *I am **aware** of all the challenges.*
bitter	amaro	Mi piace il caffè **amaro**. *I like my coffee **bitter**.*
blind	cieco	Ho un serpente **cieco**. *I have a **blind** snake.*
brave	coraggioso	Sei molto **coraggioso** a fare quel discorso. *You're very **brave** giving that speech.*
bright (light)	brillante luminoso	Giove sembra molto **brillante** nel cielo. *Jupiter looks very **bright** in the sky.*
cloudy	nuvoloso	La giornata è un po' **nuvolosa**. *The day is a bit **cloudy**.*
covered	coperto	Il pavimento è **coperto** di fango. *The floor is **covered** in mud.*
cowardly	codardo	Il mio cane è molto **codardo**. *My dog is very **cowardly**.*
dark	scuro buio	Questa foresta è molto **buia**. *This forest is very **dark**.*

---

[1] When used as an adverb, "**solo**" means *"only"* or *"just."*

deep profound	profondo	Questa è la parte **profonda** della piscina. *This is the **deep** part of the pool.*
depressing	deprimente	I funerali sono **deprimenti**. *Funerals are **depressing**.*
desirable	desiderabile	Vivere in città è molto **desiderabile**. *Living in the city is very **desirable**.*
double	doppio	Se lavoro il sabato, vengo pagato il **doppio**. *If I work on Saturday, I get paid **double**.*
drunk	ubriaco	Non devi guidare se sei **ubriaco**. *You must not drive if you are **drunk**.*
exhausted	esausto	Tagliare legna da ardere mi lascia **esausto**. *Cutting firewood leaves me **exhausted**.*
fat	grasso	Non è educato dire a qualcuno che sembra **grasso**. *It's not polite to tell someone they look **fat**.*
genius	geniale	Einstein era uno scienziato **geniale**. *Einstein was a **genius** scientist.*
historical	storico	Quella data commemora un evento **storico**. *That date commemorates a **historical** event.*
incorrect	errato scorretto	Non esiste un modo **errato** per farlo. *There is no **incorrect** way to do it.*
main principal	principale	Il punto **principale** è mantenere la calma. *The **main** point is to remain calm.*
masculine male	maschile mascolino	Quegli stivali sembrano **maschili**. *Those boots look **masculine**.*
naked bare	nudo	Voglio sapere la **nuda** verità. *I want to know the **naked** truth.*
narrow	stretto	Stai attento con quelle scale **strette**. *Be careful with those **narrow** stairs.*
own	proprio	Comprerò la mia **propria** macchina. *I'm going to buy my **own** car.*
powerful	potente	Questa macchina è molto **potente**. *This machine is very **powerful**.*
precise	preciso	Hanno un programma molto **preciso**. *They have a very **precise** schedule.*
proud	orgoglioso	Sono **orgoglioso** dei risultati del nostro team. *I'm **proud** of our team's accomplishment.*
rainy	piovoso	Sarà **piovoso** per tutto il fine settimana. *It will be **rainy** all weekend.*
raw	crudo greggio	Quel pollo è **crudo**. *That chicken is **raw**.*
relaxed	rilassato	Il sonno mi lascia **rilassato**. *Sleep leaves me **relaxed**.*
relaxing	rilassante	Dormire presto è **rilassante**. *Sleeping early is **relaxing**.*

retired	pensionato ritirato	I miei nonni sono **pensionati**. *My grandparents are **retired**.*
rude	rude maleducato scortese	Non dovresti essere **scortese** con le persone. *You shouldn't be **rude** to people.*
sensitive	sensibile	Ho la pelle molto **sensibile**. *I have very **sensitive** skin.*
spicy	speziato piccante	Adoro il cibo **piccante**! *I love **spicy** food!*
successful	riuscito di successo	Ha subito un intervento chirurgico **di successo**. *He underwent a **successful** surgery.*
tender **gentle**	tenero [1]	La carne è molto **tenera**. *The meat is very **tender**.*
thick	spesso	Non voglio una fetta di torta **spessa**. *I don't want a **thick** slice of cake.*
thin	magro [2] sottile	Sembra molto **magro** dopo la dieta. *He looks very **thin** after dieting.*
tiring	stancante faticoso	Stare svegli tutta la notte è **stacante**. *Staying up all night is **tiring**.*
united	unito	Sono **uniti** contro il nemico. *They are **united** against the enemy.*
wide	ampio largo	Il divano è molto **ampio**. *The couch is very **wide**.*
winning	vincente	Ha la ricetta **vincente**. *He has the **winning** recipe.*
wise	saggio	Il mio professore è molto **saggio**. *My professor is very **wise**.*

In addition to the above new adjectives, we add a few more English cognates that are easy to memorize.

English	Italian	Examples
approximate	approssimativo	Puoi calcolare il ritardo **approssimativo**? *Can you calculate the **approximate** delay?*
arrogant	arrogante	Non mi piacciono le persone **arroganti**. *I don't like **arrogant** people.*

---

[1] The adjective **"tenero"** *(tender)* can also refer to human behavior, e.g., **"Sono teneri con i loro figli"** *(They are tender with their children)*.

[2] Although **"magro"** and **"sottile"** both mean *"thin,"* we use **"magro"** more often with persons and animals, whereas **"sottile"** is used more often with objects.

calm	calmo	Mi sento **calmo** quando sono in spiaggia. *I feel **calm** when I am on the beach.*
defined	definito	I tuoi ricci sono molto **definiti**. *Your curls are very **defined**.*
depressed	depresso	Ascolto musica quando mi sento **depresso**. *I listen to music when I feel **depressed**.*
emotional	emozionato	I drammi mi fanno **emozionato**. *Dramas make me **emotional**.*
equivalent	equivalente	Una coppia è **equivalente** a due. *A pair is **equivalent** to two.*
financial	finanziario	La mia situazione **finanziaria** è privata. *My **financial** situation is private.*
independent	indipendente	I giovani desiderano essere più **indipendenti**. *Young people wish to be more **independent**.*
intense	intenso	Quel profumo è molto **intenso** per me. *That perfume is very **intense** to me.*
limited	limitato	Lo spazio del patio è **limitato**. *The patio's space is **limited**.*
logical	logico	Questa spiegazione non è **logica**. *This explanation is not **logical**.*
maximum	massimo	Riempio la bottiglia alla **massima** capacità. *I fill the bottle to **maximum** capacity.*
medical	medico	Ho un problema **medico**. *I have a **medical** issue.*
minimum	minimo	Non è consigliabile fare solo il **minimo**. *It's not recommended to just do the **minimum**.*
modest	modesto	Quel milionario è molto **modesto**. *That millionaire is very **modest**.*
multiple	multiplo	Ho ordinato da quel posto articoli **multipli**. *I've ordered from that place **multiple** items.*
precious valuable	prezioso	Il vaso di mia nonna è molto **prezioso**. *My grandma's vase is very **precious**.*
ridiculous	ridicolo	La mia risposta sarà **ridicola**! *My answer will be **ridiculous**!*
separate	separato	I suoi genitori sono **separati**. *His parents are **separated**.*
sexual	sessuale	Le molestie **sessuali** sono totalmente inaccettabili. ***Sexual** harassment is totally unacceptable.*
similar	simile	Io e i miei fratelli siamo molto **simili**. *My siblings and I are very **similar**.*
solid	solido	La superficie non sembra **solida**. *The surface doesn't look **solid**.*
technical	tecnico	Non capisco gli aspetti **tecnici** della macchina. *I don't understand the **technical** aspects of the car.*

traditional	tradizionale	Mi piace l'arredamento più **tradizionale**. *I like the more **traditional** decor.*
unlimited	illimitato	Ciò che può essere appreso è **illimitato**. *What can be learned is **unlimited**.*
valid	valido	Credo che abbia una ragione **valida**. *I believe that he has a **valid** reason.*

3. RELIGION I

Below is some vocabulary related to *religion*, or "**la religione**," that you may need:

God	**Dio**	*angel*	**angelo**^m
Koran	**Corano**^m	*belief*	**credenza**^f
Islam	**islam**^m	*church*	**chiesa**^f
Muslim	**musulmano**^m	*faith*	**fede**^f
Bible	**Bibbia**^f	*devil*	**diavolo**^m
Christianity	**cristianesimo**^m	*demon*	**demone**^m
Christian	**cristiano**^m	*heaven*	**paradiso**^m
Christmas	**Natale**^m	*hell*	**inferno**^m
Catholic	**cattolico**^m	*miracle*	**miracolo**^m
Catholicism	**cattolicesimo**^m	*mosque*	**moschea**^f
Protestantism	**protestantesimo**^m	*pope*	**papa**^m
Protestant	**protestante**^m	*prayer*	**preghiera**^f
Judaism	**giudaismo**^m	*prophet*	**profeta**^m
Jewish	**ebreo**^m	*sin*	**peccato**^m
Buddhism	**buddismo**^m	*soul*	**anima**^f
Buddhist	**buddista**^m	*atheism*	**ateismo**^m
Hinduism	**induismo**^m	*atheist*	**ateo**^m
Hindu	**induista**^m	*Satan*	**satana**^m

4. MEDIA I

The *media*, a singular word in English, is a plural word in Italian, that is, "**i media**." Here is some related vocabulary:

advertising	**pubblicità**^f	*press*	**stampa**^f
antenna	**antenna**^f	*public TV*	**televisione pubblica**^f
cable TV	**televisione**^f **via cavo**	*radio station*	**stazione radiofonica**^f
cinema	**cinema**^m	*rumor*	**pettegolezzo**^m
documentary	**documentario**^m	*scandal*	**scandalo**^m

fact check	conferma^f dei fatti	soap opera	telenovela^f
magazine	rivista^f	television	televisione^f
movie	film^m	TV channel	canale^m (televisivo)
news	notizie^f	TV series	serie^f (televisiva)
news report	reportage^m	TV show	programma^m (televisivo)
newspaper	giornale^m quotidiano	voice	voce^f

5. HOUSE I

Here we learn a set of vocabulary related to the *house*, or "**la casa**," in Italian:

address	indirizzo^m	glass (of water)	bicchiere^m (di acqua)
alarm clock	sveglia^f	glue	colla^f collante^m
armchair	poltrona^f	ground floor	piano^m terra
bag	busta^f	headboard	testiera^f
balcony	balcone^m	kettle	bollitore^m teiera^f
basement	seminterrato^m	key	chiave^f
basin	lavabo^m	kitchen	cucina^f
basket	cesta^f cestino^m	knife	coltello^m
bathroom	bagno^m	ladle	mestolo^m
bathtub	vasca^f da bagno	lamp	lampada^f
bed	letto^m	living room	soggiorno^m
bedroom	camera^f da letto	mail	posta^f
blanket	coperta^f	mirror	specchio^m
book	libro^m	outlet (electricity)	presa^f di corrente
bottle	bottiglia^f	oven	forno^m
bowl	ciotola^f scodella^f	painting	dipinto^m quadro^m
box	scatola^f	photo	foto^f fotografia^f
carpet	tappeto^m	pillow	cuscino^m
ceiling	soffitto^m	refrigerator	frigorifero^m
cellar	cantina^f	roof	tetto^m
chair	sedia^f	room	camera^f stanza^f
chimney	camino^m	saucepan	casseruola^f

cigar	sigaro^m	scale (kitchen)	bilancia^f da cucina
cigarette	sigaretta^f	sink	lavandino^m
clock	orologio^m	sofa	sofà^m divano^m
cup	tazza^f coppa^f	spoon	cucchiaio^m
desk	scrivania^f	stairs	scala^f
dishes plates	piatti^m	stove	fornello^m cucina^f
door	porta^f	study (room)	studio^m
extractor	estrattore^m	table	tavolo^m 1
fan	ventilatore^m	telephone	telefono^m
faucet	rubinetto^m	thing	cosa^f
floor	piano^m	towel	canovaccio^m
fork	forchetta^f	trash garbage	spazzatura^f immondizia^f
freezer	congelatore^m	wall^2	muro^m parete^f
frying pan	padella^f	wardrobe	armadio^m guardaroba^m
garage	garage^m	window	finestra^f

[1] The masculine noun "**tavolo**" is used to refer to a table as a piece of furniture. On the other hand, the feminine noun "**tavola**" is used when referring to a table set for a meal, e.g., "**La tavola è pronta per la cena**" *(The table is ready for dinner).*

[2] The word "**muro**" is often used to refer to an external wall, whereas "**parete**" is generally used to refer to an indoor wall within a building.

6. SPORTS I

Sport, or "**lo sport**," contains a lot of vocabulary that we encounter in our daily life. Here we have some commonly used ones. If you are interested in *soccer*, or "**il calcio**," you can refer to **Appendix C** for a more extensive set of vocabulary.

ball	palla^f	national team	squadra nazionale^f
baseball	baseball^m	offside	fuori gioco^m
basketball	pallacanestro^f	period	tempo^m
boxing	boxe^f	punch	pugno^m
championship	campionato^m	race	gara^f

chess	scacchi^m	referee	arbitro^m
court field	campo^m	round	giro^m
draw (tie)	parità^f	scorer	marcatore^m
entry admission	ammissione^f	shot (soccer)	tiro^m
exercise	esercizio^m	stadium	stadio^m
game	gioco^m	swimming	nuoto^m
goal	gol^m	team	squadra^f
in top shape	in piena forma^f	tennis	tennis^m
injury	lesione^f	trainer coach	allenatore^m
locker room	spogliatoio^m	training	allenamento^m
match	partita^f	wound	ferita^f

7. COLORS II

Some more colors and color-related words to add to your Italian vocabulary are:

burgundy	borgogna^{m,f}	shade	sfumatura^f ombra^f
magenta	magenta^{m,f}	tone	tono^m
pink	rosa^{m,f}	violet	viola^{m,f}

8. TECHNOLOGY

Let us go over some vocabulary related to *technology* or "**la tecnologia**":

alert	allerta^f	key (code)	chiave^f
appliance	apparato^m	keyboard	tastiera^f
atom	atomo^m	integrated circuit	circuito integrato^m
attachment	allegato^m	laboratory	laboratorio^m
backup file	file di backup	laptop	portatile^m
battery	batteria^f	network	rete^f
binary	binario^m	password	password^f parola^f d'ordine
button	bottone^m tasto^m	patent	patente^f

cable	**cavo**^m	*permission*	**permesso**^m
calculator	**calcolatrice**^f	*printer*	**stampante**^f
camera	**macchina fotografica**^f **videocamera**^f	*program*	**programma**^m
CD player	**lettore CD**^m	*reminder*	**promemoria**^m
cell phone	**cellulare**^m	*remote control*	**controllo remoto**^m
charger	**caricatore**^m	*satellite*	**satellite**^m
circuit	**circuito**^m	*search*	**ricerca**^f
code	**codice**^m	*screen*	**schermo**^m
computer	**computer**^m	*short circuit*	**corto circuito**^m
database	**base dati**^f **banca dati**^f	*speaker*	**altoparlante**^m
domain	**dominio**^m	*symbol*	**simbolo**^m
downloading	**scaricamento**^m **download**^m	*telescope*	**telescopio**^m
email	**posta elettronica**^f **email**^f	*testing*	**prova**^f
energy	**energia**^f	*transmitter*	**trasmettitore**^m
file	**archivio**^m **file**^m	*uploading*	**caricamento**^m
fuse	**fusibile**^m	*volume*	**volume**^m
headphones	**cuffie**^f **auricolari**^m	*weblink*	**collegamento web**^m
home appliances	**elettrodomestici**^m	*wire*	**filo**^m
input (device)	**ingresso**^m	*wireless*	**senza fili**^m

9. TRAVEL

Travel, or "**il viaggio,**" is another important topic with commonly used vocabulary, such as:

adventure	**avventura**^f	*outskirts*	**periferie**^f
accommodation	**alloggio**^m **sistemazione**^f	*passenger*	**passeggero**^m
arrival	**arrivo**^m	*passport*	**passaporto**^m
carry-on luggage	**bagaglio**^m **a mano**	*pharaoh*	**faraone**^m
customs	**dogana**^f	*public transportation*	**trasporto pubblico**^m
delay	**ritardo**^m	*remote zone*	**zona remota**^f
departure	**partenza**^f	*resort (vacation)*	**villaggio turistico**^m

duty (tariff)	tariffa^f tassa^f	security safety	sicurezza^f
duty-free	senza tasse doganali^f senza imposte^f	souvenir	ricordo^m
guide	guida^f	suitcase	valigia^f
holidays vacation	vacanze^f	tour	escursione^f
itinerary	itinerario^m	tourist	turista^{m,f}
journey	viaggio^m	traveler	viaggiatore^m viaggiatrice^f
luggage	bagaglio^m	trip	viaggio^m

10. LANGUAGE

There is a subtle difference between "**la lingua**" and "**il linguaggio**," both meaning *language*. Whereas "**lingua**" is used to describe the real spoken language, e.g., "**la lingua italiana**" *(the Italian language)*, "**linguaggio**" is used to describe the way and the ability of humans and other beings to communicate, e.g., "**il linguaggio parlato**" *(oral language)*. To describe computer languages, we also use "**linguaggio**," e.g., "**il linguaggio Java**" *(the Java language)*. Here is some vocabulary related to language:

acronym	acronimo^m	native	nativo^m
adjective	aggettivo^m	noun	sostantivo^m nome^m
alphabet	alfabeto^m	paragraph	paragrafo^m
Arabic	arabo^m	passage	brano^m
auxiliary	ausiliare^m	passive	passivo^m
clause	proposizione^f	phrase	frase^f
conjunction	congiunzione^f	Portuguese	portoghese^{m,f}
conjugation	coniugazione^f	preposition	preposizione^f
dialect	dialetto^m	pronoun	pronome^m
dictionary	dizionario^m	proverb	proverbio^m
discourse	discorso^m	semantics	semantica^f
emphasis	enfasi^f	sentence	frase^f
figurative	figurativo^m	slang	gergo^m
fluency	fluenza^f	subjunctive	congiuntivo^m
fluent	fluente^{m,f}	suffix	suffisso^m

grammar	**grammatica**^f	*superlative*	**superlativo**^m
Hindi	**indi**^m	*syllable*	**sillaba**^f
idiom	**idioma**^m	*tale*	**racconto**^m
indicative	**indicativo**^m	*translation*	**traduzione**^f
infinitive	**infinito**^m	*Urdu*	**urdu**^m
interjection	**interiezione**^f	*verb*	**verbo**^m
letter	**lettera**^f	*verb tense*	**tempo verbale**^m
level	**livello**^m	*vocabulary*	**vocabolario**^m
Mandarin	**mandarino**^m	*vowel*	**vocale**^f
mood	**modo**^m	*word*	**parola**^f

LEVEL IV: INTERMEDIATE

I. Introductory Topics & Grammar

At this intermediate level, we encounter new topics, some familiar thanks to our knowledge of English and some new topics that are unique to the Italian language. Use the Anki cards to reinforce these topics in your memory with reviews and exercises.

1. DEGREES OF COMPARISON

In this lesson, we will examine different ways of comparing nouns, indicating their equality, inequality, or the extreme degree of an adjective. We will study the comparison of equality, the comparison of inequality, and superlatives.

Comparatives of Equality

The most common expressions in this category are:

1. **così** + (adjective/adverb) + **come** ...   *as (adj./adv.) as ...*

Questa macchina è **così** costosa **come** una casa.	*This car is **as** expensive **as** a house.*
Lei è **così** alta **come** sua sorella.	*She is **as** tall **as** her sister.*
Parla **così** chiaro **come** un insegnante.	*He speaks **as** clearly **as** a teacher.*

2. **tanto** + (adj./adv.) + **quanto** ...   *as (adj./adv.) as ...*

Questa macchina è **tanto** costosa **quanto** una casa.	*This car is **as** expensive **as** a house.*
Lei è **tanto** alta **quanto** sua sorella.	*She is **as** tall **as** her sister.*
Parla **tanto** chiaro **quanto** un insegnante.	*He speaks **as** clearly **as** a teacher.*

Notice that it is more common, in both expressions above, to drop the first word, "**così**" or "**tanto**," in the construction in informal speech, e.g., "**Lei è alta come sua sorella**" *(She is as tall as her sister).*

3. **tanto/-a/-i/-e** + (noun) + **quanto** ...   *as much/many (noun) as ...*

Ha **tanti** soldi **quanto** un milionario.	*He has **as much** money **as** a millionaire.*
Ci sono **tante** persone qui **come** a Londra.	*There are **as many** people here **as** in London.*

Notice that "**tanto/-a/-i/-e**" in the expressions above must agree in gender and number with the noun it describes.

Comparatives of Inequality

The following formula is used to express inequality when comparing two adjectives, adverbs, or nouns:

più/meno ... di ...   *more/less ... than ...*

For example:

È **più** alta **di** sua sorella.	*She is taller than her sister.*
Parla **più** chiaro **di** un professore.	*He speaks more clearly than a teacher.*
Ha **più** soldi **del** presidente.	*He has more money than the president.*
Siamo **meno** ricchi **dei** nostri genitori.	*We are less rich than our parents.*
Parla **meno** chiaramente **di** un professore.	*He speaks less clearly than a teacher.*
Ha **meno** pazienza **di** mio fratello.	*He has less patience than my brother.*

The following adjectives have both regular and irregular forms:

buono	*good*	**migliore** or **più buono**	*better*
cattivo	*bad*	**peggiore** or **più cattivo**	*worse*
vecchio	*old*	**maggiore** or **più vecchio**	*older*
giovane	*young*	**minore** or **più giovane**	*younger*
grande	*large*	**maggiore** or **più grande**	*larger*
piccolo	*small*	**minore** or **più piccolo**	*smaller*

In the special case of comparing an adjective to another adjective of the same noun, we use "**che**" instead of "**di**" before the second adjective. For example:

Il suo discorso è **più** emotivo **che** accurato.	*His speech is **more** emotional **than** it is accurate.*

Sono **più** professionali **che** esperti.	*They are **more** professional **than** they are experienced.*

Superlatives

There are two ways to express the large or extreme degrees of an adjective.

1. Relative Superlatives

il/la/i/le + **più/meno** + (adjective)	*the + most/least + (adjective)*

Inserting a noun between the definite article and "**più/meno**" is optional.

Lei è **la più** intelligente della sua classe.	*She is **the most** intelligent in her class.*
Siamo **i meno** colpiti dalla crisi.	*We are **the least** affected by the crisis.*
È **la** <u>questione</u> **più** importante del paese.	*This is **the most** important topic in the country.*
È **il** <u>politico</u> **meno** corrotto in parlamento.	*He is **the least** corrupt politician in the parliament.*
Sono **le** <u>donne</u> **più** coraggiose che abbia mai visto.	*They are **the most** courageous women I have ever seen.*

The following adjectives from the comparison of inequality also have regular and irregular forms as relative superlatives:

buono	*good*	**il/la/i/le** + (**migliore** or **più buono**)	*best*
cattivo	*bad*	**il/la/i/le** + (**peggiore** or **più cattivo**)	*worst*
vecchio	*old*	**il/la/i/le** + (**maggiore** or **più vecchio**)	*oldest*
giovane	*young*	**il/la/i/le** + (**minore** or **più giovane**)	*youngest*
grande	*large*	**il/la/i/le** + (**maggiore** or **più grande**)	*largest*
piccolo	*small*	**il/la/i/le** + (**minore** or **più piccolo**)	*smallest*

2. Absolute Superlatives

One can express an absolute superlative by simply preceding the adjective with an adverb such as "**molto**" (*very*) or "**estremamente**" (*extremely*). For example:

Questo stadio è **molto** freddo.	*This stadium is **very** cold.*
Il caffè è **estremamente** caldo.	*The coffee is **extremely** hot.*

Another way to express absolute superlatives is by using adjectives ending in "**-issimo**" for masculine or "**-isima**" for feminine, translated as *"very"* or *"quite."* It is constructed by removing the vowel at the end of the adjective and attaching the suffix "**-isimo.**" The masculine and feminine plurals end in "**-i**" and "**-e,**" respectively.

cattivo	*bad*	cattivissimo	*very bad*
grande	*large*	grandissimo	*very large*
buono	*good*	buonissimo	*very good*
piccolo	*small*	piccolissimo	*very small*

2. PARTITIVES

To refer to an unidentified quantity of something in English, we often use words or phrases like *"some," "a few,"* and *"a little bit of."* These are called *partitives* because they refer to a part of something, whether it is countable, e.g., *"some trees,"* or uncountable, e.g., *"some water."*

In Italian, the most common way to form a partitive is using the preposition "**di**" followed by a definite article, also known as a *partitive article.* This would literally translate to *"of the."* However, it serves more as an equivalent to the partitive *"some"* in English.

Countable Nouns

Because countable nouns have a plural form, we use the preposition "**di**" followed by the plural definite article "**i**" or "**gli**" for masculine and "**le**" for feminine. This results in the three following partitive articles:

di +	gli	=	degli	Before a plural *masculine* noun that begins with a vowel, "**z**," "**gn**," "**ps**," or "**s**" + consonant
	i	=	dei	Before any other plural *masculine* noun
	le	=	delle	Before any plural *feminine* noun

Let us take some examples with countable nouns:

un ragazzo	*a boy*	dei ragazzi	*some boys*
un albero	*a tree*	degli alberi	*some trees*
una casa	*a house*	delle case	*some houses*
un porto	*a port*	dei porti	*some ports*
uno zio	*an uncle*	degli zii	*some uncles*
una stanza	*a room*	delle stanze	*some rooms*
uno sbaglio	*a mistake*	degli sbagli	*some mistakes*
un libro	*a book*	dei libri	*some books*
uno schermo	*a screen*	degli schermi	*some screens*

Remember that using partitive articles is not the only way to describe an undefined quantity of countable nouns. Other partitive words include "**alcuni/-e**" and "**qualche**," both meaning *"some."* The more specific partitive "**certi/-e**" *(certain)* can also be used depending on the context.

Let us take some examples:

una casa	*a house*	alcune case	qualche <u>casa</u>	certe case	*some houses*
un porto	*a port*	alcuni porti	qualche <u>porto</u>	certi porti	*some ports*
uno zio	*an uncle*	alcuni zii	qualche <u>zio</u>	certi zii	*some uncles*

Notice that "**qualche**" is invariable and always followed by a *singular* noun although the meaning is plural.

Uncountable Nouns

By countable nouns, we refer to nouns that are not often used in plural form, even if a plural form can be used in some contexts. For example, in English, we could say *"three fruits"* referring to three pieces of fruit. However, the word *"fruit"* is often used as an uncountable noun. Here, we discuss how to refer to an undefined quantity of such nouns when used in their uncountable form.

To refer to an uncountable noun using a partitive article, we treat it as a singular noun. Thus, we use the preposition "**di**" followed by the singular definite article "**l'**," "**il**," or "**lo**" for masculine and "**l'**" or "**la**" for feminine. This results in the three following partitive articles:

	l'	=	dell'	Before a *masculine* or *feminine* uncountable noun that begins with a vowel
di +	lo	=	dello	Before a *masculine* uncountable noun that begins with "**z**," "**gn**," "**ps**," or "**s**" + consonant
	il	=	del	Before any other *masculine* uncountable noun
	la	=	della	Before any other *feminine* uncountable noun

Let us take some examples with uncountable nouns:

l'acqua	*the water*	dell'acqua	*some water*
lo zucchero	*the sugar*	dello zucchero	*some sugar*
il pane	*the bread*	del pane	*some bread*
la pasta	*the pasta*	della pasta	*some pasta*
l'orzo	*the barley*	dell'orzo	*some barley*
il latte	*the milk*	del latte	*some milk*
la frutta	*the fruit*	della frutta	*some fruit*

As an alternative to partitive articles, one can, depending on the context, use the partitive word "**un po' di**" *(a bit of)* to refer to an undefined quantity of an uncountable noun.

Here are some examples:

l'acqua	*the water*	un po' d'acqua	*a bit of water*
lo zucchero	*the sugar*	un po' di zucchero	*a bit of sugar*
il pane	*the bread*	un po' di pane	*a bit of bread*
la pasta	*the pasta*	un po' di pasta	*a bit of pasta*

Further Notes on Partitive Articles

❖ Remember that if an adjective precedes the noun, the definite article, and thus the partitive article, must change according to the beginning of the adjective, e.g., "**dell'orzo**" *(some barley)* vs. "**del nuovo orzo**" *(some new barley)*.

❖ The partitive article is often dropped in the following cases:

1. When listing two or more items. The partitive article is often dropped rather than repeated before each item, e.g., "**Vorrei pane e zucchero**" *(I would like bread and sugar)*, "**Abbiamo**

finito il riso, la pasta, la carne e l'acqua" *(We ran out of rice, pasta, meat and water)*, etc.

2. After the preposition **"di."** Some verbs in Italian require the preposition **"di,"** e.g., **"avere bisogno di"** *(to need)*. In this case, an alternative partitive such as **"alcuni/-e"** can be used instead, e.g., **"Ho bisogno di <u>alcuni</u> libri da leggere sul tema"** *(I need <u>some</u> books to read on the subject)*.

3. In negative sentences. The partitive is omitted in negative sentences whether the noun is countable or uncountable, e.g., **"Non ho zii"** *(I don't have uncles)*, **"Non voglio zucchero"** *(I don't want sugar)*, **"Non c'è pane"** *(There isn't bread)*, etc.

❖ In negative sentences with countable nouns, the negative meaning of *"any,"* as in *"There isn't any bread,"* can be rendered by the use of **"nessuno"** and its variants. The word **"nessuno"** is treated like an indefinite article. It conveys the meaning of *"not one"* or *"not any,"* and is always followed by a singular noun even if the meaning is plural. Here are some examples:

Non c'è **nessun** albero nel deserto.	*There aren't **any** trees in the desert.*
Non ho **nessuno** zio.	*I don't have **any** uncles.*
Non c'è **nessuna** casa in questa zona.	*There aren't **any** houses in this area.*
Lei non ha **nessun'**amica.	*She doesn't have **any** friends.*

Remember, however, that **"nessuno"** cannot be used with uncountable nouns.

3. REFLEXIVE PRONOUNS & VERBS

A verb is considered reflexive if the subject and the object of the verb are the same. This means that the subject is doing the action to itself, not to something or someone else. For instance, *"I wash myself"* is reflexive, while *"I wash my car"* is not reflexive.

Some verbs in Italian are commonly used in the reflexive form. Let us take one example that we are familiar with. The verb **"chiamare"** means *"to call,"* e.g., **"mia madre, mi chiama ogni**

venerdì" (*My mom calls me every Friday*). However, the reflexive form of the verb **"chiamarsi,"** which literally means *"to call oneself,"* is used to express one's name. For instance, **"Mi chiamo Carlo"** means *"My name is Carlo,"* which is literally *"I call myself Carlo."* A reflexive verb in formed by replacing the final "**-e**" in the infinitive with "**-si,**" often translated as *"oneself."*

There are many verbs in Italian that have reflexive forms. We will discuss some examples; however, let us first learn how to conjugate reflexive verbs.

	Object Personal Pron.	e.g., chiamarsi
io	mi	chiamo
tu	ti	chiami
lui/lei	si	chiama
noi	ci	chiamiamo
voi	vi	chiamate
loro	si	chiamano

As shown in the table, we add the object personal pronoun before the verb. Note that the subject and object personal pronouns are of the same gender and number because the subject and the object are essentially the same.

Remember that when the verb is used in reflexive form, the infinitive ends in "**si,**" e.g., **"chiamarsi."** Here are more examples of reflexive verbs.

alzarsi	*to get up*	**annoiarsi**	*to get bored*
arrabbiarsi (con)	*to get mad (at)*	**distrarsi**	*to distract oneself*
divertirsi	*to have fun*	**farsi la doccia**	*to take a shower*
farsi male	*to hurt oneself*	**fermarsi**	*to stop*
innamorarsi	*to fall in love*	**lavarsi**	*to wash oneself*
occuparsi	*to take care of oneself*	**mettersi**	*to put on*
pettinarsi	*to comb one's hair*	**perdersi**	*to get lost*
prepararsi	*to get ready*	**preoccuparsi**	*to worry*
pulirsi	*to clean oneself*	**radersi** **farsi la barba**	*to shave*
ricordarsi	*to remember*	**rallegrarsi**	*to rejoice*
sbrigarsi	*to hurry*	**riprendersi**	*to recover*

sedersi	*to sit down*	**sentirsi**	*to feel*
slogarsi	*to twist or sprain*	**spogliarsi**	*to undress oneself*
stancarsi	*to get tired*	**svegliarsi**	*to wake up*
ubriacarsi	*to get drunk*	**vestirsi**	*to get dressed*

Let us look at some examples:

Mi annoio velocemente a casa.	*I **get bored** fast at home.*
Lei **si sveglia** sempre presto.	*She always **wakes up** early.*
Ci divertiamo molto insieme.	*We **have** a lot of **fun** together.*
Mi rado due volte a settimana.	*I **shave** twice a week.*

One can add the reflexive pronoun to verbs that are not usually reflexive to make them reflexive, for example:

parlarsi	*to speak to each other*	**vedersi**	*to see each other*
capirsi	*to understand each other*	**visitarsi**	*to visit each other*
comprarsi	*to buy oneself something*	**ascoltarsi**	*to listen to oneself*

Some verbs are used *only* in reflexive form, such as "**suicidarsi**" *(to commit suicide)*.

Some verbs change their meaning when they are used in reflexive form, for example:

annoiare	*to bore*	**annoiarsi**	*to get bored*
coricare	*to lay down*	**coricarsi**	*to lie down or go to bed*
sposare	*to join in marriage*	**sposarsi**	*to get married*
addormentare	*to put to sleep*	**addormentarsi**	*to fall asleep*

Finally, keep in mind that all reflexive verbs use the auxiliary "**essere**" when conjugated in the present perfect tense, regardless of the auxiliary used by the non-reflexive form of the verb. For example:

Ieri sera **mi <u>sono</u> annoiato**.	*I **got bored** last night.*
Lei **si <u>è</u> svegliata** presto oggi.	*She **woke up** early today.*
Ieri **ci <u>siamo</u> divertiti** molto.	*We **had** a lot of **fun** yesterday.*
Mi <u>sono</u> rasato la scorsa settimana.	*I **shaved** last week.*
Si <u>sono</u> visti per caso.	*They **saw each other** by accident.*

Remember that when "**essere**," is used as an auxiliary, the past participle takes the treatment of an adjective and must agree in gender and number with the subject.

4. EXPRESSIONS USING "AVERE" & "FARE"

Some expressions in Italian do not make sense if literally translated into English. For example, the expression "**dare un esame**," meaning *"to take an exam,"* uses the verb "**dare**" *(to give)* rather than "**prendere**" *(to take).* In this section, we will learn some expressions using "**avere**" *(to have)* and "**fare**" *(to do or to make)* that are common in Italian.

1.   Expressions using "**Avere**"

In addition to the obvious use of "**avere**" to indicate possession, e.g., "**Ho due gatti**" (*I have two cats*), there are some less obvious uses of the verb "**avere**" in Italian.

In English, we use the verb *"to be"* to describe age, as in *"how old are you?"* and *"I am 30 years old."* In Italian, the verb "**avere**" is used instead; that is, we literally say, *"I have 30 years old"* rather than, *"I am 30 years old."* Here are a few more examples:

Quanti anni **hai**?	*How old are you?*
Ho 40 anni.	*I am 40 years old.*
Lui **ha** 20 anni.	*He is 20 years old.*

Some expressions in Italian describe a feeling or desire using the verb "**avere**," while their equivalents in English use the verb *"to be,"* e.g., "**Ho paura**" *(I am afraid).* The word "**paura**" means *"fear."* Thus, we literally say, *"I have fear."* Some other examples include:

avere fame	*to be hungry*	avere sete	*to be thirsty*
avere freddo	*to be cold*	avere caldo	*to be hot*
avere sonno	*to be sleepy*	avere allergie	*to be allergic*

Finally, there are many other idioms and expressions that use the verb "**avere**." One common expression is "**Ha senso**," which means *"It makes sense."* Some other expressions include:

avere ragione	*to be right*	avere torto	*to be wrong*
avere successo	*to be successful*	avere luogo	*to take place*
avere fretta	*to be in a hurry*	avere fortuna	*to be lucky*
avere inizio	*to begin*	avere la parola	*to have the floor*
avere a che fare con	*to have to do with*	avere da fare	*to be busy*
avere dolore	*to have pain*	avere bisogno di	*to need*

2. Expressions using "**Fare**"

There are many expressions that use the verb "**fare**" *(to do or to make)* in Italian, when similar expressions in English would not. We have encountered the verb "**fare**" used with weather expressions in **Level III, Lesson 7**, e.g., "**fa freddo**" *(It is cold)*. Similarly, the verb "**fare**" in "**Il tè fa bene/male**" simply replaces the verb *"to be"* to mean: *"The tea is good/bad."*

Let us examine some other expressions that use the verb "**fare**." In general, we use the verb "**fare**" when referring to sports and hobbies. Here are some examples:

fare sport	*to play sports*	fare ginnastica	*to exercise*
fare una corsa	*to go for a run*	fare una passeggiata	*to take a walk*
fare surf	*to do surfing*	fare snowboard	*to snowboard*
fare ciclismo	*to go cycling*	fare yoga	*to do yoga*

The verb "**fare**" is also used with many house chores and day-to-day tasks. Examples include:

fare i compiti	*to do homework*	fare il bucato	*to do laundry*
fare il letto	*to make the bed*	fare una telefonata	*to make a call*
fare la spesa	*to buy groceries*	fare il pieno	*to fill up on gas*
fare le faccende	*to do the chores*	fare spese	*to go shopping*
fare colazione	*to have breakfast*	fare le pulizie	*to do the cleaning*
fare la doccia	*to take a shower*	fare il bagno	*to take a bath*

There are many other idioms and expressions that use the verb **"fare"** that do not fall under any of the aforementioned categories, such as:

fare la fila fare la coda	to wait in line	fare in tempo	to do something in time
fare presto	to be early	fare tardi	to be late
fare una domanda	to ask a question	fare una pausa	to take a break
fare male	to hurt or to be painful	fare una foto	to take a photo
fare da sé	to do on your own	fai da te	DIY
fare di tutto	to do everything possible	fare un pisolino	to take a nap

Finally, the verb **"fare"** can be used in many causative expressions meaning *"to have someone do something."* For example:

fare vedere a qualcuno	to have someone see (to show someone)
fare cucinare a qualcuno	to have someone cook

5. Present Subjunctive Tense I

All the tenses we have encountered so far were in the indicative mood. The indicative mood is what we use to express facts. This is the mood we encounter often. There are five moods in total in Italian: infinitive, indicative, subjunctive, imperative, and conditional. The subjunctive mood is used to express opinion, possibility, and feelings, such as fear, doubt, hope, desire, etc. Generally speaking, the indicative describes facts, whereas the subjunctive describes non-facts.

To conjugate verbs in the present subjunctive, we begin from the *first-person singular in the present indicative*, i.e., **"parlo,"** **"vendo,"** **"parto,"** **"finisco,"** etc., and we extract the stem **"parl-,"** **"vend-,"** **"part-,"** **"finisc-,"** etc., by dropping the last **"-o."** Then, we add the endings shown in the following table. The **"noi"** and **"voi"** forms are conjugated differently. The **"noi"** form is the same as the indicative, and the "**voi**" form has "**-iate**" ending regardless of the verb group.

	-are ending parlare *(to speak)*	-ere ending vendere *(to sell)*	-ire ending (Type I) partire *(to leave)*	-ire ending (Type II) finire *(to finish)*
io	parli	venda	parta	finisca
tu	parli	venda	parta	finisca
lui/lei	parli	venda	parta	finisca
noi	parliamo	vendiamo	partiamo	finiamo
voi	parliate	vendiate	partiate	finiate
loro	parlino	vendano	partano	finiscano

From the examples in the table, notice that:

1. The forms "**io**," "**tu**," and "**lui/lei**" have identical conjugation. This makes them, unlike in the indicative mood, indistinguishable if the subject is omitted. Thus, we often include the subject if one of these three forms is used.

2. The "**noi**" form of regular verbs has identical conjugation in both the indicative and subjunctive moods.

3. The "**voi**" form has the same conjugation ending in all verb groups in the present subjunctive.

4. All verbs with "**-ere**" and "**-ire**" endings have the same conjugation patterns in the present subjunctive.

Finally, you must remember to use the stem from the first-person "**io**" form in the present indicative, not the stem from the infinitive. This is especially important with verbs that are irregular in the "**yo**" form in the present indicative. For example, the stem from "**io bevo**" is used for the verb "**bere**" *(to drink)* in the present subjunctive. Here are some examples:

	bere bev-	dire dic-	potere poss-	uscire esc-	volere vogli-
io	beva	dica	possa	esca	voglia
tu	beva	dica	possa	esca	voglia
lui/lei	beva	dica	possa	esca	voglia

noi	beviamo	diciamo	possiamo	usciamo	vogliamo
voi	beviate	diciate	possiate	usciate	vogliate
loro	bevano	dicano	possano	escano	vogliano

There are only few irregular verbs that do not follow the aforementioned conjugation patterns. These include the following:

1. Verbs with "**-are**" ending that follow the conjugation pattern of "**-ere**" and "**-ire**" verbs. There are two common verbs in this group: "**andare**" *(to go)* and "**fare**" *(to do or to make)*. The "**noi**" form is the same as the indicative. The "**voi**" form of "**andare**" is irregular and uses the stem from the *infinitive*.

	andare vad-	fare facci-
io	vada	faccia
tu	vada	faccia
lui/lei	vada	faccia
noi	andiamo	facciamo
voi	andiate	facciate
loro	vadano	facciano

2. Verbs that use the stem from the "**noi**" form instead of the "**io**" form, by dropping the last "**-amo.**" There are a few common verbs in this category. The "**noi**" form is the same as the indicative, and the "**voi**" form drops one "**i**" to avoid the double "**i**" sound.

	avere abbi-	dare di-	essere si-	sapere sappi-	stare sti-
io	abbia	dia	sia	sappia	stia
tu	abbia	dia	sia	sappia	stia
lui/lei	abbia	dia	sia	sappia	stia
noi	abbiamo	diamo	siamo	sappiamo	stiamo
voi	abbiate	diate	siate	sappiate	stiate
loro	abbiano	diano	siano	sappiano	stiano

3. Contracted infinitive verbs with "**-rre**" endings are all conjugated like "**-ere**" and "**-ire**" verbs. The "**noi**" form is the same as the indicative, and the "**voi**" form uses the stem from the *infinitive* with the "**-iate**" ending.

	trarre *(to pull)* tragg-	porre *(to put)* pong-	tradurre *(to translate)* traduc-
io	tragga	ponga	traduca
tu	tragga	ponga	traduca
lui/lei	tragga	ponga	traduca
noi	traiamo	poniamo	traduciamo
voi	traiate	poniate	traduciate
loro	traggano	pongano	traducano

4. Finally, the same orthographic changes applied to verbs ending in "-care," "-gare," "-ciare," "-giare," and "-gliare" in the present indicative tense are applied here to maintain the proper pronunciation.

The subjunctive is usually used in subordinate clauses that use the conjunction "che" *(that)*, where the main clause expresses opinions and feelings such as fear, doubt, hope, desire, etc.

	Examples
Impersonal opinion	È importante che tu mangi bene. *It is important that you eat well.*
Happiness	Sono contento che stiano bene. *I'm glad they are well.*
Doubt	Dubito che oggi ci sia il sole. *I doubt that it is sunny today.*
Hope	Spero che lei sia felice. *I hope that she is happy.*
Desire	Voglio che lui studi bene. *I want him to study well.*

Expressing Opinions

Knowing when to use the indicative mood and when to use the subjunctive mood when expressing an opinion in Italian can be a little tricky. Nevertheless, these are the main guidelines:

1. Impersonal Opinions

For impersonal opinions, such as *"it is important that ...,"* *"it is good that ...,"* and *"it is bad that ...,"* we generally use the subjunctive mood, for example:

È importante che tu visiti la tua famiglia.	It is important that you visit your family.
È bello che tu sia qui oggi.	It is good that you are here today.

However, if the impersonal opinion expresses some sense of certainty, such as "*it is true that* ..." or "*it is obvious that* ...," the indicative mood is used, for example:

È chiaro che possono vincere questa partita.	It is clear that they can win this match.
È ovvio che non sono interessato.	It is obvious that I am not interested.
È vero che voglio uscire oggi.	It is true that I want to go out today.

If any of the above expressions is used to express doubt, the subjunctive mood must be used, for example:

Non è chiaro se possano vincere questa partita.	It is not clear whether they can win this match.

2. Personal Opinions

If the main clause expresses an opinion that is not asserted as a fact, the subordinate clause is in the subjunctive mood, for example:

Penso che questa casa sia molto grande.	I think that this house is too big.
Non penso che questa casa sia molto grande.	I don't think that this house is too big.
Credo che ci siano persone che vivono lì.	I believe that there are people living there.
Non credo che ci siano persone che vivono lì.	I don't believe that there are people living there.

If the main clause indicates certainty or the assertion of a fact, the subordinate clause must be in the indicative, not in the subjunctive mood, for example:

Sono sicuro che questa casa è troppo grande.	I am sure that this house is too big.
Sa che ci sono persone che vivono lì.	He knows that there are people living there.

Expressing Possibilities

Most expressions that express the possibility or probability of something being one way or the other use the subjunctive mood. For example:

È possibile che io non trovi le mie chiavi.	*It is possible that* I don't find my keys.
È probabile che domani sia nuvolo.	*It is probable that* it is cloudy tomorrow.
Può darsi che Marco sia bloccato nel traffico.	*It could be that* Marco is stuck in traffic.
Potrebbe essere che Anna dorma presto.	*It could be that* Anna sleeps early.

Some notable exceptions that use the indicative are **"forse"** and **"magari."** Both words mean *"perhaps"* or *"maybe,"* but **"magari"** indicates more excitement or hope. For example:

Forse Anna dorme presto.	*Maybe* Anna sleeps early.
Magari domani c'è il sole.	*Maybe* it is sunny tomorrow.

Expressing Desires, Wishes, Feelings, and Requests

In general, desires, wishes, feelings, and requests are expressed in the subjunctive mood, for example:

Voglio che mangi con noi.	*I want you to* eat with us.
Spero che ci rivedremo presto.	*I hope that* we see each other soon.
Sono contento che tu stia bene.	*I'm glad* you are well.

Note that when the verb in the main clause is used to express desire, the subjunctive mood is only used if the subject and the performer of the action are not the same. For example:

Voglio che tu **studi** bene.	*I want you to **study** well.*

If the subject and the performer of the action are the same, we use the infinitive following the verb. For example:

Voglio **studiare** bene.	*I want to **study** well.*

When the verb in the main clause expresses an opinion, feeling, demand, or doubt, and the subject and the performer of the action are the same, we use the infinitive preceded by "**di**." For example:

| Penso che tu **guidi** molto. | *I think that you **drive** a lot.* |
| Penso **di guidare** molto. | *I think that I **drive** a lot.* |

| Crede che lei **corra** veloce. | *He believes that she **runs** fast.* |
| Crede **di correre** veloce. | *He believes that he **runs** fast.* |

6. PRESENT PROGRESSIVE TENSE

The present progressive tense, similar to its use in English, describes an event that continues to take place in the present, e.g., "**Io sto parlando**" *(I am speaking)*. The present progressive tense, in Italian, uses the auxiliary verb "**stare**" in the present indicative tense, followed by the present participle, also known as the *gerund*. The gerund is formed by attaching "**-ando**" to the stem of "**-are**" ending verbs and "**-endo**" to the stem of "**-ere**" and "**-ire**" ending verbs.

"**-are**" verbs	subject pronoun + "**stare**" in present tense + (verb stem+ **ando**)
"**-ere**" verbs	subject pronoun + "**stare**" in present tense + (verb stem+ **endo**)
"**-ire**" verbs	subject pronoun + "**stare**" in present tense + (verb stem+ **endo**)

Let us look at some examples:

		-ar ending e.g., parlare	-er ending e.g., vivere	-ir ending e.g., finire
io	sto			
tu	stai			
lui/lei	sta	parl**ando**	viv**endo**	fin**endo**
noi	stiamo			
voi	state			
loro	stanno			

Unlike in English, it is possible to use the present simple tense to describe something happening continuously at the moment to convey the same meaning as the present progressive tense. For example, "**Cosa fai adesso?**" and "**Cosa stai facendo adesso?**" can both mean *"What are you doing now?"* Similarly, "**Parlo con il**

mio amico" and **"Sto parlando con il mio amico"** both can mean *"I am talking to my friend."*

The present progressive can also be in the subjunctive. In this case, **"stare"** must be conjugated in the subjunctive and followed by the gerund, e.g., **"Penso che lui stia parlando con il suo amico"** *(I think that he is talking to his friend).*

Irregular Gerunds

There are only a few irregular gerunds. The most common ones are: **"bere"** *(to drink)*, **"dare"** *(to give)*, **"dire"** *(to say)*, **"fare"** *(to do or to make)*, and **"stare"** *(to stay or to be).* Notice that, with these irregular verbs, the gerund is often formed from the stem of the first-person **"io"** form in the present indicative.

	bere	dare	dire	fare	stare
"io" Form	bevo	do	dico	faccio	sto
Gerund	bevendo	dando	dicendo	facendo	stando

7. FUTURE PERFECT TENSE

The future perfect tense, similar to its use in English, describes events that will happen and be completed in the future by a certain time or happen after another event is completed in the future.

We use the auxiliary **"avere"** or **"essere"** in the future tense followed by a past participle. The auxiliary **"avere"** or **"essere"** in future tense serves a similar function to the auxiliary *"will have"* in English, e.g., *"I will have done my homework by the time they come."*

The verb **"avere"** in the future form is conjugated as follows:

		-are ending parlare	-ere ending vendere	-ire ending dormire
io	avrò			
tu	avrai			
lui/lei	avrà	parlato	venduto	dormito
noi	avremo			
voi	avrete			
loro	avranno			

On the other hand, the verb **"essere"** in the future form is conjugated as follows:

		-are ending e.g., andare	-ere ending e.g., cadere	-ire ending e.g., partire
io	sarò	andato/-a	caduto/-a	partito/-a
tu	sarai	andato/-a	caduto/-a	partito/-a
lui	sarà	andato	caduto	partito
lei	sarà	andata	caduta	partita
noi	saremo	andati/-e	caduti/-e	partiti/-e
voi	sarete	andati/-e	caduti/-c	partiti/-c
loro	saranno	andati/-e	caduti/-e	partiti/-e

Recall from **Level III, Lesson 5** that some verbs have irregular past participle forms.

Let us look at some examples of the future perfect tense:

Avrò visitato l'Egitto a gennaio.	I **will have visited** Egypt in January.
Avrai bevuto il caffè.	You **will have drunk** the coffee.
Avrà parlato con sua madre.	She **will have spoken** to her mother.
Noi **avremo mangiato**.	We **will have eaten**.
Voi **sarete arrivati**.	You **will have arrived**.
Saranno guariti per allora.	They **will have healed** by then.

8. INTERJECTIONS

Interjections are mere exclamation words or expressions that usually represent feelings like surprise or anger. Interjections are often followed by an exclamation mark.

		Examples
Che ...!	*What...!*	**Che** bel gatto! **What** *a beautiful cat!*
Come ...!	*How...!*	**Come** canta! **How** *he sings!*
Quanto...!	*How much...!*	**Quanto** la amo! **How** *much I love her!*
Aiuto!	*Help!*	Per favore, **aiuto**! *Please,* **help me**!

Attenti!	*Attention!*	**Attenti**! È buio qui. ***Attention**! It's dark here.*
Attenzione!	*Careful!*	**Attenzione**! È scuro. ***Careful**! It's dark.*
Basta! Piantala!	*Stop it!*	**Basta**! Sono stanco. ***Enough**! I'm tired.*
Beato/-a te!	*Lucky you!*	Tu eri lì? **Beato te**! *You were there? **Lucky you**!*
Bene!	*Alright!*	**Bene**! Aspettiamo e vediamo. ***Alright**! Let's wait and see.*
Boh! Mah!	*Who knows?!*	**Boh**! forse inizierò un'attività. ***Who knows**? Maybe I'll start a business.*
Bravo!	*Well done!*	**Bravo**! Hanno giocato bene. ***Well done**! They played well.*
Buon appetito!	*Bon appétit!*	Ecco qui. **Buon appetito**! *Here you go. **Bon appétit**!*
Buona fortuna!	*Good luck!*	Ci vediamo. **Buona fortuna**! *See you soon. **Good luck**!*
Buon Viaggio!	*Have a nice trip!*	Divertiti! **Buon viaggio**! *Enjoy! **Have a nice trip**!*
Certo!	*Of course!*	-Hai fame? -**Certo**! *-Are you hungry? -**Of course**.*
Che barba!	*How boring!*	Sto ancora aspettando. **Che barba**! *I'm still waiting. **How boring**!*
Che figo! Che figata!	*Cool!*	Ci sono fuochi d'artificio. **Che figo**! *There are fireworks. **Cool**!*
Che orrore!	*How awful!*	È stato brutto. **Che orrore**! *It was bad. **How awful**!*
Che peccato!	*What a pity!*	Abbiamo perso. **Che peccato**! *We lost. **What a pity**!*
Che scemo!	*How silly!*	È uno scherzo? **Che scemo**! *Is this a joke? **How silly**!*
Che schifo!	*How gross!*	**Che schifo** questo dolce! ***How gross** this dessert!*
Che sfiga!	*What a bad luck!*	Il viaggio è annullato. **Che sfiga**! *The trip is canceled. **Bummer**!*
Dai!	*Come on!*	**Dai**! Possiamo vincere. ***Come on**! We can win.*
Davvero?!	*For real?!*	**Davvero**?! È successo? ***For real**?! This happened?*

Evviva! Viva!	Hurray!	Sì, è ora. **Evviva!** *Yes, it's time.* ***Hurray!***
Figurati!	*Don't worry about it!*	Non c'è problema, **figurati!** *No problem,* ***don't worry about it!***
Grazie a Dio!	*Thank God!*	**Grazie a Dio** non è venuto! ***Thank God*** *he didn't come!*
Magari!	*I wish!*	-Vincerai. -**Magari!** *-You will win.* ***-I wish!***
Meno male!	*(Relief)*	**Meno male** che non mi ha visto! ***Good thing*** *he didn't see me!*
Mi raccomando!	*Don't forget!* *Please!*	Portalo con te, **mi raccomando!** *Bring it with you,* ***please!***
Neanche per sogno!	*No way!*	Non ci credo. **Neanche per sogno!** *I don't believe it.* ***No way!***
Ovvio!	*Obviously!*	-Ti piace? -**Ovvio!** *-Do you like it?* ***-Obviously!***
Per l'amor di Dio!	*For God's sake!*	Cos'è successo, **per l'amor di Dio?** *What happened,* ***for God's sake?***
Salute!	*Cheers!*	A tutti voi, grazie e **alla salute!** *To all of you, thanks and* ***cheers!***
Sei fuori!	*Are you crazy?!*	È troppo caro. **Sei fuori!** *It's too expensive.* ***Are you crazy?***
Via! **Andate via!**	*Go away!*	Non ho tempo. **Andate via!** *I don't have time.* **Go away!**
Zitto!	*Shut up!*	**Zitto!** Ho del lavoro da fare. ***Shut up!*** *I have work to do.*

II. Vocabulary Building

Go over the vocabulary in this section. You could use Anki to study and memorize the new vocabulary efficiently.

1. VERBS IV

Below is a list of verbs that we need at this level:

English	Italian	Examples
achieve	raggiungere	**Ha raggiunto** i suoi obiettivi per quel mese. *He* ***achieved*** *his goals for that month.*
act	agire	**Agisco** sempre in maniera educata. *I always* ***act*** *in a polite manner.*

add	aggiungere	**Ho aggiunto** una tazza di acqua alla miscela. *I **added** a cup of water to the mixture.*
adjust	regolare	Vuole **regolare** la luce nella stanza. *He wants to **adjust** the light in the room.*
advise	consigliare avvisare	Il mio amico mi **ha consigliato** delle università l'anno scorso. *My friend **advised** me about the universities last year.*
apologize	scusarsi	**Mi scuso,** l'ho fatto senza volerlo. *I **apologize,** I did it unintentionally.*
avenge	vendicare	L'eroe voleva **vendicare** la morte di suo padre. *The hero wanted to **avenge** his father's death.*
avoid	evitare [1]	Volevo **evitare** di vederlo al caffè. *I wanted to **avoid** seeing him in the café.*
bake	infornare cuocere	Ho appena **infornato** questa torta. *I **have just baked** this pie.*
bathe	bagnarsi fare il bagno	**Fare il bagno** nella vasca è rilassante. ***Bathing** in the tub is relaxing.*
bounce	rimbalzare	I palloni da basket **rimbalzano** molto. *Basketballs **bounce** a lot.*
brush	spazzolare	Devi **spazzolare** il mantello per eliminare sporco e polvere. *You have to **brush** the coat to get rid of dirt and dust.*
burn	bruciare	Non ero lì quando **ha bruciato** il cibo. *I wasn't there when he **burned** the food.*
catch up reach	raggiungere	Lo **raggiungerò** al prossimo round. *I **will catch up** with him in the next round.*
challenge	sfidare	Ti **sfido** a duello. *I **challenge** you to a duel.*
charm	incantare	Mi ha **incantato** fin dall'inizio. *It **charmed** me from the beginning.*
chase pursue	inseguire	Un cane in strada mi **ha inseguito** la scorsa notte. *A dog from the street **chased** me last night.*
cheat (in exam)	imbrogliare barare	**Ha imbrogliato** sulle domande dell'ultimo esame. *He **cheated** on the last exam's questions.*
cheat (deceive)	ingannare truffare	I maghi **ingannano** i loro spettatori. *Magicians **cheat** their spectators.*
check (information)	controllare verificare	Puoi **controllare** prima le tue risposte? *Can you **check** your answers first?*

---

[1] The verb "**evitare**" can also mean *"to prevent"* depending on the context.

claim	reclamare	**Reclamerò** un rimborso per il volo mancante. *I **will claim** a reimbursement for the missing flight.*
comb	pettinare	Sai **pettinare** i tuoi ricci? *Can you **comb** your curls?*
congratulate	congratularsi con	Non **si è congratulata con** me per il giorno della mia laurea. *She didn't **congratulate** me on my graduation day.*
connect	connettere(-si)	Devi **connetterti** al server. *You have to **connect** to the server.*
cut	tagliare	Mi **taglierò** i capelli molto corti. *I **will cut** my hair really short.*
decrease	diminuire ridurre	Se spendi per questo, i tuoi fondi **diminuiranno**. *If you spend on that, your funds **will decrease**.*
delay	ritardare tardare	Le spedizioni sono **ritardate**. *The shipments are **delayed**.*
deserve	meritare	**Meriti** quel premio. *You **deserve** that award.*
develop	sviluppare	Recentemente **ho sviluppato** un gusto per il caffè amaro. *I recently **developed** a taste for bitter coffee.*
dial compose	comporre	**Ha composto** il numero sbagliato. *He **dialed** the wrong number.*
digest	digerire	È difficile per me **digerire** il lattosio. *It's hard for me to **digest** lactose.*
dismantle	smantellare smontare	Ho provato a **smantellare** il mio orologio. *I tried to **dismantle** my clock.*
doubt	dubitare	**Dubito** che tu riesca a finire una pizza intera. *I **doubt** you can finish a whole pizza.*
dress	vestire(-si)	È bello che **si vesta** in modo sobrio. *It's good that he **dresses** soberly.*
embarrass	imbarazzare	Mio figlio mi **imbarazza** sempre in pubblico. *My kid always **embarrasses** me in public.*
enjoy	godere(-si) gustare	**Mi godrò** la mia vacanza. *I **will enjoy** my vacation.*
entertain	intrattenere	Quella recita di ieri sera mi **ha intrattenuto** molto. *That play last night **entertained** me a lot.*
erase	cancellare	**Ho cancellato** i miei messaggi per sbaglio. *I **erased** my messages by accident.*
escape	scappare fuggire scampare	Il mio topo **scappa** sempre dalla sua gabbia. *My mouse **escapes** from its cage all the time.*

fall	cadere	**Sono caduto** dalle scale la scorsa settimana. I *fell down the stairs last week.*
fast (food)	digiunare	Ci sono persone che **digiunano** per giorni interi. *There are people who* **fast** *for whole days.*
feel	sentire(-si)	**Mi sento** felice e contento. I **feel** *happy and content.*
fight **struggle** **wrestle**	lottare	Il guerriero **sta lottando** per la sua libertà. *The warrior is **fighting** for his freedom.*
fight **combat** **quarrel**	combattere	I fratelli **combattono** sempre. *Siblings always* **quarrel.**
float	galleggiare fluttuare	L'anatroccolo **galleggia** nella vasca da bagno. *The duckling **floats** in the bathtub.*
focus **concentrate**	concentrare focalizzare	**Mi concentro** meglio se non ho fame. I **focus** *better if I'm not hungry.*
freeze	congelare	Non dimenticare di **congelare** le verdure. *Don't forget to* **freeze** *the vegetables.*
fry	friggere	**Friggerò** quelle patate domani. I **will fry** *those potatoes tomorow.*
gamble	giocare (d'azzardo)	**Ha giocato** e ha perso. *He* **gambled** *and lost.*
get up	alzare(-si)	Puoi **alzarti?** *Can you* **get up?**
grill **roast**	grigliare	**Grigliamo** le verdure sul barbecue. *We* **grill** *vegetables on the barbecue.*
guide	guidare	**Mi guiderò** con la mappa. I **will guide myself** *with the map.*
have fun	divertire(-si)	La gente va al parco per **divertirsi.** *People go to the park to* **have fun.**
heal	guarire(-si) curare(-si)	Spero che l'ustione **guarisca** presto. I hope the burn **heals** soon.
hide	nascondere (-si) occultare(-si)	**Nascondo** i miei soldi nell'armadio. I **hide** *my money in the closet.*
hit **strike**	colpire	Un'auto lo **ha colpito** mentre attraversava la strada. *A car* **hit** *him while he was crossing the street.*
hug **embrace**	abbracciare	Lo **ha abbracciato** nel momento in cui l'ha visto. *He* **hugged** *him the moment he saw him.*
improve	migliorare ottimizzare	**Ho migliorato** molto il mio stile durante quest'ultimo anno. I **improved** *my style a lot during this last year.*

increase	aumentare incrementare	In estate la temperatura **aumenta** molto. *In the summer, the temperature **increases** a lot.*
introduce (oneself)	presentare(-si)	Puoi **presentarti**? *Can you **introduce yourself**?*
involve	coinvolgere comportare	Non voglio **coinvolgere** altre persone in questo. *I don't want to **involve** other people in this.*
launch throw	lanciare	Il 16 luglio 1969 fu **lanciato** l'Apollo 11. *On July 16, 1969, Apollo 11 was **launched**.*
lift raise	sollevare alzare	**Solleverò** il divano per controllare. *I **will lift** the couch to check.*
look after	badare	Puoi **badare** a tuo nipote oggi? *Can you **look after** your nephew today?*
lower reduce	abbassare	Puoi **abbassare** il volume? *Can you **lower** the volume?*
manage to	riuscire a	**Sono riuscito** a finire il mio lavoro in tempo. *I **have managed** to finish my work on time.*
maintain	mantenere	Il frigorifero aiuta a **mantenere** il cibo. *The fridge helps in **maintaining** food.*
marry	sposare(-si)	Mio cugino **si è sposato** in primavera. *My cousin **got married** in the spring.*
measure	misurare	**Misurerò** la lunghezza del tuo piede. *I **will measure** your foot's length.*
melt	sciogliere fondere	Devi **sciogliere** il cioccolato per usarlo. *You have to **melt** the chocolate to use it.*
miss (emotionally)	mancare[1]	Gli **sei mancato**, quindi è venuto a trovarti. *He **missed** you, so he came to see you.*
object	obiettare opporsi	Devo **obiettare** a quello che stai dicendo. *I have to **object** to what you're saying.*
obtain	ottenere	L'anno prossimo **otterrò** la certificazione. *Next year I **will obtain** the certification.*
occur	verificarsi avvenire	Lo schianto **si verificherà** sicuramente. *The crash **will** surely **occur**.*
order	ordinare	Buonasera, voglio **ordinare** da mangiare. *Good evening, I want to **order** food.*
paint	dipingere	Gli piace **dipingere** bei paesaggi. *He likes to **paint** beautiful landscapes.*

---

[1] The verb "**mancare**" works like the verb "**piacere**." It essentially means *"to be missing or lacking,"* e.g., "**Mi mancano i miei amici**" *(I miss my friends)*. Notice that "**i miei amici**" *(my friends)* is the subject.

park (car)	parcheggiare	È vietato **parcheggiare** qui? *Is it prohibited to **park** here?*
produce	produrre	Le api **producono** il miele. *Bees **produce** honey.*
protect	proteggere	Le mamme orse **proteggono** la loro prole. *Mother bears **protect** their offspring.*
prove	provare [1]	Devi **provare** di poterlo fare. *You must **prove** you can do it.*
punish	punire castigare	L'**ho punito** per il suo cattivo comportamento ieri sera. *I **punished** him due to his bad behavior last night.*
put up with **endure**	sopportare	Odio dover **sopportare** il freddo. *I hate having to **put up with** the cold.*
recognize **acknowledge**	riconoscere	Non ti **ho riconosciuto** con quella pettinatura. *I didn't **recognize** you with that hairstyle.*
reduce	ridurre diminuire	Devi **ridurre** la velocità nelle strade del quartiere. *You must **reduce** your speed on neighborhood streets.*
remember	ricordare(-si)	**Ricordo** il lago che abbiamo visitato. *I **remember** the lake we visited.*
replace	rimpiazzare sostituire	**Ho rimpiazzato** la mia vecchia macchina del caffè con una nuova. *I **replaced** my old coffee machine with a new one.*
retire	ritirare(-si) andare in pensione	**Andrò in pensione** tra due anni. *I **will retire** in two years.*
return	ritornare	Mio cugino **è tornato** ieri dal suo viaggio. *My cousin **returned** from his trip yesterday.*
review **revise**	rivedere riesaminare	**Rivedremo** insieme quel capitolo. *We **will go over** that chapter together.*
ruin	rovinare	Il tabacco **rovina** la tua salute. *Tobacco **ruins** your health.*
run away	fuggire scappare	Ai bambini piace **scappare** nei negozi. *Children like to **run away** in stores.*
save **rescue**	salvare	Non sono riuscito a **salvare** la torta dopo che è bruciata. *I couldn't **save** the pie after it burned.*
save **spare**	risparmiare	**Risparmierò** più soldi per questo viaggio. *I **will save** more money for this trip.*

---

[1] The verb "**provare**" can also mean *"to test"* or *"to taste."*

scratch (oneself)	graffiare grattare	**Ho graffiato** la puntura di zanzara quasi all'istante. *I scratched the mosquito bite almost instantly.*
scratch (surface)	graffiare grattare	Il mio gatto **gratta** le poltrone. *My cat scratches the armchairs.*
scream yell	gridare urlare	Non è giusto che tu **gridi** contro tuo figlio. *It's not right for you to yell at your son.*
shave	radere(-si)	**Mi raderò** domani. *I will shave tomorrow.*
shine	brillare	Quel diamante **brilla** molto! *That diamond shines a lot!*
shoot fire	sparare tirare	**Tira** molto bene. *He shoots very well.*
sink	affondare	Penso che quel giocattolo non **affonderà**. *I think that toy will not sink.*
sit	sedere(-si)	Puoi **sederti** accanto a me. *You can sit next to me.*
skate	pattinare	Adoro **pattinare** in inverno. *I love to skate in winter.*
ski	sciare	È divertente **sciare** in montagna. *It's fun to ski in the mountains.*
spend (money)	spendere	È fantastico che tu non **spenda** così tanto in vestiti. *It's great that you don't spend so much on clothes.*
spend (time)	passare trascorrere	Amo **passare** il tempo in spiaggia. *I love to spend time on the beach.*
spy	spiare	Non è carino da parte tua **spiare** i tuoi fratelli. *It's not nice of you to spy on your siblings.*
stand	stare in piedi	Non mi piace **stare in piedi** mentre sono sull'autobus. *I don't like to stand while on the bus.*
stay remain	rimanere restare	Vuoi **restare** a dormire? *Do you want to stay over?*
stop [1]	fermare(-si)	Devi **fermarti** all'angolo. *You have to stop at the corner.*
succeed	riuscire avere successo	Ci **sono riuscito** dopo tanti tentativi. *I succeeded after many tries.*
suck	succhiare	Devi **succhiare** attraverso la cannuccia. *You have to suck through the straw.*

[1] To use the verb *"stop"* to refer to quitting or ceasing an activity, **"smettere di"** is used instead, e.g., **"Dovresti smettere di fumare"** (*You should stop smoking*).

suggest	suggerire	Mi **ha suggerito** di mangiare quattro frutti al giorno. *He **suggested** that I eat four fruits a day.*
suppose	supporre	**Suppongo** che tu non abbia programmi oggi. *I **suppose** you don't have any plans today.*
survive	sopravvivere	Le mie piante **sono sopravvissute** lo scorso inverno. *My plants **survived** last winter.*
sustain	sostenere	Una vita sana è facile da **sostenere**. *A healthy life is easy to **sustain**.*
swear	giurare imprecare	Il testimone **ha giurato** di dire la verità. *The witness **has sworn** to tell the truth.*
sweat	sudare	**Sudo** molto in palestra. *I **sweat** a lot at the gym.*
switch off	spegnere	Puoi **spegnere** la luce? *Can you **switch off** the light?*
tackle **address**	affrontare	**Affronterò** questo argomento nella prossima lezione. *I **will address** this subject in the next class.*
take a **shower**	fare la doccia	**Ti sarai fatto la doccia** quando sarò arrivato? *Will you **have showered** by the time I arrive?*
take apart	smontare	**Smonterò** l'armadio per il trasloco. *I **will take apart** the closet for the move.*
take out	portare fuori	Puoi **portare fuori** la spazzatura? *Can you **take out** the trash?*
take (photo)	fare una foto	Puoi **farmi una foto**? *Can you **take** a photo of me?*
throw	lanciare gettare	Smettila di **lanciare** sassi! *Stop **throwing** rocks!*
throw away	buttare gettare	Voglio **buttare** via i vecchi mobili. *I want to **throw away** the old furniture.*
tire **exhaust**	stancare affaticare	Prendermi cura dei bambini mi **stanca**. *Taking care of children **tires** me.*
tour **roam**	girare	Vorrei **girare** la città. *I'd like to **tour** the city.*
treat	trattare	**Tratto** sempre gli altri con rispetto. *I always **treat** others with respect.*
trip **stumble**	inciampare	Bisogna stare attenti a non **inciampare**. *You have to be careful not to **trip**.*
twist	torcere(-si)	**Mi sono torto** la caviglia mentre giocavo a tennis. *I **twisted** my ankle while playing tennis.*
upload	caricare	**Caricherò** i video tra un'ora. *I **will upload** the videos in an hour.*

wake up	svegliare(-si)	È difficile per me **svegliarmi** presto. *It's hard for me to **wake up** early.*
wear put on	indossare portare vestire	Non dimenticare di **indossare** una sciarpa. *Don't forget to **wear** a scarf.*
weigh	pesare	Lunedì mi **peserò**. *I **will weigh** myself on Monday.*
wet	bagnare	Devi prima **bagnare** il pavimento per pulirlo. *You have to **wet** the floor first to clean it.*
whistle	fischiare	**Fischio** sempre mentre mi lavo. *I always **whistle** while I bathe.*
worry	preoccupare(-si)	**Mi preoccupo** sempre per gli esami. *I always **worry** about exams.*
worsen	peggiorare	La malattia di mio nonno **è peggiorata** l'anno scorso. *My grandfather's disease **worsened** last year.*

In addition to the above new verbs, we add a few more English cognates that are easy to memorize.

English	Italian	Examples
adapt	adattare(-si)	I bambini **si adattano** rapidamente a scuola. *Children **adapt** quickly in school.*
affirm	affermare	**Ha affermato** di essere lì. *He **affirmed** he is there.*
alter	alterare	**Altererò** un po' il vestito. *I **will alter** the dress a bit.*
arrest	arrestare	Lo **hanno arrestato** per furto. *They **arrested** him for stealing.*
assemble	assemblare	**Assembleremo** il tavolo più tardi. *We **will assemble** the table later.*
assign allocate	assegnare	Mi **hanno assegnato** questo compito tre volte. *They **assigned** me this task three times.*
capture	catturare	**Hanno catturato** velocemente il ladro ieri notte. *They **captured** the thief quickly last night.*
cause	causare	Non volevo **causare** confusione. *I didn't want to **cause** a fuss.*
communicate	comunicare	È più facile **comunicare** con Internet. *It's easier to **communicate** with the internet.*
console	consolare	Doveva **consolar**la quando piangeva. *He had to **console** her when she was crying.*
debate	dibattere	**Dibatteranno** sul budget. *They **will debate** the budget.*

dedicate **devote**	dedicare	**Dedico** il mio tempo libero alla scrittura. *I dedicate my free time to writing.*
deteriorate	deteriorare(-si)	Se non ti prendi cura della vernice, può **deteriorarsi**. *If you don't take care of the paint, it can deteriorate.*
determine	determinare	Il governo **determina** il budget annuale. *The government determines the annual budget.*
differ	differire	Il prezzo **differisce** da quello sul cartellino. *The price differs from that on the sign.*
dispense	dispensare	Questa farmacia **dispensa** prescrizioni tutto il giorno. *This pharmacy dispenses prescriptions all day long.*
dispute	disputare(-si)	**Si stanno disputando** l'eredità. *They are disputing the inheritance.*
dissolve	dissolvere(-si)	Il sale **si dissolve** bene nell'acqua. *The salt dissolves well in water.*
exhibit	esibire	**Hanno esibito** le sue opere in una galleria l'anno scorso. *They exhibited her works in a gallery last year.*
generate	generare	La diga **genera** elettricità per la città. *The dam generates electricity for the city.*
imagine	immaginare	Non riesco a **immaginare** come debba essere. *I can't imagine how it must be.*
incorporate	incorporare	Cerco di **incorporare** più esercizi nella mia routine. *I try to incorporate more exercises into my routine.*
insist	insistere	**Ha insistito** così tanto che l'hanno fatto entrare. *He insisted so much, they let him in.*
invade	invadere	L'esercito temeva di **invadere** la città. *The army feared invading the city.*
invent	inventare	Chi **ha inventato** questa tecnologia? *Who invented this technology?*
negotiate	negoziare	I paesi **negoziano** un accordo commerciale. *The countries negotiate a trade agreement.*
occupy	occupare	L'ultima volta **hanno occupato** due posti al tavolo. *They occupied two seats at the table last time.*
offend	offendere	Non volevo **offenderti**. *I didn't mean to offend you.*
operate	operare	Il chirurgo **opera** i pazienti il giovedì. *The surgeon operates on patients on Thursdays.*
prepare	preparare(-si)	Devo **prepararmi** per l'esame di domani. *I have to prepare for the exam tomorrow.*
provoke	provocare	Non va bene **provocare** gli animali selvatici. *It's not good to provoke wild animals.*

publish	pubblicare	**Pubblicherò** questa poesia. *I **will publish** this poem.*
qualify	qualificare(-si)	Non **ti qualifichi** per questo programma. *You do not **qualify** for this program.*
refrigerate	refrigerare	Devi **refrigerare** la soda. *You have to **refrigerate** the soda.*
register	registrare(-si)	Puoi **registrarti** qui. *You can **register** here.*
resist	resistere	Non posso **resistere** alla torta. *I can't **resist** cake.*
reveal disclose	rivelare	**Rivela** come è veramente. *He **reveals** how he truly is.*
simulate	simulare	La realtà virtuale cerca di **simulare** la vita reale. *Virtual reality tries to **simulate** real life.*

2. Adjectives IV

Below is a list of adjectives that we need at this level. Adding them to your vocabulary will improve your comprehension of Italian speech and writing.

English	Italian	Examples
accustomed	abituato	Sono **abituato** al clima freddo. *I'm **accustomed** to the cold weather.*
advantageous	vantaggioso	È **vantaggioso** essere organizzati. *It's **advantageous** to be organized.*
alive	vivo	Quel calamaro è ancora **vivo**! *That squid is still **alive**!*
angry	arrabbiato rabbioso	Ero molto **arrabbiato**. *I was very **angry**.*
asleep	addormentato	Mi sono **addormentato** sul divano. *I fell **asleep** on the couch.*
capable of	capace di	Sono **capace di** superare l'esame. *I'm **capable of** passing the exam.*
confused confusing	confuso	Quella domanda mi ha lasciato **confuso**. *That question left me **confused**.*
conservative	conservatore	Oggi il partito **conservatore** ha vinto. *Today, the **conservative** party won.*
costly	costoso	Quel ristorante è molto **costoso**. *That restaurant is very **costly**.*
crushed smashed	schiacciato fracassato	Per questa ricetta usi l'aglio **schiacciato**. *You use **crushed** garlic for this recipe.*

daily	quotidiano giornaliero	Comincio la mia routine **quotidiana** con la colazione. *I start my **daily** routine with breakfast.*
dangerous	pericoloso	È **pericoloso** uscire di notte. *It's **dangerous** to go out at night.*
dead	morto	Il mio bisnonno è **morto** da molti anni. *My great-grandfather has been **dead** for many years.*
defeated	sconfitto	Sono stato **sconfitto** nel gioco. *I was **defeated** in the game.*
destroyed	distrutto	Gli antichi imperi furono **distrutti**. *The ancient empires were **destroyed**.*
developed	sviluppato	La trama del libro è ben **sviluppata**. *The book's plot is nicely **developed**.*
disadvantageous	svantaggioso	È **svantaggioso** non avere risparmi. *It's **disadvantageous** to not have savings.*
disappointed	deluso	Mi ha **deluso** vedere che non sei venuto. *I was **disappointed** to see you didn't come.*
disgusting	disgustoso	Questo zaino ha un odore **disgustoso**. *This backpack has a **disgusting** smell.*
distinctive	distintivo	Le mucche hanno un odore **distintivo**. *Cows have a **distinctive** smell.*
doubtful	dubbio dubbioso	Ho risposto in modo **dubbioso**. *I answered in a **doubtful** manner.*
enormous	enorme	Quell'elefante è **enorme**! *That elephant is **enormous**!*
entertaining	divertente	Lo spettacolo è stato **divertente**. *The show was **entertaining**.*
enthusiastic	entusiasta	Questo insegnante è molto **entusiasta**. *This teacher is very **enthusiastic**.*
entire	intero	Voglio vedere il mondo **intero**. *I want to see the **entire** world.*
environmental	ambientale	L'inquinamento ha un impatto **ambientale**. *Pollution has an **environmental** impact.*
excited	eccitato emozionato	Sono **eccitato** per il nuovo film. *I'm **excited** for the new movie.*
exciting	eccitante emozionante	Le montagne russe sono **eccitanti**. *Roller coasters are **exciting**.*
exhausting	estenuante	L'escursionismo è **estenuante**. *Hiking is **exhausting**.*
flat	piatto piano	Il pavimento è molto **piatto** lì. *The floor is very **flat** there.*
foreign	straniero	Mi piacciono i condimenti **stranieri**. *I like **foreign** condiments.*

free (liberty)	libero	Sei **libero** di fare quello che vuoi. *You are free to do whatever you want.*
free (money)	gratuito[1]	Ottieni un articolo **gratuito** con il buono sconto. *Get a free item with the discount coupon.*
furnished	arredato ammobiliato	L'appartamento è completamente **arredato**. *The apartment is completely furnished.*
grateful	grato	Sono **grato** ai miei genitori per tutto. *I am grateful to my parents for everything.*
guilty	colpevole	Mi sono sentito **colpevole** dopo aver mangiato il biscotto. *I felt guilty after eating the cookie.*
handmade	fatto a mano	Questa coperta è stata **fatta a mano**. *This blanket was handmade.*
hated	odiato	Quel personaggio è molto **odiato**. *That character is very hated.*
heavy	pesante	Questo zaino è troppo **pesante**. *This backpack is too heavy.*
hidden	nascosto occulto	Era **nascosto** tra le rocce. *It was hidden between the rocks.*
humble	umile	L'attore era molto **umile**. *The actor was very humble.*
incredible	incredibile	Lo spettacolo è stato **incredibile**. *The show was incredible.*
jealous	geloso	La sorella maggiore era **gelosa** della minore. *The older sister was jealous of the younger one.*
known	conosciuto	È un autore molto **conosciuto**. *He is a very well-known author.*
lazy	pigro	Il mio cane è molto **pigro**. *My dog is very lazy.*
loved	amato	Questo è il mio **amato** orsacchiotto. *This is my beloved teddy.*
offended	offeso	Alla fine si è molto **offeso** per quello che è successo. *He ended up very offended by what happened.*
opposite	opposto	Lui è dalla parte **opposta**. *He's on the opposite side.*
oppressive	opprimente oppressivo	È difficile vivere sotto un regime **oppressivo**. *It is difficult to live under an oppressive regime.*

---

[1] The word "**gratis**" is used when referring to the word *"free"* as an adverb, e.g., "**Ha lavorato gratis**" *(He worked for free).*

picky	esigente	Mia sorella è molto **esigente**. *My sister is very **picky***.
portable	portatile	È una console **portatile**. *It's a **portable** console.*
pregnant	incinta	Mia cugina ha annunciato di essere **incinta**. *My cousin announced that she's **pregnant**.*
quiet	tranquillo	Mi piacciono i posti **tranquilli** per rilassarmi. *I like **quiet** places to relax.*
satisfied	soddisfatto	Ho mangiato fino a quando non sono stato **soddisfatto**. *I ate until I was **satisfied**.*
silent (person)	silenzioso	È rimasto **silenzioso** durante l'incontro. *He remained **silent** during the meeting.*
sour	acido	Adoro le caramelle gommose **acide**. *I love **sour** gummies.*
sunny	soleggiato	Ieri è stato molto **soleggiato**. *It was very **sunny** yesterday.*
tasty	gustoso saporito	Questa torta è molto **gustosa**. *This cake is very **tasty**.*
unknown	sconosciuto	È un ristorante **sconosciuto**. *It's an **unknown** restaurant.*
used	usato	A volte compro vestiti **usati**. *I sometimes buy **used** clothes.*
warm tepid	tiepido	Vorrei un caffè **tiepido**. *I would like to have a **warm** coffee.*
weekly	settimanale	Avremo incontri **settimanali**. *We'll have **weekly** meetings.*

In addition to the above new adjectives, we add a few English cognates that are easy to memorize.

English	Italian	Examples
acceptable	accettabile	Il cibo era **accettabile**. *The food was **acceptable**.*
ample broad	ampio	Ha **ampia** conoscenza in materia. *He has **broad** knowledge on the matter.*
cellular	cellulare	Il cambiamento è a livello **cellulare**. *The change is at a **cellular** level.*
concise	conciso	L'articolo è **conciso**. *The article is **concise**.*
content pleased glad	contento	Era molto **contento** di vederti bene. *He was very **pleased** to see you well.*

credible	credibile	Mi sembrava una storia **credibile**. *It seemed like a **credible** story to me.*
effective	effettivo	È un farmaco molto **effettivo**. *It's a very **effective** medication.*
efficient	efficiente	Lavora in modo molto **efficiente**. *He works in a very **efficient** way.*
electrical	elettrico	Devi stare attento con il collegamento **elettrico**. *You must be careful with the **electrical** connection.*
exaggerated	esagerato	Credo che le loro stime dei costi siano **esagerate**. *I believe that their cost estimates are **exaggerated**.*
existent **existing**	esistente	Questo è l'unico thermos **esistente** qui. *This is the only **existing** thermos here.*
genuine	genuino	La nostra amicizia è **genuina**. *Our friendship is **genuine**.*
impressed	impressionato	Sono rimasto **impressionato** dalla sua voce. *I was **impressed** with his voice.*
impressive	impressionante	La dimensione dell'edificio è **impressionante**. *The size of the building is **impressive**.*
influenced	influenzato	Il suo stile artistico è stato **influenzato** da altri. *His art style was **influenced** by others.*
legal	legale	Ho bisogno di una consulenza **legale**. *I need **legal** advice.*
lethal	letale	Fumare molto può essere **letale**. *Smoking a lot can be **lethal**.*
modern	moderno	La tecnologia **moderna** mi stupisce sempre. ***Modern** technology always amazes me.*
nuclear	nucleare	La città si basa su una centrale **nucleare**. *The town relies on a **nuclear** plant.*
obese	obeso	Il veterinario mi ha detto che il mio gatto è **obeso**. *The vet told me that my cat is **obese**.*
obligatory **mandatory**	obbligatorio	Hanno una divisa **obbligatoria**. *They have an **obligatory** uniform.*
offensive	offensivo	Non uso mai un linguaggio **offensivo**. *I never use **offensive** language.*
pathetic	patetico	Mi sentivo **patetico** in questo vestito. *I felt **pathetic** in this outfit.*
preventive	preventivo	È meglio prendere misure **preventive**. *It's better to take **preventive** measures.*
prosperous	prospero	Credo che questo raccolto sarà molto **prospero**. *I believe this harvest will be very **prosperous**.*
psychological	psicologico	Le sue paure sono tutte **psicologiche**. *His fears are all **psychological**.*
punctual	puntuale	È importante essere **puntuali** al lavoro. *It's important to be **punctual** at work.*

pure	puro	Questo è **puro** miele dell'alveare. *This is **pure** honey from the hives.*
realistic	realistico	Mi pongo sempre obiettivi **realistici**. *I always set **realistic** goals for myself.*
representative	rappresentativo	La statua è **rappresentativa** della persona reale. *The statue is **representative** of the real person.*
severe	severo	Le pene in questo caso sono **severe**. *The punishments are **severe** in this case.*
specific	specifico	Mi piaceva in quel colore **specifico**. *I liked it in that **specific** color.*
stupendous **terrific**	stupendo	Abbiamo trascorso un periodo **stupendo** al parco. *We had a **stupendous** time at the park.*
supreme	supremo	Ha fatto uno sforzo **supremo** per avere successo. *He has made a **supreme** effort to succeed.*
temporary	temporaneo	Devo richiedere un visto di soggiorno **temporaneo**. *I must apply for a **temporary** residence visa.*
unacceptable	inaccettabile	Il comportamento del suo gatto era **inaccettabile**. *His cat's behavior was **unacceptable**.*
unique	unico	Il suo talento è davvero **unico**. *His talent is truly **unique**.*
vacant	vacante [1]	Quella posizione è **vacante** da anni. *That position has been **vacant** for years.*
various **several**	vario	Ho **vari** vasi di quello stile. *I have **several** pots of that style.*
visual	visivo visuale	Il dipinto ha buoni effetti **visivi**. *The painting has good **visual** effects.*

[1] The word "**vacante**" often refers to a seat or position. To refer to a vacant room or apartment, we use "**libero**" *(free)* or "**disponibile**" *(available)*.

3. PEOPLE II

We go over more vocabulary to describe people in our daily life.

accountant	**contabile**[m,f] **ragioniere**[m]	*leader*	**leader**[m]
actor	**attore**[m]	*owner*	**proprietario**[m]
actress	**attrice**[f]	*pharmacist*	**farmacista**[m,f]
architect	**architetto**[m]	*philosopher*	**filosofo**[m]
artist	**artista**[m,f]	*poet*	**poeta**[m]
author	**autore**[m]	*police station*	**commissariato**[m]

business partner	socio^m in affari	policeman	poliziotto^m
butcher	macellaio^m	programmer	programmatore^m
cashier	cassiere^m	reporter	reporter^m
chauffeur	autista^m	researcher	investigatore^m
chef	cuoco^m	retirement	pensione^f
chief	capo^m	scientist	scienziato^m
colleague	collega^{m,f}	secretary	segretario^m
crowd	folla^f	singer	cantante^{m,f}
dancer	ballerino^m ballerina^f	society	società^f
designer	disegnatore^m	soldier	soldato^m
director	direttore^m	speaker	oratore^m
doctor	dottore^m medico^m	spy	spia^f
employee	impiegato^m	statue	statua^f
employer	datore^m di lavoro	teacher	insegnante^m maestro^m professore^m
engineer	ingegnere^m	union	sindacato^m
interview	intervista^f	veterinarian	veterinario^m
journalist	giornalista^{m,f}	victim	vittima^f
lawyer	avvocato^m	waiter	cameriere^m

4. HEALTH I

Health, or "**la salute**," is always an important topic in any language. Here is some related vocabulary in Italian:

burn	bruciatura^f	mind	mente^f
disorder (medical)	disturbo^m	narcotic	narcotico^m
drug (narcotic)	droga^f	needle	ago^m
drug (medicine)	medicina^f medicinale^m farmaco^m	pain	dolore^m
fever	febbre^f	painkiller	antidolorifico^m analgesico^m
floss	filo interdentale^m	pill lozenge	pastiglia^f
flu	influenza^f	public health	sanità pubblica^f
illness	malattia^f	surgery	chirurgia^f
insurance	assicurazione^f	symptom	sintomo^m

medical coverage	copertura sanitaria[f]	vaccine	vaccino[m]
medication	medicazione[f]	well-being	benessere[m]

5. LAW

The law, or "**la legge**," usually has its specific set of vocabulary. We go over some important vocabulary here:

acceptance	accettazione[f]	lie	bugia[f] menzogna[f]
accomplice	complice[m,f]	murder	assassinio[m]
background check	verifica[f] dei precedenti[m]	murderer	assassino[m]
bail bond	cauzione[f]	offense	offesa[f]
case	caso[m]	pickpocket	borseggiatore[m]
clue	pista[f]	prosecutor	procuratore[m]
court	tribunale[m] corte[f]	lieutenant	tenente[m] luogotenente[m]
crime	crimine[m] delitto[m]	meeting	riunione[f]
delinquency	delinquenza[f]	mistake	errore[m] sbaglio[m]
evidence	evidenza[f]	patrol	pattuglia[f]
fault guilt blame	colpa[f]	punishment	punizione[f] castigo[m]
fingerprint	impronta digitale[f]	quarrel	bisticcio[m] litigio[m]
footprint	impronta[f] orma[f]	raid (police)	sopralluogo[m]
fraud	frode[f] truffa[f]	records	registri[m]
gang	banda[f]	report	report[m] relazione[f]
harassment	molestia[f]	request	richiesta[f] sollecitazione[f]
hearing	udienza[f]	right	diritto[m]
hit blow	colpo[m]	scammer swindler	truffatore[m]
judge	giudice[m]	sentence	sentenza[f]
jury	giuria[f]	suicide	suicidio[m]

justice	**giustizia**^f	*trial*	**processo**^m
lawsuit	**causa**^f	*witness*	**testimone**^m

6. MEASUREMENTS

The verb *"to measure"* in Italian is "**misurare**," and *measurement* is "**la misura**." Below is some useful vocabulary related to measurements:

angle	**angolo**^m	*line*	**linea**^f
average	**media**^f	*meter*	**metro**^m
barrel	**barile**^m	*mile*	**miglio**^m
bundle	**fardello**^m **malloppo**^m	*piece*	**pezzo**^m
centimeter	**centimetro**^m	*pound*	**libbra**^f
circle	**cerchio**^m	*quantity* *amount*	**quantità**^f
contents	**contenuti**^m	*rectangle*	**rettangolo**^m
degree	**grado**^m	*sphere*	**sfera**^f
diameter	**diametro**^m	*square*	**quadrato**^m
edge	**bordo**^m	*step*	**passo**^m
form *shape*	**forma**^f	*temperature*	**temperatura**^f
fragment	**frammento**^m	*ton*	**tonnellata**^f
height	**altezza**^f	*unit*	**unità**^f
hole	**buco**^m	*weight*	**peso**^m
inch	**pollice**^m	*width*	**larghezza**^f
kilometer	**chilometro**^m	*yard*	**iarda**^f

7. HOUSE II

Here, we add more vocabulary related to *the house*, or "**la casa**."

air conditioner	**aria condizionata**^f **condizionatore**^m	*light*	**luce**^f
ashtray	**posacenere**^m	*lighter*	**accendino**^m
ax	**ascia**^f	*lock*	**chiusura**^f **lucchetto**^m
bench	**panca**^f	*mattress*	**materasso**^m
blender	**miscelatore**^m **frullatore**^m	*microwave*	**microonde**^m
bucket	**secchio**^m	*napkin*	**tovagliolo**^m

calendar	**calendario**^m	*nail (hardware)*	**chiodo**^m
candle	**candela**^f **cero**^m	*pantry*	**dispensa**^f
chest (container)	**baule**^m	*paper tissue*	**fazzoletto**^m **di carta**
chores	**doveri**^m **faccende**^f	*paper towel*	**tovagliolo**^m **di carta**
clay	**argilla**^f	*plug*	**spina**^f
cleaning cleanliness	**pulizia**^f	*plumbing*	**idraulica**^f
cloth	**panno**^m	*plunger*	**sturalavandino**^m
coal	**carbone**^m	*pool*	**piscina**^f
column	**colonna**^f	*porcelain*	**porcellana**^f
cottage	**casa**^f **di campagna**	*portrait*	**ritratto**^m
crease	**piega**^f	*pot (cookware)*	**pentola**^f
curtain drape	**tenda**^f	*project*	**progetto**^m
dining room	**sala**^f **da pranzo**	*property*	**proprietà**^f
drain	**scarico**^m	*rice cooker*	**cuociriso**^m
driveway	**vialetto**^m	*saw*	**sega**^f
dryer	**asciugatrice**^f	*screw*	**vite**^f
elevator	**ascensore**^m	*shelf*	**mensola**^f
fence	**recinto**^m	*shower*	**doccia**^f
fire (incident)	**incendio**^m	*soap*	**sapone**^m
flashlight	**torcia**^f	*strap*	**laccio**^m **cinghia**^f
frame	**cornice**^f	*tangle*	**groviglio**^m
furniture	**mobili**^m	*teaspoon*	**cucchiaino**^m
garden	**giardino**^m	*tenant*	**inquilino**^m
gift	**regalo**^m	*tent*	**tenda**^f **da campeggio**
grill	**griglia**^f	*tray*	**vassoio**^m
hallway	**corridoio**^m	*toaster*	**tostapane**^m
heating	**riscaldamento**^m	*toilet paper*	**carta igienica**^f
hut	**capanna**^f	*toilet*	**gabinetto**^m
instrument	**strumento**^m	*tool*	**attrezzo**^m
ironing board	**asse**^f **da stiro**	*toothbrush*	**spazzolino**^m
iron	**ferro**^m **da stiro**	*toothpaste*	**dentifricio**^m
item	**articolo**^m **oggetto**^m	*trashcan*	**cestino**^m **della spazzatura**
jewelry	**gioielli**^m	*tube*	**tubo**^m
kit	**kit**^m	*utensil*	**utensili**^m

ladder	**scala**^f	*utilities*	**servizi pubblici**^m
landlord *owner*	**proprietario**^m **padrone**^m	*vacuum cleaner*	**aspirapolvere**^m
laundry *dirty clothes*	**panni sporchi**^m **biancheria sporca**^f	*view*	**vista**^f
lawn	**erba**^f **prato**^m	*wall (external)*	**muro**^m
lawn mower	**tagliaerba**^m	*wall (internal)*	**parete**^f
leak	**fuga**^f **perdita**^f	*washing machine*	**lavatrice**^f
letter	**lettera**^f	*wax*	**cera**^f
light bulb	**lampadina**^f	*yard* *patio*	**patio**^m **veranda**^f

8. FOOD II

Here is more vocabulary related to *food*, or "**il cibo**":

almond	**mandorla**^f	*melon*	**melone**^m
appetizer	**aperitivo**^m **antipasto**^m	*nuts*	**noci**^f
avocado	**avocado**^m	*onion*	**cipolla**^f
bacon	**pancetta**^f	*peanut*	**arachide**^f
beans	**fagioli**^m	*pear*	**pera**^f
blueberry	**mirtillo**^m	*pepper*	**peperoncino**^m
breakfast	**colazione**^f	*pistachio*	**pistacchio**^m
burger	**hamburger**^m	*pomegranate*	**melograno**^m
butter	**burro**^m	*potato*	**patata**^f
cabbage	**cavolo**^m	*raspberry*	**lampone**^m
cake	**torta**^f	*recipe*	**ricetta**^f
can	**lattina**^f	*sandwich*	**panino**^m
coconut	**cocco**^m	*seafood*	**frutti**^m **di mare**
corn	**mais**^m	*shrimp*	**gambero**^m
cranberry	**mirtillo rosso**^m	*soup*	**zuppa**^f
cucumber	**cetriolo**^m	*spice*	**spezia**^f
currant	**ribes**^m	*straw*	**cannuccia**^f
dessert	**dolce**^m	*strawberry*	**fragola**^f
fries	**patatine fritte**^f	*sweet potato*	**patata dolce**^f
lentils	**lenticchie**^f	*takeaway*	**da asporto**^m
meal	**pasto**^m	*watermelon*	**anguria**^f

9. CLOTHES II

Here we add more vocabulary related to *clothes*, or "**i vestiti.**"

accessories	**accessori**^m	*perfume*	**profumo**^m
attire	**abbigliamento**^m	*raincoat*	**impermeabile**^m
blouse	**camicetta**^f	*sandals*	**sandali**^m
bow (knot) *ribbon*	**nastro**^m	*scarf*	**sciarpa**^f
bracelet	**braccialetto**^m	*shoes*	**scarpe**^f
checkered shirt	**camicia**^f **a quadri**	*sideburn*	**basetta**^f
cleavage	**scollatura**^f	*size (clothes)*	**taglia**^f
diaper	**pannolino**^m	*size (shoes)*	**misura**^f
disguise	**travestimento**^m	*sleeve*	**manica**^f
dress	**vestito**^m	*socks*	**calze**^f **calzini**^m
fabric	**tessuto**^m	*stain*	**macchia**^f
fitting room	**camerino**^m	*stockings*	**collant**^m
garment	**indumento**^m	*striped shirt*	**camicia**^f **a righe**
haircut	**taglio**^m **di capelli**	*suit*	**completo**^m
mask	**maschera**^f	*sweater*	**maglione**^m
necklace	**collana**^f	*swimsuit*	**costume**^m **da bagno**
pajamas	**pigiama**^m	*tie*	**cravatta**^f
pattern	**modello**^m	*watch*	**orologio**^m **da polso**

10. DIRECTIONS II

Below is some useful vocabulary to describe directions:

alley	**vicolo**^m	*destination*	**destinazione**^f
around the corner	**dietro l'angolo**^m	*downstairs*	**sotto** **al piano inferiore**^m
arrow	**freccia**^f	*highway*	**autostrada**^f
at the beginning of	**all'inizio**^m **di**	*in the middle of*	**nel mezzo**^m **di** **a metà**^f **di**
at the corner	**all'angolo**	*neighborhood*	**vicinato**^m
at the end of	**alla fine**^f **di**	*next block*	**prossimo isolato**^m
avenue	**viale**^m	*side*	**lato**^m
bottom	**fondo**^m	*somewhere*	**da qualche parte**^f
corner	**angolo**^m	*upstairs*	**sopra** **al piano superiore**^m

I. Introductory Topics & Grammar

As you plow through the language to reach this advanced level, take your time to go over the new topics, which will become a little more challenging but much more interesting. You can Anki cards to reinforce these topics in your memory with reviews and exercises.

1. THE PRONOUNS "CI" & "NE"

The two pronouns "**ci**" and "**ne**" are a constant source of confusion to many learners of Italian. We will look at the most common uses of these pronominal particles in different contexts.

Uses of "Ci"

Here we discuss two important uses of the pronoun "**ci**":

1. Meaning *"there"* when referring to a place.

For example, in the sentence: "**Vado in quella caffetteria tutte le mattine**" *(I go to that coffee shop every morning)*, we can eliminate "**in quella caffetteria**" *(to that coffee shop)* and say: "**Ci vado tutte le mattine**" *(I go there every morning)*.

Notice that "**ci**" is placed before the verb. Here are more examples:

Vado sempre **al mare** d'estate.	*I always go **to the beach** in summer.*
Ci vado sempre d'estate.	*I always go **there** in summer.*
Vivremo **a Napoli** per due anni.	*We will live **in Naples** for two years.*
Ci vivremo per due anni.	*We will live **there** for two years.*
Sei stato **a Roma**?	*Have you been **to Rome**?*
Ci sei stato?	*Have you been **there**?*

2. Some verbs are usually followed by the preposition "**a**," "**in**," or "**su**," such as: "**pensare a**" *(to think about)*, "**credere in**" *(to believe in)*, "**contare su**" *(to count on)*, etc.

For example, in the sentence "**Stai pensando <u>al lavoro</u>?**" *(Are you thinking <u>about work</u>?)*, we can replace "**al lavoro**" *(about work)* with "**ci**" and place it before the verb, that is, "**<u>Ci</u> stai pensando?**" *(Are you thinking <u>about it</u>?)*. Notice that "**ci**" here is placed before the verb and is translated as *"about it."*

Here are some more examples:

Penserò **<u>a questo problema</u>**. **<u>Ci</u>** penserò.	*I will think **<u>about that problem</u>**.* *I will think **<u>about it</u>**.*
Puoi contare **<u>sul loro aiuto</u>.** **<u>Ci</u>** puoi contare.	*You can count **<u>on their help</u>**.* *You can count **<u>on it</u>**.*
Credo **<u>in ciò di cui è capace</u>.** **<u>Ci</u>** credo.	*I believe in **<u>what he is capable of</u>**.* *I believe **<u>in it</u>**.*

Notice that "**ci**" is always placed before the verb, unless the verb is in the infinitive or the imperative. For example:

È importante pensare **<u>al futuro</u>**. È importante pensar**<u>ci</u>**.	*It is important to think **<u>about the future</u>**.* *It is important to think **<u>about it</u>**.*
Non contare **<u>sul loro aiuto</u>**. Non contar**<u>ci</u>**.	*Don't count **<u>on their help</u>**.* *Don't count **<u>on it</u>**.*
Pensa **<u>all'offerta</u>**. Pensa**<u>ci</u>**.	*Think about **<u>the offer</u>**.* *Think about **<u>it</u>**.*

3. The pronoun "**ci**" is used in the expressions "**c'è**" *(there is)* and "**ci sono**" *(there are)*, as we have encountered in **Level III, Lesson 7**. For example:

C'è solo un modo per risolvere questo problema.	***There is*** *only one way to solve this problem.*
Ci sono molti modi per risolvere questo problema.	***There are*** *many ways to solve this problem.*
Non **c'è** nessuno qui.	***There is*** *no one here.*
Non **ci sono** abbastanza sedie nella stanza.	***There aren't*** *enough chairs in the room.*

Uses of "Ne"

The pronoun "**ne**" has some similar functions to the pronoun "**ci**." It often precedes the verb unless the verb is in the infinitive or the imperative. The pronoun "**ne**" has the following uses in Italian:

1. Meaning *"from here"* or *"from there"* when referring to a place.

For example, in the sentence: "**È appena arrivato da Milano**" *(He has just arrived from Milan)*, we can eliminate "**da Milano**" *(from Milan)* and say: "**Ne è appena arrivato**" *(He has just arrived from there)*.

Notice that "**ne**" is placed before the verb. It is also common to use "**ne**" with the verb "**andare**." Here are more examples:

Me **ne** vado domani.	*I am leaving (**from here**) tomorrow.*
Se **n'**è andato.	*He's gone (**from here**).*
Devo andarme**ne**.	*I must get out (**of here**).*
È uscito salvo **dall'incidente.**	*He got out **of the accident** safely.*
Ne è uscito salvo.	*He got out (**of there**) safely.*

2. Some verbs and expressions are followed by the preposition "**di**," such as: "**parlare di**" *(to talk about)*, "**avere bisogno di**" *(to need)*, "**felice di**" *(happy about)*, "**sicuro di**" *(sure of)*, etc. In these expressions, "**ne**" can replace *"of it"* or *"about it."*

For example, in the sentence "**Sono felice del risultato**" *(I am happy about the result)*, we can replace "**del risultato**" *(about the result)* with "**ne**" and place it before the verb, that is, "**Ne sono felice**" *(I am happy about it)*. Notice that "**ne**" here is placed before the verb and is translated as *"about it."*

Here are some more examples:

Sta parlando **del nuovo progetto**.	*He is talking **about the new project**.*
Ne sta parlando.	*He is talking **about it**.*
Ho bisogno **di soldi** per uscire.	*I need **the money** to go out.*
Ne ho bisogno per uscire.	*I need **it** to go out.*
Sei sicuro **della risposta**?	*Are you sure **of the answer**?*
Ne sei sicuro?	*Are you sure **of it**?*

There are also some idiomatic expressions that use the pronoun "ne," even though it may sometimes seem redundant. For example:

Ne vale la pena.	*It is worth **it**.*
Chi se **ne** importa di …?	*Who cares **about** …?*
Non me **ne** importa niente.	*I don't care at all (**about it**).*
Non **ne** posso più.	*I can't stand **it** anymore.*

3. The pronoun "**ne**" is used with quantities and amounts, and is often translated as *"of it"* or *"of them."* It usually replaces a number or a partitive such as *"some"* or *"a little."*

For example, in the sentence "**Voglio del latte**" *(I want some milk)*, we can replace "**del latte**" *(some milk)* with "**ne**" and place it before the verb, that is, "**Ne voglio**" *(I want some of it)*. Notice that "**ne**" here is placed before the verb and is translated as *"some of it."*

Similarly, in the sentence "**Ho due biscotti**" *(I have two cookies)*, we can replace "**biscotti**" *(cookies)* with "**ne**" and place it before the verb, that is, "**Ne ho due**" *(I have two "of them")*. Notice that "**ne**" here is placed before the verb and is translated as *"of them."*

Here are some more examples:

Vuoi **un po' d'acqua?**	*Do you want **some water?***
Ne vuoi?	*Do you want **some?***
Ho preso la metà **dello zucchero**.	*I took half **the sugar**.*
Ne ho preso la metà.	*I took half **of it**.*
Ci sono tre **mele** sul tavolo.	*There are three **apples** on the table.*
Ce **ne** sono tre sul tavolo.	*There are three **of them** on the table.*

Notice that in the last example "**ci sono**" *(there are)* is changed to "**ce ne sono**" *(there are "of them")* because "**ci**" is often changed to "**ce**" when followed by another pronoun. Also, notice that the noun that "**ne**" replaces can be countable or uncountable.

In case there is a reflexive or indirect pronoun in the sentence, the reflexive or indirect pronoun is placed before "**ne**." For example:

Ti darò due **libri**.	*I will give <u>you</u> two* **books**.
Ti **ne** darò due.	*I will give <u>you</u> two* (**of them**).
Gli darò due libri.	*I will give <u>him</u> two* **books**.
Glie**ne** darò due.	*I will give <u>him</u> two* (**of them**).

Notice that, in the last example, the indirect pronoun "**gli**" is combined with "**ne**" to form the contraction "**gliene**."

| gli | + | ne | = | gliene |

The pronoun "**ne**" can also attach to the verb in the infinitive or the imperative. This is more common with pronominal verbs which we will cover in **Level VI, Lesson 7**.

2. PAST ABSOLUTE TENSE

The past absolute tense is often used to refer to the distant or remote past. It is often used in reference to past events or narrations. However, since defining a certain past event as distant is something relative, one can use both the present perfect and the past absolute to refer to events that have been completed in the past. Nevertheless, the past absolute cannot be used to refer to past events that have not been completed at the present moment. In this case, only the present perfect can be used. Thus, words such as "**già**" *(already)* and "**appena**" *(just)* are often not seen in the past absolute tense, but only in the present perfect tense.

In general, the past absolute finds more use in the southern part of Italy, whereas the present perfect is more common in other parts of Italy in daily spoken language.

Conjugation

The stem is formed by removing the final "**-are**," "**-ere**," or "**-ire**," and attaching the conjugation suffix according to the personal pronoun, as shown in the following table:

	-are ending parlare *(to speak)*	-ere ending vendere *(to sell)*	-ire ending partire *(to leave)*
io	parl**ai**	vend**ei** (or) vend**etti**	part**ii**
tu	parl**asti**	vend**esti**	part**isti**
lui/lei	parl**ò**	vend**é** (or) vend**ette**	part**ì**
noi	parl**ammo**	vend**emmo**	part**immo**
voi	parl**aste**	vend**este**	part**iste**
loro	parl**arono**	vend**erono** (or) vend**ettero**	part**irono**

Many, but not all, regular verbs in the "**-ere**" group have an alternative form in the "**io**," "**lui/lei**," and "**loro**" forms. These have the endings: "**-etti**," "**-ette**," and "**-ettero**," respectively.

There are many irregular verbs in the past absolute, especially verbs with the "**-ere**" ending. Note that most of these irregular verbs have regular "**tu**," "**noi**," and "**voi**" forms. Here, we list the most common ones:

	io	tu	lui/lei	noi	voi	loro
avere *to have*	ebbi	avesti	ebbe	avemmo	aveste	ebbero
bere *to drink*	bevvi	bevesti	bevve	bevemmo	beveste	bevvero
cadere *to fall*	caddi	cadesti	cadde	cademmo	cadeste	caddero
chiedere *to ask*	chiesi	chiedesti	chiese	chiedemmo	chiedeste	chiesero
chiudere *to close*	chiusi	chiudesti	chiuse	chiudemmo	chiudeste	chiusero
conoscere *to know*	conobbi	conoscesti	conobbe	conoscemmo	conosceste	conobbero
correggere *to correct*	corressi	correggesti	corresse	correggemmo	correggeste	corressero
dare *to give*	diedi	desti	diede	demmo	deste	diedero
decidere *to decide*	decisi	decidesti	decise	decidemmo	decideste	decisero
dire *to say or tell*	dissi	dicesti	disse	dicemmo	diceste	dissero
discutere *to discuss*	discussi	discutesti	discusse	discutemmo	discuteste	discussero

essere *to be*	fui	fosti	fu	fummo	foste	furono
fare *to do or make*	feci	facesti	fece	facemmo	faceste	fecero
leggere *to read*	lessi	leggesti	lesse	leggemmo	leggeste	lessero
mettere *to put*	misi	mettesti	mise	mettemmo	metteste	misero
nascere *to be born*	nacqui	nacesti	nacque	nascemmo	naceste	nacquero
perdere *to lose*	persi	perdesti	perse	perdemmo	perdeste	persero
piacere *to please*	piacqui	piacesti	piacque	piacemmo	piaceste	piacquero
prendere *to take*	presi	prendesti	prese	prendemmo	prendeste	presero
ridere *to laugh*	risi	ridesti	rise	ridemmo	rideste	risero
sapere *to know*	seppi	sapesti	seppe	sapemmo	sapeste	seppero
scegliere *to choose*	scelsi	scegliesti	scelse	scegliemmo	sceglieste	scelsero
scendere *to descend*	scesi	scendesti	scese	scendemmo	scendeste	scesero
scrivere *to write*	scrissi	scrivesti	scrisse	scrivemmo	scriveste	scrissero
stare *to stay or be*	stetti	stesti	stette	stemmo	steste	stettero
vedere *to see*	vidi	vedesti	vide	vedemmo	vedeste	videro
venire *to come*	venni	venisti	venne	venimmo	veniste	vennero
vincere *to win*	vinsi	vincesti	vinse	vincemmo	vinceste	vinsero
volere *to want*	volli	volesti	volle	volemmo	voleste	vollero

Notice that the verbs in the list above are all "-**ere**" verbs except for "**dare**," "**dire**," "**fare**," and "**stare**." [1]

---

[1] The treatment of the verbs "**fare**" and "**dire**" as "-**ere**" verbs can be attributed to the fact that both verbs are derived from the Latin verbs "facere" and "dicere," respectively.

Examples

Let us examine some examples that use the past absolute tense:

Servivano pasti deliziosi in questo ristorante.	*They **served** delicious meals in this restaurant.*
Perse le chiavi qui molto tempo fa.	*He **lost** his keys here a long time ago.*
Comprammo questa casa prima dell'ultima recessione.	*We **bought** this house before the last recession.*
Scrivesti molti bei libri.	*You **wrote** many great books.*
Lei **lesse** molti articoli sull'argomento.	*She **read** many articles on the topic.*
Vinsi molti premi per le mie ricerche in questo campo.	*I **won** many awards for my research in this field.*

3. IMPERATIVE MOOD & GIVING COMMANDS

The imperative mood is generally used to give commands or instructions in the affirmative or the negative. We have so far encountered the indicative and the subjunctive moods. The imperative is considered a separate mood in Italian.

The imperative mood can be used in the singular or plural form and can be formal or informal. Thus, we have four cases:

1. Singular informal (i.e., "**tu**" **form**)
2. Singular formal (i.e., "**Lei**" **form**)
3. Plural informal (i.e., "**voi**" **form**)
4. Plural formal (i.e., "**Loro**" **form**)

Each of the above can be used in the affirmative or the negative. In addition to these four cases of imperative commands, we will study commands using "**noi.**"

Singular Informal Imperative

To give commands to a single person in an informal way, we use the *present indicative* in the second-person singular form, i.e., "**tu**," in the affirmative and the *infinitive* in the negative. The only exception is the "**-are**" verbs in the affirmative, which use the present indicative in the third-person singular form, i.e., "**Lei**," for example:

Comprami un caffè.	**Buy** *me a coffee.*
Cammina piano.	**Walk** *slowly.*
Lavati le mani.	**Wash** *your hands.*
Non mentirmi.	**Don't lie** *to me.*
Non parlare velocemente.	**Don't speak** *fast.*

Notice that if there is a pronoun related to the verb, e.g., reflexive or indirect object pronoun, it is attached to the affirmative imperative or the infinitive in case of the negative imperative.

There are a few common irregular verbs in the affirmative singular informal command form.

Infinitive	Command	Example		
essere	sii	**Sii** educato.	**Be** *polite.*
andare	vai (or) va'	**Vai** a scuola.	**Go** *to school.*
avere	abbi	**Abbi** tutto.	**Have** *it all.*
dire	di'	**Di'** la verità.	**Tell** *the truth.*
fare	fai (or) fa'	**Fai** i tuoi compiti.	**Do** *your homework.*
stare	stai (or) sta'	**Stai** tranquillo!	**Calm down!**

Singular Formal Imperative

To give commands to a single person in a formal way, we use the *present subjunctive* in the third-person singular form, i.e., "**Lei**" form, in both the affirmative and the negative, for example:

Signora, **entri** da qui, per favore.	*Ma'am,* **enter** *from here, please.*
Signore, **non fumi** qui, per favore.	*Sir,* **don't smoke** *here, please.*

There are a few common irregular verbs in the affirmative singular formal command form.

Infinitive	Command	Example		
essere	sia	**Sia** educato.	**Be** *polite.*
andare	vada	**Vada** a Londra.	**Go** *to London.*
avere	abbia	**Abbia** tutto.	**Have** *it all.*
dare	dia	**Dia** quello che può.	**Give** *what you can.*
dire	dica	**Dica** la verità.	**Tell** *the truth.*

fare	faccia	**Faccia** la cosa giusta.	*Do the right thing.*
stare	stia	**Stia** tranquillo!	*Calm down!*
uscire	esca	**Esca** da questa parte.	*Exit this way.*
venire	venga	**Venga** con noi.	*Come with us.*

Plural Informal Imperative

To give commands to a group of people, we use the *present indicative* in the second-person plural informal form in both the affirmative and the negative; that is, the form used with "**voi**," for example:

| Ragazzi, **fate** i compiti. | *Boys, **do** the homework.* |
| **Non fumate** qui. | ***Don't smoke** here.* |

The verbs "**essere**" and "**avere**" are irregular. The plural informal imperative forms of "**essere**" and "**avere**" are "**siate**" and "**abbiate**," respectively.

Plural Formal Imperative

To give commands to a group of people, we use the *present subjunctive* in the second-person plural formal (or polite) form in both the affirmative and the negative; that is, the form used with "**Loro**," for example:

| Signore, **seguano** le istruzioni. | *Ladies, **follow** the instructions.* |
| Signori, **non fumino** qui, per favore. | *Gentlemen, **don't smoke** here, please.* |

The verbs "**essere**" and "**avere**" are also irregular here. The plural formal imperative forms of "**essere**" and "**avere**" are "**siano**" and "**abbiano**," respectively.

Commands using "Noi"

Similar to the expression *"let's do something"* in English, commands using "**noi**" in Italian express the same idea and can be affirmative or negative. Both use the *present indicative*, for example:

Facciamo i compiti.	***Let's do** our homework.*
Non fumiamo.	***Let's not smoke.***
Andiamo!	***Let's go!***

4. The Conditional Tenses

The simple conditional tense is used to describe a hypothetical situation, express wishes, give advice, or make a polite request. It is similar in its use to the simple conditional tense in English, for example, "I *would do* the laundry if I had time."

To form the stem of the verb needed for regular verb conjugation, we drop the final "e" of the verb and change the final "-ar" to "-er" in the case of "-are" verbs. The endings are the same for the three types of verbs.

	-are ending parlare *(to speak)*	-ere ending vendere *(to sell)*	-ire ending partire *(to leave)*
io	parlerei	venderei	partirei
tu	parleresti	venderesti	partiresti
lui/lei	parlerebbe	venderebbe	partirebbe
noi	parleremmo	venderemmo	partiremmo
voi	parlereste	vendereste	partireste
loro	parlerebbero	venderebbero	partirebbero

Irregular Verbs

The same verbs that are irregular in the simple future tense are also irregular in the simple conditional tense. Thus, we summarize these verbs here in a similar fashion:

1. Some verbs, in addition to dropping the final "e," drop the vowel before the final "r" from the infinitive to form the stem. For example, the stem from the verb "**andare**" becomes "**andr-**" instead of "**andar-.**" Other examples from this group are: "**avere**" *(to have)*, "**cadere**" *(to fall)*, "**dovere**" *(must)*, "**potere**" *(can)*, "**sapere**" *(to know)*, "**vedere**" *(to see)*, and "**vivere**" *(to live)*.

	andare **andr-**	avere **avr-**	cadere **cadr-**	dovere **dovr-**	potere **potr-**
io	andrei	avrei	cadrei	dovrei	potrei
tu	andresti	avresti	cadresti	dovresti	potresti
lui/lei	andrebbe	avrebbe	cadrebbe	dovrebbe	potrebbe
noi	andremmo	avremmo	cadremmo	dovremmo	potremmo
voi	andreste	avreste	cadreste	dovreste	potreste
loro	andrebbero	avrebbero	cadrebbero	dovrebbero	potrebbero

2. Some short verbs with the "**-are**" ending do not change the "**-ar**" to "**-er**" after dropping the final "**e**" to form the stem. The most common verbs in this group are: "**dare**" *(to give)*, "**fare**" *(to do or to make)*, and "**stare**" *(to stay or to be)*.

	dare dar-	fare far-	stare star-
io	darei	farei	starei
tu	daresti	faresti	staresti
lui/lei	darebbe	farebbe	starebbe
noi	daremmo	faremmo	staremmo
voi	dareste	fareste	stareste
loro	darebbero	farebbero	starebbero

3. Some verbs, in addition to dropping the final "**e**," replace both the consonant and the vowel preceding the final "**r**" of the infinitive with an extra "**r**" to form the stem. For example, the stem from "**tenere**" *(to hold)* is "**terr-**" instead of "**tener-**." The most common verbs in this group are: "**tenere**" *(to hold)*, "**volere**" *(to want)*, and "**venire**" *(to come)*.

	tenere terr-	volere vorr-	venire verr-
io	terrei	vorrei	verrei
tu	terresti	vorresti	verresti
lui/lei	terrebbe	vorrebbe	verrebbe
noi	terremmo	vorremmo	verremmo
voi	terreste	vorreste	verreste
loro	terrebbero	vorrebbero	verrebbero

4. Some verbs are completely irregular, such as "**essere**" *(to be)* and "**bere**" *(to drink)*, whose stems are "**sar-**" and "**berr-**," respectively.

	essere sar-	bere berr-
io	sarei	berrei
tu	saresti	berresti
lui/lei	sarebbe	berrebbe
noi	saremmo	berremmo
voi	sareste	berreste
loro	sarebbero	berrebbero

5. Finally, the same orthographic changes applied to verbs ending in "**-care**," "**-gare**," "**-ciare**," "**-giare**," and "**-gliare**" in the present indicative tense and the simple future tense are applied here to maintain the proper pronunciation.

Examples

Here are some examples that use the simple conditional tense:

Viaggerei ogni anno se avessi soldi.	I **would travel** *every year if I had money.*
Se fossi in te, oggi non **andrei** in palestra.	*If I were you,* I **wouldn't go** *to the gym today.*
Se avessi molti soldi, **comprerei** un palazzo.	*If I had a lot of money,* I **would buy** *a palace.*
Potresti studiare più ore per l'esame.	*You* **could** *study more hours for the exam.*
Potresti passarmi il pepe?	**Could** *you pass me the pepper?*
Vivremmo in una piccola città?	**Would** *we* **live** *in a small city?*
Dormirebbero tutto il giorno se non avessero un lavoro.	*They* **would sleep** *all day if they didn't have work.*
Direbbe la verità se glielo chiedessero.	*He* **would tell** *the truth if they asked him.*

The Conditional Perfect: "Would/Could/Should have"

To convey the meaning of *"would/could/should have ..."* in Italian, we resort to the conditional perfect tense.

❖ *"Would have"* + past participle = "**avere**" or "**essere**" in conditional tense + past participle, for example:

Io l'**avrei fatto**.	*I* **would have done** *it.*
Loro **avrebbero pagato**.	*They* **would have paid**.
Noi **saremmo venuti**.	*We* **would have come**.

❖ *"Could have"* + past participle = "**avere**" or "**essere**" in conditional tense + "**potere**" in past participle + infinitive, for example:

Io **avrei potuto farlo**.	*I* **could have done** *it.*
Loro **avrebbero potuto pagare**.	*They* **could have paid**.
Noi **saremmo potuti venire**.	*We* **could have come**.

❖ *"Should have"* + past participle = **"avere"** or **"essere"** in conditional tense + **"dovere"** in past participle + infinitive, for example:

Io **avrei dovuto farlo.**	*I **should have done** it.*
Loro **avrebbero dovuto pagare.**	*They **should have paid**.*
Noi **saremmo dovuti venire.**	*We **should have come**.*

5. PRESENT SUBJUNCTIVE TENSE II

We discussed some of the uses of the subjunctive mood in **Level IV, Lesson 7**, mainly expressing opinions, possibilities, desires, wishes, feelings, and requests. Here, we will cover other cases in which the subjunctive mood ought to be used.

Expressions Starting with "Che"

The conjunction **"che"** can be used to express a wish or hope if placed in the beginning of an expression followed by the subjunctive. For example:

Che la neve ci **copra** tutti.	*Let the snow **cover** us all.*
Che **trovino** la strada alla fine.	*Hopefully, they **find** the way eventually.*

Expressions with Conjunctions ending in "-ché" or "che"

Let us examine the following expressions:

affinché perché in modo che	*so that, in order that*
purché a patto che sempre che	*provided (that), as long as*
a meno che	*unless*
senza che	*without (that)*
prima che	*before (that)*
nel caso che	*in the event that*
benché	*although, despite that*

Notice that the above expressions are either simple conjunctions ending in "**-ché**" or compound conjunctions ending in "**che.**" Such expressions are often followed by the subjunctive, for example:

Dammi la chiave <u>in modo che</u> **possa** entrare.	*Give me the key <u>so that</u> he **can** get in.*
Farò del mio meglio <u>affinché</u> tu **ti diverta**.	*I will do my best <u>so that</u> you **enjoy** your time.*
Le persone lavorano sodo <u>perché</u> i loro figli **abbiano** una buona vita.	*People work hard <u>so that</u> their kids **have** a good life.*
Va bene <u>purché</u> **finisca** bene.	*That's fine <u>as long as</u> it **ends** well.*
<u>A meno che</u> tu (non) **abbia** molti soldi, sarà difficile vivere qui.	*<u>Unless</u> you **have** enough money, it will be difficult to live here.*
Lascerò la chiave <u>senza che</u> lui **veda**.	*I will leave the key <u>without</u> him **seeing**.*
<u>Prima che</u> **inizi** il gioco, facciamo shopping.	*<u>Before</u> the game **starts**, let's go shopping.*
Andrò in palestra <u>benché</u> **sia** stanco.	*I'll go to the gym <u>although</u> I **am** tired.*

Notice that the "**non**" after "**a meno che**" is redundant and does not affect the meaning of *"unless."*

In a sense, all the expressions above indicate either doubt or a hypothetical situation, that is, non-fact statements that require the use of the subjunctive mood.

Expressions with Some Conjunctions ending in "-que"

Some conjunctions that end in "**-que**" or convey the meaning of *"any"* require the use of the subjunctive. Examples of these conjunctions include:

qualsiasi qualunque	*any, whatever, whichever*
chiunque	*whoever*
dovunque	*wherever*

Let us take examples with these conjunctions:

Qualunque opzione tu **scelga**, devi stare attento.	_Whichever option you **choose**, you have to be careful._
Potrei invitare chiunque tu **voglia** alla riunione.	_I could invite whoever you **want** to the meeting._
Ti incontrerò dovunque tu **sia** in questo momento.	_I will meet you wherever you **are** right now._

Negative Conjunctions followed by "che"

Some compound conjunctions that end in "**che**" and convey a negative meaning such as _"nothing," "nobody," "the only one,"_ etc., require the use of the subjunctive. Examples of these conjunctions include:

niente che nulla che	_nothing that, anything that_
nessuno che	_nobody who, anybody who_
l'unico che	_the only one who_

Here are some examples with these conjunctions:

Niente che io **voglia** è disponibile qui.	_Nothing that I **want** is available here._
Non fare nulla che **sia** offensivo.	_Do nothing that **is** offensive._
Non conosco nessuno che **voglia** questo.	_I don't know anyone who **wants** this._
Sei l'unico che **possa** leggerlo.	_You are the only one who **can** read that._

Superlative Expressions with "che" followed by a Verb

If a superlative expression has a verb in the subordinate clause that follows "**che**," the verb should be in the subjunctive. For example:

È la persona più onesta che **conosca**.	_He is the most honest person that I **know**._
Questo è lo strumento più utile che **abbia**.	_This is the most useful tool that I **have**._
È il momento migliore che ci **sia** per andare al mare.	_It's the best time there **is** to go to the beach._

Expressions meaning "Although" or "Despite (that)"

The Italian conjunctions "**benché**," "**sebbene**," "**malgrado**," "**nonostante**," and "**anche se**" all have the meaning of *"although," "even though,"* or *"despite (that),"* and all of them, except "**anche se**," require the use of the verb in the subjunctive. Here are some examples:

Viaggia molto <u>benché</u> non **sia** ricco.	
Viaggia molto <u>sebbene</u> non **sia** ricco.	
Viaggia molto <u>malgrado</u> non **sia** ricco.	*He travels a lot <u>although</u> he **is** not rich.*
Viaggia molto <u>nonostante</u> non **sia** ricco.	
Viaggia molto <u>anche se</u> non è ricco.	

Notice that "**anche se**" is the only conjunction that requires the indicative to convey the same meaning of *"although"* or *"despite that."*

Another possible conjunction that conveys the same meaning is "**pur**" which is often followed by the *gerund*. For example:

Viaggia molto <u>pur</u> non **essendo** ricco.	*He travels a lot <u>despite</u> not **being** rich.*

Finally, if "**anche se**" is followed by the imperfect subjunctive, the meaning would change to *"even if"* and the preceding phrase is often in the conditional tense, that is, for example:

Viaggerebbe molto <u>anche se</u> non **fosse** ricco.	*He would travel a lot <u>even if</u> he **were** not rich.*

6. PRESENT PERFECT SUBJUNCTIVE TENSE

We have previously studied the subjunctive mood and the present subjunctive tense. The subjunctive mood is used to express opinion, possibilities, and feelings such as fear, doubt, hope, desire, etc.

We have also studied the present perfect tense in the indicative mood. The present perfect tense is used to describe events that happened and completed in the past or happened in the past and continue in the present.

Now, we will study the cases when we want to express opinions, possibilities, and feelings, such as fear, doubt, hope, desire, etc., about something that happened and was completed in the past or happened in the past and continues in the present. In other words, we want to describe the present perfect but in the subjunctive mood, i.e., the present perfect subjunctive tense.

The present perfect subjunctive, similar to the present perfect in the indicative, uses the past participle. However, the only difference is that the auxiliary verb, whether it is **"avere"** or **"essere,"** is conjugated in the subjunctive.

Let us look at some examples of verbs conjugated using the auxiliary **"avere"**:

		-are ending e.g., parlare	-ere ending e.g., vendere	-ire ending e.g., dormire
io	abbia			
tu	abbia			
lui/lei	abbia	parlato	venduto	dormito
noi	abbiamo			
voi	abbiate			
loro	abbiano			

Similarly, these are some examples of verbs conjugated using the auxiliary **"essere"**:

		-are ending e.g., andare	-ere ending e.g., cadere	-ire ending e.g., partire
io	sia	andato/-a	caduto/-a	partito/-a
tu	sia	andato/-a	caduto/-a	partito/-a
lui	sia	andato	caduto	partito
lei	sia	andata	caduta	partita
noi	siamo	andati/-e	caduti/-e	partiti/-e
voi	siate	andati/-e	caduti/-e	partiti/-e
loro	siano	andati/-e	caduti/-e	partiti/-e

Here are some more examples in context:

Examples	
È importante che tu ti **sia riposato** dopo la partita.	*It is good that you* **have relaxed** *after the match.*
Spero ti **sia piaciuto** il tuo viaggio.	*I hope that you* **have enjoyed** *your trip.*
Mi rattrista che non mi **abbia chiamato**.	*It makes me sad that he* **hasn't called** *me.*
Dubito che **abbiamo visto** casa tua prima di oggi.	*I doubt that we* **have seen** *your house before today.*
Sono felice che voi **siate arrivato**.	*I am happy that you* **have arrived.**
Non credo che **abbiano vissuto** qui.	*I don't believe they* **have lived** *here.*

7. IMPERFECT INDICATIVE TENSE

The imperfect indicative tense is used to describe:

1. Habitual or repeated actions in the past, e.g., *"I used to play volleyball when I was young."*
2. Actions that continued in the past for undefine period, especially those interrupted by or in the background of another action, e.g., *"While you were studying, I was watching TV."*
3. Descriptions of people, places, and objects in the past, e.g., *"Da Vinci was a famous painter and scientist."*
4. Time and age in the past, e.g., *"When I was 15 years old, I lived in a village."*

Notice that, depending on the context, the imperfect indicative tense can correspond to the simple past tense or the past progressive tense in English. In some contexts, it can also be translated to *"used to"* + *infinitive* or *"would"* + *infinitive*.

Conjugation

To form the stem of the verb needed for regular verb conjugation, we drop the final "**-re**" of the verb and attach the conjugation suffix. The suffixes are the same for the three types of verbs.

	-are ending parlare *(to speak)*	-ere ending vendere *(to sell)*	-ire ending partire *(to leave)*
io	parlavo	vendevo	partivo
tu	parlavi	vendevi	partivi
lui/lei	parlava	vendeva	partiva
noi	parlavamo	vendevamo	partivamo
voi	parlavate	vendevate	partivate
loro	parlavano	vendevano	partivano

Irregular Verbs

There are a few verbs in the imperfect indicative tense that are irregular. These should be practiced and memorized. The most common ones are: "**essere**" *(to be)*, "**bere**" *(to drink)*, "**dire**" *(to say)*, and "**fare**" *(to do)*.

	io	tu	lui/lei	noi	voi	loro
bere *(to drink)*	bevevo	bevevi	beveva	bevevamo	bevevate	bevevano
dare *(to give)*	davo	davi	dava	davamo	davate	davano
dire *(to say/tell)*	dicevo	dicevi	diceva	dicevamo	dicevate	dicevano
essere *(to be)*	ero	eri	era	eravamo	eravate	erano
fare *(to do/make)*	facevo	facevi	faceva	facevamo	facevate	facevano
stare *(to stay/be)*	stavo	stavi	stava	stavamo	stavate	stavano

Examples

Let us now look at some examples of the imperfect in different contexts:

*As a child, I **used to live** in a village.* Da bambino, **vivevo** in un villaggio.	Habit in the past, indicated by *"used to"*
*In the past, I **would sleep** only few hours.* In passato, **dormivo** solo poche ore.	Habit in the past, indicated by *"would"*
*My school professor **was** tall.* Il mio insegnante di scuola **era** alto.	Description in the past
*When I **was** 15 years old, I used to play tennis.* Quando **avevo** 15 anni, giocavo a tennis.	Time and age in the past
*I **was** at work when you called me.* **Ero** al lavoro quando mi hai chiamato.	Actions continuously happening in the past when interrupted by another action

In general, use the imperfect when the sentence is in the *past* and you see words such as: "**di solito**" *(usually)*, "**sempre**" *(always)*, "**mentre**" *(while)*, "**a volte**" *(at times)*, "**tutti i giorni**" *(every day)*, "**ogni tanto**" *(every so often)*, etc., or phrases such as: "**da piccolo**" *(as a child)*, "**quando ero giovane**" *(when I was young)*, "**quando avevo 15 anni**" *(when I was 15 years old)*, etc.

Quando ero giovane, potevo correre molto.	***When I was young**, I could run a lot.*
Da bambino, mi piaceva la frutta.	***When I was a child**, I used to like fruits.*
Quando ero adolescente, bevevo caffè.	***When I was a teenager**, I used to drink coffee.*

Also, use the imperfect when comparing the present to the past, for example:

Oggi è facile viaggiare, **ma prima** <u>era</u> molto difficile.	*Today it is easy to travel, **but before**, it <u>used to be</u> difficult.*

Another important use of the imperfect tense is to express a past intention of doing something that does not end up being done in the present. These are expressions such as *"I was going to …,"* *"I was thinking of …,"* and *"I wanted to …."*

The general formula of such expressions is as follows:

Imperfect tense of ("**stare per**," "**pensare a**," or "**volere**") + *infinitive*

For example:

Stavo per chiamarti, ma mi sono addormentato.	***I was going to** call you, but I fell asleep.*
Pensavo di uscire, ma è già troppo tardi.	***I was thinking** of going out, but it's already too late.*
Volevo venire, ma ho avuto un incidente.	***I wanted to** come, but I had an accident.*

On the other hand, use the present perfect or the past absolute if you are talking about actions with a defined time or period in the past. Look for expressions such as: *yesterday, last night, last week, ago, in 1994, from… to…, two times, for three hours, the other day*, etc. These expressions may not be explicitly used, but the meaning can implicitly refer to a defined time or period in the past, which necessitates the use of the present perfect or the past absolute.

*I **visited** my mother last night.* Ieri sera **ho fatto visita** a mia madre.	Action with defined time in the past (last night)
*I **was** at the gym for two hours.* **Sono stato** in palestra per due ore.	Action with defined time in the past (for two hours)
*I **talked** to her the other day.* Le **ho parlato** l'altro giorno.	Action with defined time in the past (the other day [1])
In 1922, Alexander Bell invented the telephone. Nel 1922 Alexander Bell **inventò** il telefono.	Action with defined time in the past (in 1922)

---

[1] Although *"the other day"* may seem vague and undefined, it is considered a defined time from a grammatical viewpoint. In addition, the sentence does not imply any habit or continuous action in the past.

8. PAST & CONDITIONAL PROGRESSIVE TENSES

The past progressive tense, similar to its use in English, describes an event that continued to take place in the past, e.g., "**Io stavo parlando**" (*I was speaking*). It is formed by adding the imperfect tense of the auxiliary verb "**stare**" to the present participle, also known as the *gerund*.

subject pronoun + imperfect tense of the verb "**stare**" + *gerund*

		-are ending parlare	-ere ending vendere	-ire ending finire
io	stavo			
tu	stavi			
lui/lei	stava	parlando	vendendo	finendo
noi	stavamo			
voi	stavate			
loro	stavano			

For example:

Mia madre **stava cucinando** quando mio padre è entrato in casa.	*My mom **was cooking** when my dad entered the house.*
Stavamo nuotando mentre tu studiavi.	*We **were swimming** while you were studying.*

Remember that the imperfect indicative tense can also correspond to the past progressive tense in English when describing continuous actions in the past. For example, *"I was cooking"* can be translated to either **"Cucinavo"** or **"Stavo cucinando."** The past progressive tense may be interpreted as giving more focus on the action than the imperfect. However, in most contexts, both are valid options to express continuous actions in the past.

On the other hand, the conditional progressive tense is used to describe an event that would be happening now had another event happened earlier, e.g., **"Io starei giocando se non fossi infortunato"** (*I would be playing if I weren't injured*). It is constructed from the conditional form of the auxiliary verb **"stare"** followed by the gerund.

subject pronoun + conditional form of the verb **"stare"** + *gerund*

		-are ending parlare	-ere ending vendere	-ire ending finire
io	starei			
tu	staresti			
lui/lei	starebbe	parl**ando**	vend**endo**	fin**endo**
noi	staremmo			
voi	stareste			
loro	starebbero			

For example:

Starei parlando con mio fratello se fossi andato a casa sua.	*I **would be talking** to my brother had I gone to his house.*
Non starei mangiando molto se fossi a dieta.	*I **wouldn't be eating** much if I were on a diet.*

II. Vocabulary Building

Go over the vocabulary in this section. You could use Anki to study and memorize the new vocabulary efficiently.

1. VERBS V

Below is a list of some important verbs that we need at this level:

English	Italian	Examples
accomplish	realizzare compiere[1]	**Ho realizzato** il mio obiettivo di diventare sano. *I have accomplished my goal of becoming healthy.*
admonish	ammonire	Ho dovuto **ammonire** i miei studenti oggi. *I had to admonish my students today.*
advertise	pubblicizzare	Puoi **pubblicizzare** la tua attività in TV. *You can advertise your business on TV.*
afford	permettersi	È ricco e può **permettersi** qualsiasi spesa. *He is rich and can afford any expense.*
age	invecchiare	Questa carne **è invecchiata** molto bene. *This meat has aged very well.*
agree	essere d'accordo	**Ero d'accordo** con il suo discorso dopo averlo ascoltato. *I agreed with his speech upon listening to him.*
amaze	stupire	La tecnologia moderna mi **stupisce** sempre. *Modern technology always amazes me.*
anger	fare arrabbiare	Il modo in cui tratta i clienti mi **fa arrabbiare**. *His treatment of customers angers me.*
announce	annunciare	Mia zia **annuncerà** la sua gravidanza sabato. *My aunt will announce her pregnancy on Saturday.*
approach (motion)	avvicinarsi	Ho visto come lo scoiattolo **si è avvicinato** alle mie piante. *I saw how the squirrel approached my plants.*
assure ensure	assicurare garantire	Ti **assicuro** che ti piacerà. *I assure you that you will like it.*
attract	attrarre attirare	I poli opposti si **attraggono**. *Opposite poles attract one another.*
babysit	fare da babysitter	Di tanto in tanto **faccio da babysitter** ai figli del mio vicino. *I babysit my neighbor's kids from time to time.*

---

[1] The verb **"compiere"** can also mean *"to turn a certain age,"* e.g., **"Domani compio 30 anni"** *(I'll turn 30 tomorrow).*

bark	abbaiare latrare	Il mio cane **abbaia** molto. *My dog **barks** a lot.*
be born	nascere	Mio nipote **nascerà** con un taglio cesareo. *My nephew **will be born** through a C-section.*
be worth	valere	Quella versione del libro **vale** una fortuna. *That version of the book **is worth** a fortune.*
beg	mendicare elemosinare	Non vorrei dover **mendicare**. *I wouldn't like to have **to beg**.*
bend	piegare	**Ha** inavvertitamente **piegato** la forchetta con la mano. *He inadvertently **bent** the fork with his hand.*
benefit	beneficiare	Puoi **beneficiare** di tale accordo. *You can **benefit** from that arrangement.*
bet	scommettere puntare	**Scommetteva** sempre un sacco di soldi. *He **used to** always **bet** a lot of money.*
bite	mordere	**Ha morso** il formaggio perché aveva fame. *He **bit off** the cheese because he was hungry.*
blackmail	ricattare	**Ha ricattato** i suoi amici quando lo hanno affrontato. *He **blackmailed** his friends when they confronted him.*
blame	biasimare incolpare	Non lo **biasimo** per aver voluto andarsene. *I don't **blame** him for wanting to leave.*
bleed	sanguinare	Non mi piace vedere le persone **sanguinare**. *I don't like to see people **bleed**.*
blink	battere le ciglia	Devi **battere le ciglia** per idratare i tuoi occhi. *You have to **blink** to hydrate your eyes.*
bloom blossom	fiorire	Le rose **fioriscono** in primavera. *Roses **bloom** in the spring.*
boil	bollire	L'acqua **bolle** a 100 gradi Celsius. *The water **boils** at 100 degrees Celsius.*
borrow	prendere in prestito	Posso **prendere in prestito** il tuo pennello? *Can I **borrow** your brush?*
bow	inchinarsi	In Giappone è consuetudine **inchinarsi** quando si saluta. *In Japan it's customary to **bow** when saluting.*
break down	guastarsi rompersi	La mia macchina **si è guastata** ieri. *My car **broke down** yesterday.*
breastfeed	allattare	La gatta **sta allattando** i suoi piccoli. *The cat **is breastfeeding** its babies.*
bribe	corrompere	Non dovresti mai **corrompere** la polizia. *You should never **bribe** the police.*
burst	scoppiare	La bottiglia **è scoppiata** a causa della pressione. *The bottle **burst** because of the pressure.*

cage	ingabbiare	Nel circo **ingabbiano** gli animali. *In the circus they **cage** the animals.*
carry out	svolgere	Venerdì **svolgeranno** i restanti compiti. *On Friday, they **will carry out** the remaining tasks.*
catch **capture**	catturare	La polizia è riuscita a **catturare** il ladro. *The police managed to **catch** the thief.*
chew	masticare	È maleducazione **masticare** gomme in classe. *It's bad manners to **chew** gum in class.*
clap **applaud**	applaudire	Tutti **hanno applaudito** quando ha finito di cantare. *Everyone **applauded** when he finished singing.*
clarify	chiarire chiarificare	Puoi **chiarire** questa risposta? *Can you **clarify** this answer?*
classify **sort**	classificare	Puoi **classificare** queste cartelle? *Can you **classify** these folders?*
climb	salire scalare	Non **salire** sull'albero! *Don't **climb** the tree!*
complain	lamentare(-si)	Non **lamentarti** così tanto. *Don't **complain** so much.*
conceal	nascondere celare	Il suo amico ha cercato di **nascondere** ciò che aveva rubato. *His friend tried to **conceal** what he had stolen.*
cool down	raffreddare	Devi far **raffreddare** il pane. *You have to let the bread **cool down**.*
cough	tossire	**Ho tossito** molto con l'influenza il mese scorso. *I **coughed** a lot with the flu last month.*
crack	spezzarsi	**Si spezzerà** se ci versi dentro dell'acqua calda. *It **will crack** if you pour hot water into it.*
crawl	gattonare strisciare	Ha imparato a **gattonare** quando era molto piccolo. *He learned how to **crawl** when he was very little.*
curl	arricciare	Mi **arriccerò** i capelli per uscire. *I **will curl** my hair to go out.*
dare	osare	**Oserò** parlare davanti a un pubblico. *I **will dare** to talk in front of an audience.*
deal with	trattare con	È difficile **trattare con** persone crudeli. *It is difficult to **deal with** cruel people.*
declare	dichiarare	**Hanno dichiarato** la loro indipendenza 50 anni fa. *They **declared** their independence 50 years ago.*
demand **require**	esigere richiedere	Il mio lavoro precedente **esigeva** che indossassi un'uniforme. *My previous job **demanded** that I wear a uniform.*
dent	ammaccare	L'incidente **ha ammaccato** la mia macchina. *The accident **dented** my car.*

deprive	privare	Non è bene **privare** te stesso tutto il tempo. *It's not good to **deprive** yourself all the time.*
discourage	scoraggiare	Non voglio **scoraggiarti** dal continuare. *I don't want to **discourage** you from continuing.*
disturb	disturbare turbare	Non dovresti **disturbare** i cani del vicino. *You shouldn't **disturb** the neighbor's dogs.*
download	scaricare	In passato **scaricavo** musica illegalmente. *In the past, I used to **download** music illegally.*
drag	trascinare	**Ho** accidentalmente **trascinato** una scatola con la mia macchina. *I accidentally **dragged** a box with my car.*
drag & drop	trascinare e rilasciare	**Trascina e rilascia** gli elementi sulla pagina. ***Drag and drop** the elements on the page.*
drop	cadere	La pioggia **è caduta** improvvisamente dal cielo. *The rain suddenly **dropped** from the sky.*
empty	vuotare svuotare	Puoi **svuotare** le tasche? *Can you **empty** your pockets?*
encourage	incoraggiare	Mia madre mi **incoraggia** molto nella mia vita. *My mom **encourages** me a lot in my life.*
enrich	arricchire	Non credo che mi **arricchirò**, ma ci proverò. *I don't believe I **will enrich** myself, but I'll try.*
envy	invidiare	**Invidio** il suo stile. *I **envy** her style.*
erupt	eruttare	Il vulcano **ha eruttato** lo scorso mese. *The volcano **erupted** last month.*
evaluate assess	valutare	Devo **valutare** i danni. *I have to **assess** the damages.*
execute	eseguire	Il soldato **ha eseguito** immediatamente l'ordine. *The soldier **executed** the order right away.*
exhaust deplete	esaurire	Devo **esaurire** tutte le possibilità. *I have to **exhaust** all the chances.*
explode	esplodere	Ho sentito come **esplodevano** i chicchi di popcorn. *I heard how the popcorn kernels **were exploding**.*
exploit	sfruttare	In quell'azienda **sfruttano** i loro dipendenti. *In that company, they **exploit** their employees.*
extract	estrarre	Mi **hanno estratto** i denti del giudizio. *They **extracted** my wisdom teeth.*
familiarize acquaint	familiarizzare	Devi **familiarizzare** con i passaggi. *You have to **familiarize yourself** with the steps.*
flirt	flirtare	Non è bello **flirtare** con i colleghi. *It's not good to **flirt** with colleagues.*
flow	scorrere fluire	L'acqua **scorre** nel condotto per generare energia. *The water **flows** in the duct to generate power.*

graduate	diplomarsi laurearsi	**Mi diplomerò** quest'anno. *I **will graduate** this year.*
grant concede	concedere	Mi **concederanno** una borsa di studio completa. *They **will grant** me a full scholarship.*
greet	salutare	Devi **salutare** i tuoi ospiti quando arrivano. *You have to **greet** your guests when they arrive.*
haggle bargain	mercanteggiare	**Ho mercanteggiato** sul prezzo della mia macchina quando l'ho comprata. *I **haggled** over the price of my car when I bought it.*
heat	riscaldare	La stufa a legna **riscaldava** meglio in passato. *The wood stove **heated** better in the past.*
hinder	ostacolare	L'altezza della collina **ostacola** l'atterraggio. *The height of the hill **hinders** landing.*
hold	tenere	Puoi **tenere** il mio bambino per un secondo? *Can you **hold** my baby for a second?*
hook	agganciare	Ieri **ha agganciato** un pesce al primo tentativo. *He **hooked** a fish on the first try yesterday.*
hunt	cacciare	Non mi piace **cacciare**. *I don't like to **hunt**.*
induce	indurre	I medici hanno deciso di **indurre** il travaglio. *The doctors decided to **induce** the labor.*
inhabit	abitare	Molti orsi **abitano** questa zona. *Many bears **inhabit** this zone.*
inherit	ereditare	**Ha ereditato** la casa di sua nonna. *He **inherited** his grandmother's house.*
insert	inserire	Quello era uno slot per **inserire** i dischi. *That was a slot to **insert** disks.*
inspect	ispezionare	**Ha ispezionato** la mia macchina in dettaglio. *He **inspected** my car in detail.*
interrupt	interrompere	Non **interrompermi** mentre parlo. *Do not **interrupt** me when I'm talking.*
interview	intervistare	**Intervisterò** la celebrità. *I **will interview** the celebrity.*
invest	investire	Non **investire** denaro dal budget della famiglia. *Don't **invest** money from the household's budget.*
judge	giudicare	Non mi piace che mi **giudichino** senza conoscermi. *I don't like that they **judge** me without knowing me.*
kidnap	rapire	Ho sentito che **hanno rapito** un'altra persona. *I heard they **kidnapped** another person.*
knock (door)	bussare	**Bussa** alla porta prima di entrare. ***Knock** on the door before you enter.*
land	atterrare sbarcare	L'aereo è **atterrato** in anticipo. *The airplane **landed** early.*

legislate	legiferare	Stanno cercando di **legiferare** su questo tema. *They are trying to **legislate** on this issue.*
lend	prestare	Puoi **prestar**mi dei soldi? *Can you **lend** me money?*
lie down	sdraiarsi coricare(-si)	Devo **sdraiarmi** per riposare. *I have to **lie down** to rest.*
locate	localizzare	Sei riuscito a **localizzare** tua madre? *Were you able to **locate** your mom?*
make a mistake	sbagliare	**Ho sbagliato** a comprare questa marca di tè. *I **made a mistake** buying this brand of tea.*
make sense	avere senso	Adesso tutto **ha senso** per me. *It all **makes sense** to me now.*
mark	contrassegnare	**Hanno contrassegnato** il suo passaporto all'aeroporto all'ingresso. *They **marked** his passport at the airport upon entering.*
mature	maturare	Quell'avocado deve **maturare** di più. *That avocado needs to **mature** more.*
misinterpret	interpretare male	**Ha interpretato male** quello che ho detto l'ultima volta. *He **misinterpreted** what I said last time.*
moan	gemere	Il mio gatto mi spaventa quando **geme**. *My cat scares me when she **moans**.*
move (emotionally)	commuovere	Quel film mi **commuove** sempre. *That movie always **moves** me.*
move (direction)	muovere(-si) spostare(-si)	Puoi **muovere** un po'? *Can you **move** a spot?*
move (residence)	trasferire(-si)	Il mio vicino **si trasferirà** il messe prossimo. *My neighbor **will move** next month.*
obey	obbedire	Il mio cane mi **obbedisce** sempre. *My dog always **obeys** me.*
obstruct	ostruire ostacolare	Quel palo **ostruisce** la strada. *That post **obstructs** the way.*
oppose to	opporsi a	**Si oppone** sempre alle mie proposte. *He always **opposes** my proposals.*
overcome exceed	superare	Voglio **superare** il mio miglior voto. *I want to **surpass** my best mark.*
pardon	perdonare	Dovrai **perdonare** i suoi modi. *You'll have to **pardon** his manners.*
participate	partecipare	Vorrei **partecipare** alla sfilata. *I'd like to **participate** in the parade.*
paste	incollare	**Incolla** quel bordo con l'altro. *Paste that edge with the other one.*
pedal	pedalare	**Pedalo** sempre molto quando uso la bicicletta. *I always **pedal** a lot when I use the bicycle.*

play (instrument)	suonare	Da bambino **suonavo** il flauto. *As a child, I **played** the flute.*
polish	lucidare	**Ha lucidato** tutte le posate l'anno scorso. *She **polished** all the cutlery last year.*
pour	versare	**Ha versato** il succo nella sua tazza e se n'è andata. *She **poured** the juice in her cup and left.*
preach	predicare	Dobbiamo **predicare** la pace tra le persone. *We must **preach** peace among people.*
prevent	prevenire impedire evitare[1]	Essere prudenti **previene** molti incidenti. *Being cautious **prevents** lots of accidents.*
proceed	procedere	**Procedi** con cautela. ***Proceed** with caution.*
promise	promettere	Mi **ha promesso** che questa volta si sarebbe comportato bene. *He **promised** me he'd behave well this time.*
propose	proporre	**Propongo** di mettere un semaforo. *I **propose** they put a stoplight.*
quit	lasciare abbandonare	Ha detto che vuole **lasciare** la band. *She said she wants to **quit** the band.*
recover	recuperare riprendere(-si)	Devo **recuperare** dopo la corsa. *I have to **recover** after running.*
reflect	riflettere	È così pulito che **riflette** tutto. *It's so clean it **reflects** everything.*
refresh freshen up	rinfrescare	Ho dovuto **rinfrescare** l'aria più volte. *I had to **refresh** the air several times.*
refuse reject	rifiutare(-si) negare	**Mi rifiuto** di pagare tale importo. *I **refuse** to pay that amount.*
refute	confutare	Nel dibattito, **ha confutato** tutto ciò che ho detto. *In the debate, he **refuted** everything I said.*
reimburse	rimborsare	L'azienda non **rimborsa** le spese di spedizione. *The company doesn't **reimburse** the shipping costs.*
reinforce	rafforzare rinforzare	Il suo libro ha contribuito a **rafforzare** il nuovo concetto. *His book helped **reinforce** the new concept.*
release	rilasciare liberare	**Ha rilasciato** la sua farfalla da compagnia ieri notte. *He **released** his pet butterfly last night.*
repent	pentirsi	È importante **pentirsi** per imparare. *It's important to **repent** in order to learn.*

---

[1] The verb "**evitare**" can also mean *"to avoid"* depending on the context.

reprimand	rimproverare	Non mi piace doverlo **rimproverare**. *I don't like having to **reprimand** him.*
resign	dimettersi rinunciare	**Si è dimesso** dal suo incarico in azienda. *He **resigned** from his position in the company.*
restrict	restringere	L'accesso a quella zona è **ristretto**. *Access to that zone is **restricted**.*
rhyme	rimare	Cerco di far **rimare** le mie poesie. *I try to make my poems **rhyme**.*
roll	rotolare	**È rotolato** giù per la collina per caso. *He **rolled** down the hill by accident.*
rub	strofinare sfregare	Devi **strofinare** la crema perché funzioni. *You have to **rub** the cream on for it to work.*
sail **navigate**	navigare	Amava **navigare** attraverso il mare. *He loved to **sail** across the sea.*
scare	spaventare impaurire	I fantasmi mi **spaventano**. *Ghosts **scare** me.*
scatter	disperdere spargere	Il vento **ha disperso** tutte le mie carte. *The wind **scattered** all of my papers.*
schedule	programmare	Ti **programmerò** per la prossima settimana. *I **will schedule** you for next week.*
scold	sgridare	**Sgridano** il figlio tutto il tempo. *They **scold** their son all the time.*
sculpt	scolpire	Ha imparato a **scolpire** figure da suo padre. *He learned to **sculpt** figures from his father.*
sew	cucire	**Cucirò** i miei calzini. *I **will sew** my socks.*
slim down	dimagrire	**È dimagrito** molto quest'anno. *He **slimmed down** a lot this year.*
sneeze	starnutire	In primavera **starnutisco** molto. *In the spring I **sneeze** a lot.*
spin	girare roteare	Le ruote hanno iniziato a **girare** subito. *The wheels started to **spin** right away.*
stroll **go for a walk**	passeggiare	Mi sento calmo quando **passeggio** sulla spiaggia. *I feel calm when I **go for a walk** on the beach.*
subscribe	iscriversi abbonarsi	**Si sono iscritti** alla palestra per un anno. *They **subscribed** to the gym for a year.*
substitute	sostituire	**Sostituirò** lo zucchero con il dolcificante. *I **will substitute** the sugar for sweetener.*
subtract	sottrarre	Devi **sottrarre** $ 100 dal debito. *You have to **subtract** $100 from the debt.*
sue	citare in giudizio	Vogliono **citare in giudizio** l'azienda. *They want to **sue** the company.*
suspect	sospettare	**Sospettavo** che il vecchio fosse l'assassino. *I **suspected** the old man was the killer.*

swing	oscillare	Il pendolo dell'orologio **oscilla** correttamente. *The clock's pendulum **swings** correctly.*
take advantage of	approfittare	**Approfitterò** dell'offerta e ne comprerò tre. *I **will take advantage of** the offer and I'll buy three.*
take off	decollare	**Decolleremo** tra mezz'ora. *We **will take off** in half an hour.*
tempt	tentare	Quelle torte mi **tentano** sempre. *Those cakes always **tempt** me.*
tie	legare	Devi sapere come **legare** i lacci delle scarpe da solo. *You have to know how to **tie** your shoelaces by yourself.*
trap	intrappolare	Ha usato una nuova tecnica per **intrappolare** il suo avversario. *He used a new technique to **trap** his opponent.*
turn	girare	**Gira** a destra e poi prosegui dritto. ***Turn** right and then keep going straight ahead.*
update	aggiornare	Devo **aggiornare** il sistema operativo. *I have to **update** the operating system.*
validate	convalidare	Deve **convalidare** il suo diploma. *She has to **validate** her diploma.*
wander roam	girovagare	Mi piace **girovagare** per il centro commerciale. *I like to **wander** through the mall.*
welcome	accogliere	I consiglieri ci **hanno accolto** ieri. *The advisors **welcomed** us yesterday.*
whisper	sussurrare	Per favore **sussurra** per non svegliare il bambino. *Please **whisper** to not wake up the baby.*
witness	testimoniare	**Ho testimoniato** all'incidente di persona. *I **witnessed** the accident in person.*
wrap	incartare avvolgere	Non sono bravo a **incartare** i regali. *I'm bad at **wrapping** gifts.*
yield	cedere	Devi **cedere** il tuo posto in quell'angolo. *You have to **yield** your spot in that corner.*

In addition to the above new verbs, we add a few more English cognates that are easy to memorize.

English	Italian	Examples
absorb	assorbire	Il terreno **ha assorbito** immediatamente tutta l'acqua. *The soil **absorbed** all the water immediately.*
adhere	aderire	Il magnete **ha aderito** al frigorifero. *The magnet **adhered** to the fridge.*
administer	amministrare	Devo **amministrare** un gruppo di 10. *I have to **administer** a group of 10.*
authorize	autorizzare	**Ha autorizzato** l'uso della sua immagine. *She **authorized** the use of her image.*

automate	automatizzare	Sto cercando di **automatizzare** i processi. *I am seeking to automate the processes.*
coincide	coincidere	I nostri programmi **coincidono** ogni giorno. *Our schedules coincide every day.*
collaborate	collaborare	**Hanno collaborato** per comprare questa macchina. *They collaborated to buy this car.*
compile	compilare	**Ho compilato** le foto della mia infanzia l'altro giorno. *I compiled photos of my childhood the other day.*
cooperate	cooperare	**Hanno collaborato** per costruire quella casa. *They cooperated to build that house.*
coordinate	coordinare	Dobbiamo **coordinare** la gita. *We have to coordinate the outing.*
denote	denotare	Questo risultato **denota** un fallimento generale. *This result denotes a general failure.*
derive	derivare	Questa parola **deriva** dal latino. *This word derives from Latin.*
deviate	deviare	È pericoloso **deviare** dal sentiero. *It's dangerous to deviate from the trail.*
disperse	disperdere(-si)	Il gruppo **si è disperso** immediatamente. *The group dispersed immediately.*
distinguish	distinguere	Non riesce a **distinguere** tra verde e rosso. *He can't distinguish between green and red.*
emerge	emergere	**È emerso** dopo mesi di isolamento. *He emerged after months isolated.*
emit	emettere	**Hanno emesso** un avviso per il maltempo di ieri sera. *They emitted an alert about the bad weather last night.*
err	errare	Preferisce **errare** per essere cauto. *He prefers to err for being cautious.*
forge	forgiare	Mio nonno **forgia** spade. *My grandfather forges swords.*
improvise	improvvisare	Non mi piace **improvvisare** al volo. *I don't like to improvise on the fly.*
inhale	inalare	Amo **inalare** aria fresca. *I love to inhale fresh air.*
inhibit	inibire(-si)	**Si inibiscono** quando sono in pubblico. *They get inhibited when in public.*
insinuate	insinuare	**Stai insinuando** qualcosa che non ho detto. *You are insinuating something I didn't say.*
inspire	ispirare	È stato **ispirato** dai grandi scrittori. *He was inspired by the great writers.*

mobilize	mobilitare(-si)	La resistenza **si mobilitò** immediatamente contro l'occupazione. *The resistance **mobilized** against the occupation immediately.*
narrate	narrare	Mi piace **narrare** storie. *I like to **narrate** stories.*
oblige compel	obbligare	Le leggi ci **obbligano** a comportarci bene. *Laws **oblige** us to behave.*
persist	persistere	Queste erbacce **persistono** anche se le taglio. *These weeds **persist** even if I cut them.*
personalize	personalizzare	**Personalizzo** sempre i miei taccuini. *I always **personalize** my notebooks.*
persuade	persuadere	Devi **persuadere** la mamma così me lo lascerà. *You have to **persuade** mom so she'll let me.*
present	presentare	L'azienda **ha presentato** il suo nuovo progetto. *The company **presented** its new project.*
prolong	prolungare	Ho cercato di **prolungare** la mia routine. *I tried to **prolong** my routine.*
recite	recitare	Dovrà **recitare** una poesia completa. *She will have to **recite** a complete poem.*
scan (computer)	scansionare	Puoi **scansionare** queste pagine, per favore? *Can you **scan** these pages, please?*
stimulate	stimolare	Il caffè mi **stimola** a lavorare di più. *Coffee **stimulates** me to work more.*
subsist	sussistere	Sono riuscito a **sussistere** nella natura. *I've managed to **subsist** in nature.*
theorize	teorizzare	Gli esperti **hanno teorizzato** la possibile soluzione lo scorso anno. *The experts **theorized** the possible solution last year.*
transform	trasformare(-si)	**Si è trasformato** quasi in un'altra persona di recente. *He **transformed** almost into another person recently.*
transplant	trapiantare	Gli **hanno trapiantato** un rene nel corpo. *They **transplanted** a kidney into his body.*

2. ADJECTIVES V

Below is a list of some common adjectives that we need at this level. You could use Anki to study and memorize the new vocabulary efficiently. Notice that an adjective must agree with the noun in number and gender.

English	Italian	Examples
alleged	presunto	È un **presunto** ladro. *He's an **alleged** thief.*

astonished	stupito	Ero **stupito** dal mio voto. *I was **astounded** by my grade.*
astonishing	stupefacente	È stato **stupefacente**! *That was **astonishing**!*
bald	calvo	Il mio professore universitario era **calvo**. *My university teacher was **bald**.*
based on	basato su	Il libro era **basato su** eventi reali. *The book was **based on** real events.*
beaten (defeated)	sconfitto picchiato	Mi sono sentito **sconfitto** dopo il combattimento. *I felt **beaten** after the fight.*
beaten (whipped)	montato	Metti la panna **montata** sopra la torta. *You put **whipped** cream on top of the pie.*
blurry	sfocato	Vedo tutto **sfocato** senza i miei occhiali. *I see everything **blurry** without my glasses.*
brief	breve	Mi scuserò per un **breve** momento. *I'll excuse myself for a **brief** moment.*
brunette	brunetta mora	Quella donna è **mora**. *That woman is a **brunette**.*
cautious	cauto prudente	Sono sempre **cauto** per strada. *I'm always **cautious** on the street.*
challenging	impegnativo sfidante	La gara è molto **impegnativa**. *The race is very **challenging**.*
charitable	caritatevole	È un lavoro **caritatevole**. *It's a **charitable** job.*
clumsy awkward	goffo impacciato	Da bambino ero molto **goffo**. *As a child I was very **clumsy**.*
committed	impegnato	Sono **impegnati** nella causa ora. *They're **committed** to the cause now.*
cruel	crudele	È difficile avere a che fare con persone **crudeli**. *It is difficult to deal with **cruel** people.*
deaf	sordo	Mio cugino è nato **sordo**. *My cousin was born **deaf**.*
dear	caro	Era una persona molto **cara** per me. *He was a very **dear** person to me.*
dented	ammaccato	L'auto è stata **ammaccata** dopo l'incidente. *The car was **dented** after the accident.*
dizzy	vertiginoso	Le montagne russe mi lasciano **vertiginoso**. *Roller coasters leave me **dizzy**.*
edible	commestibile	Che tu ci creda o no, quei fiori sono **commestibili**. *Believe it or not, those flowers are **edible**.*

embarrassed	imbarazzato	Ero molto **imbarazzato** da quello che ha detto. *I was very **embarrassed** by what he said.*
embarrassing	imbarazzante	È stato un momento un po' **imbarazzante**. *It was a moment that was a bit **embarrassing**.*
envious	invidioso	È molto brutto essere **invidiosi**. *It's very ugly to be **envious**.*
fidgety **restless**	inquieto irrequieto	Sei **irrequieto** oggi. *You're **fidgety** today.*
flattered	lusingato	Sono **lusingato** dal tuo interesse. *I am **flattered** by your interest.*
flawed	difettoso	Ho dovuto restituirlo perché **difettoso**. *I had to return it because it was **flawed**.*
floating	galleggiante	Adoravo quell'anatra **galleggiante**. *I loved that **floating** duck.*
following	seguente successivo	Non vedo l'ora che arrivi il **seguente** episodio. *I can't wait for the **following** episode.*
former	ex precedente	L'ha dipinto l'**ex** proprietario della casa. *The **former** owner of the house painted it.*
grated	grattugiato	Uso molto formaggio **grattugiato**. *I use a lot of **grated** cheese.*
hospitable	ospitale	Mio cugino è sempre molto **ospitale**. *My cousin is always very **hospitable**.*
immigrant	immigrato immigrante	Sono figlio di genitori **immigrati**. *I'm the child of **immigrant** parents.*
injured	infortunato ferito	Si è **infortunato** durante la gara. *He was **injured** during the race.*
in order	in ordine ordinato	Mi piace tenere **in ordine** la mia casa. *I like to keep my house **in order**.*
linked	collegato	Lui è **collegato** a molte voci. *He is **linked** to many rumors.*
long-lasting **durable**	duraturo	Hanno una relazione molto **duratura**. *They have a very **long-lasting** relationship.*
loose	sciolto largo	Mi piacciono i vestiti **larghi** e confortevoli. *I like **loose** and comfortable clothes.*
luxurious	lussuoso	Il ristorante era molto **lussuoso**. *The restaurant was very **luxurious**.*
pale	pallido	Sembri molto **pallido**. *You look very **pale**.*
picturesque	pittoresco	È un paesaggio **pittoresco**. *It's a **picturesque** landscape.*
populated	popolato	Questa città non è molto **popolata**. *This town isn't very **populated**.*

reliable	affidabile	Sai che è una persona **affidabile**. *You know he's a reliable person.*
round	rotondo	La bolla sembra **rotonda**. *The bubble looks round.*
sacred	sacro	Questo terreno è **sacro** per molte persone. *This ground is sacred to many people.*
safe	sicuro	Si sente al **sicuro** con te. *He feels safe with you.*
scared **frightened**	impaurito spaventato	Il mio cucciolo era **spaventato** quando l'ho visto. *My puppy was scared when I saw him.*
scary **frightening**	pauroso spaventoso	Gli zombie sono **spaventosi**. *Zombies are scary.*
shredded	triturato	Ho visto dei fogli **triturati** nel cestino. *I saw shredded papers in the basket.*
square	quadrato	Ho cercato di rendere la serra **quadrata**. *I tried to make the greenhouse squared.*
steep	ripido scosceso	La montagna è molto **ripida**. *The mountain is very steep.*
stingy	avaro taccagno	Una persona **avara** non è un buon amico. *A stingy person is not a good friend.*
subtle	sottile impercettibile	Mi piace indossare un trucco **sottile**. *I like to wear subtle makeup.*
sudden	improvviso repentino	Il cambiamento è stato molto **improvviso**. *The change was very sudden.*
suitable	adatto appropriato idoneo	È un insegnante **adatto** per quei bambini. *He's a suitable teacher for those children.*
surprised	sorpreso	Fece una faccia **sorpresa**. *He put on a surprised face.*
surprising	sorprendente	È stato un evento **sorprendente**. *It was a surprising event.*
suspicious	sospetto	Il suo comportamento è molto **sospetto**. *His behavior is very suspicious.*
theoretical	teorico	Non sono bravo nelle scienze **teoriche**. *I'm not good at theoretical sciences.*
tight	stretto	È molto **stretto** all'interno di questa macchina. *It is very tight inside this car.*
trivial	banale	Non preoccuparti per cose **banali**. *Don't worry over trivial things.*
unbearable	insopportabile	Il dolore era **insopportabile**. *The pain was unbearable.*

unbeatable	imbattibile	È stato **imbattibile** per molto tempo. *He was **unbeatable** for a long time.*
unprecedented	senza precedenti	È stato un risultato **senza precedenti**. *It was an **unprecedented** result.*
unworthy	indegno	È **indegno** della mia fiducia. *He's **unworthy** of my trust.*
veiled	velato	La sposa si avvicinò all'altare **velata**. *The bride walked to the altar **veiled**.*
wavy	ondulato	Lo sfondo ha un aspetto **ondulato**. *The background has a **wavy** appearance.*
wicked **evil**	malvagio	Il cattivo era molto **malvagio**. *The villain was very **wicked**.*
wild **savage**	selvaggio selvatico	Questa pianta è un fiore **selvatico**. *This plant is a **wild** flower.*
willing to	disposto a	Sono **disposto** ad aiutarti con tutto. *I'm **willing to** help you with everything.*
wooden	di legno	Aveva molti giocattoli **di legno**. *He had a lot of **wooden** toys.*
worthy of	degno di	È **degno** del titolo che si è guadagnato. *He's **worthy of** the title he earned.*
woven	intrecciato	È un bel cardigan **intrecciato**. *It's a nice **woven** cardigan.*
wrinkled	stropicciato rugoso	Quella camicia è molto **stropicciata**. *That shirt is very **wrinkled**.*
zealous	zelante	Era molto **zelante** nella sua ideologia. *He was very **zealous** in his ideology.*

In addition to the above new adjectives, we add a few English cognates that are easy to memorize.

English	Italian	Examples
absurd	assurdo	La trama mi sembrava **assurda**. *The plot seemed **absurd** to me.*
acute **sharp**	acuto	Odio i rumori **acuti**. *I hate **sharp** noises.*
adequate	adeguato	Ha un prezzo **adeguato**. *It has an **adequate** price.*
aggregate	aggregato	Dice che non ha zucchero **aggregato**. *It says it doesn't have **aggregated** sugar.*
agitated	agitato	Ti senti **agitato**? *Are you feeling **agitated**?*
ambitious	ambizioso	Mio fratello è sempre stato **ambizioso**. *My brother has always been **ambitious**.*

anonymous	anonimo	Quel dipinto è stato realizzato da un artista **anonimo**. *That painting was made by an anonymous artist.*
appropriate	appropriato	Questo outfit vi sembra **appropriato**? *Does this outfit seem appropriate to you?*
archeological	archeologico	Questa reliquia **archeologica** è di un'altra epoca. *This archeological relic is from another era.*
balanced	bilanciato equilibrato	Ho una dieta **bilanciata**. *I have a balanced diet.*
conscientious	coscienzioso	Mio padre è molto **coscienzioso**. *My father is very conscientious.*
consecutive	consecutivo	Sono in ordine **consecutivo**. *They are in consecutive order.*
cosmopolitan	cosmopolita	Non mi considero una persona **cosmopolita**. *I don't consider myself a cosmopolitan person.*
curved	curvo	La mia casa ha un muro **curvo**. *My house has a curved wall.*
deliberate	deliberato	Lo ha fatto in modo **deliberato**. *He did it in a deliberate manner.*
delicate	delicato	Lavo i capi **delicati** a mano. *I wash delicate clothes by hand.*
desperate	disperato	Ero **disperato** per ottenere il lavoro. *I was desperate to obtain the job.*
erroneous	erroneo	La prima volta, ha avuto un risultato **erroneo**. *The first time, he had an erroneous result.*
essential	essenziale	L'acqua è **essenziale** per la vita. *Water is essential for life.*
explicit	esplicito	Il film ha una violenza **esplicita**. *The movie has explicit violence.*
federal	federale	La violazione del diritto d'autore è un reato **federale**. *Copyright infraction is a federal offense.*
homogenous	omogeneo	Mescola fino a quando l'impasto è **omogeneo**. *Stir until the dough is homogeneous.*
humanitarian	umanitario	Partecipo a varie opere **umanitarie**. *I participate in various humanitarian works.*
immersed	immerso	Ero completamente **immerso** nella trama. *I was completely immersed in the plot.*
immune	immune	Oggi nessuno è **immune** alle critiche. *Today no one is immune to criticism.*
intimate	intimo	Hanno appena avuto un matrimonio **intimo**. *They just had an intimate wedding.*

individual [1]	individuale	Ecco un dolce **individuale**. *Here you have an **individual** dessert.*
involuntary **inadvertent**	involontario	Il singhiozzo è un riflesso **involontario**. *A hiccup is an **involuntary** reflex.*
legitimate	legittimo	Alla fine, aveva un **legittimo** erede. *In the end, he had a **legitimate** heir.*
mere	mero	Era una **mera** spettatrice dell'evento. *She was a **mere** spectator of the event.*
meticulous	meticoloso	Sono molto **meticoloso** quando cucino. *I am very **meticulous** when I cook.*
metropolitan	metropolitano	È nell'area **metropolitana** del paese. *It's in the **metropolitan** area of the country.*
pertinent **relevant**	pertinente	Ho bisogno di informazioni **pertinenti**. *I need **pertinent** information.*
pioneer	pioniere	Fu un **pioniere** nel suo campo. *He was a **pioneer** in his field.*
privileged	privilegiato	Non è una persona **privilegiata**. *He's not a **privileged** person.*
reciprocal	reciproco	L'amore che avevano era **reciproco**. *The love they had was **reciprocal**.*
sinister	sinistro	La sua risata **sinistra** mi spaventò. *His **sinister** laugh scared me.*
spontaneous	spontaneo	Mi piace scattare foto **spontanee**. *I like to take **spontaneous** photos.*
sterile	sterile	Devi pulirlo con una garza **sterile**. *You have to clean it with a **sterile** gauze.*
synthetic	sintetico	Preferisco usare tessuti **sintetici**. *I prefer to use **synthetic** fabrics.*
tremendous	tremendo	L'educazione ha un impatto **tremendo** sulla nostra vita. *Upbringing has a **tremendous** impact on our lives.*
urban	urbano	Questa zona ha diverse leggende **urbane**. *This zone has various **urban** legends.*
vague	vago	La descrizione del libro è troppo **vaga**. *The book's description is too **vague**.*
vigorous	vigoroso	Ho fatto un allenamento **vigoroso**. *I did **vigorous** training.*
visionary	visionario	Da Vinci è considerato un pensatore **visionario**. *Da Vinci is considered a **visionary** thinker.*

---

[1] The adjective *"individual"* in English is referred to using the adjective **"individuale"** in Italian, whereas the noun *"individual"* referring to a person uses the Italian word **"individuo^m."**

3. Animals II

Here we add more animal vocabulary to our list.

alligator	**alligatore**^m	*hunting*	**caccia**^f
ant	**formica**^f	*insect*	**insetto**^m
bark (of a dog)	**abbaio**^m	*ivory*	**avorio**^m
bat (animal)	**pipistrello**^m	*kangaroo*	**canguro**^m
bear	**orso**^m	*lion*	**leone**^m
beaver	**castoro**^m	*monkey*	**scimmia**^f
bee	**ape**^f	*octopus*	**polpo**^m
beehive	**alveare**^m	*ostrich*	**struzzo**^m
breed	**razza**^f	*owl*	**gufo**^m
cage	**gabbia**^f	*oyster*	**ostrica**^f
camel	**cammello**^m	*parrot*	**pappagallo**^m
caterpillar	**bruco**^m	*paw*	**zampa**^f
cattle	**bestiame**^m	*peacock*	**pavone**^m
cheetah	**ghepardo**^m	*penguin*	**pinguino**^m
chick	**pulcino**^m	*petting*	**carezza**^f
cockroach	**scarafaggio**^m	*pigeon*	**piccione**^m
creature	**creatura**^f	*poaching*	**bracconaggio**^m
crocodile	**coccodrillo**^m	*predator*	**predatore**^m
deer	**cervo**^m	*prey*	**preda**^f
dinosaur	**dinosauro**^m	*seagull*	**gabbiano**^m
dove	**colomba**^f	*seal*	**foca**^f
eagle	**aquila**^f	*shark*	**squalo**^m
elephant	**elefante**^m	*slaughterhouse*	**macello**^m
extinction	**estinzione**^f	*snake*	**serpente**^m
falcon	**falco**^m	*spider*	**ragno**^m
feather	**piuma**^f	*spiderweb*	**ragnatela**^f
fishing rod	**canna**^f **da pesca**	*squirrel*	**scoiattolo**^m
fox	**volpe**^f	*tail*	**coda**^f
frog	**rana**^f	*tiger*	**tigre**^f
gill	**branchia**^f	*turtle* *tortoise*	**tartaruga**^f
giraffe	**giraffa**^f	*vulture*	**avvoltoio**^m
goat	**capra**^f	*wasp*	**vespa**^f
goose	**oca**^f	*whale*	**balena**^f
herd	**gregge**^m	*wing*	**ala**^f
hippopotamus	**ippopotamo**^m	*wolf*	**lupo**^m

| *howl (of a wolf)* | **ululato**^{m} | *worm* | **verme**^{m} |

4. POLITICS

Politics, in Italian, is "**la politica**," and it is singular. Below is some related vocabulary:

agenda	**agenda**^{f}	*grant* *subsidy*	**sussidio**^{m}
ambassador	**ambasciatore**^{m}	*heritage*	**patrimonio**^{m}
anthem	**inno**^{m}	*mayor*	**sindaco**^{m}
awareness	**conoscenza**^{f}	*mayoress*	**sindaca**^{f}
ballot box	**urna elettorale**^{f}	*measures*	**misure**^{f}
bill (law)	**progetto**^{m} **di legge**	*minister*	**ministro**^{m}
candidate	**candidato**^{m}	*ministry*	**ministero**^{m}
citizen	**cittadino**^{m}	*monarchy*	**monarchia**^{f}
citizenship	**cittadinanza**^{f}	*nomination*	**nomina**^{f}
congress	**congresso**^{m}	*official* *(government employee)*	**funzionario**^{m}
constitution	**costituzione**^{f}	*parliament*	**parlamento**^{m}
controversy	**polemica**^{f} **controversia**^{f}	*podium*	**podio**^{m}
council (committee)	**consiglio**^{m}	*policy*	**politica**^{f}
coup d'état	**colpo**^{m} **di stato**	*political party*	**partito politico**^{m}
crown	**corona**^{f}	*political post*	**carica politica**^{f}
democracy	**democrazia**^{f}	*power*	**potere**^{m}
demonstration	**manifestazione**^{f}	*prince*	**principe**^{m}
dictatorship	**dittatura**^{f}	*princess*	**principessa**^{f}
donor	**donatore**^{m}	*protocol*	**protocollo**^{m}
dual-citizenship	**doppia nazionalità**^{f}	*province*	**provincia**^{f}
dynasty	**dinastia**^{f}	*rebel*	**ribelle**^{m,f}
election	**elezione**^{f}	*referendum*	**referendum**^{m}
electoral campaign	**campagna elettorale**^{f}	*republic*	**repubblica**^{f}
embassy	**ambasciata**^{f}	*senate*	**senato**^{m}
emperor	**imperatore**^{m}	*senator*	**senatore**^{m}
empire	**impero**^{m}	*skeptic*	**scettico**^{m}
ethics	**etica**^{f}	*slip of the tongue*	**lapsus**^{m}
exit polls	**sondaggi elettorali**^{m}	*trick*	**trucco**^{m}
flag	**bandiera**^{f}	*unrest*	**disordine**^{m}
government	**governo**^{m}	*vice president*	**vicepresidente**^{m}
governor	**governatore**^{m}	*vote*	**voto**^{m}

5. COUNTRIES & NATIONALITIES II

More vocabulary to expand our knowledge about countries and nationalities is in the table below:

Algeria	**Algeria**[f]	*Algerian*	algerino/-a
Austria	**Austria**[f]	*Austrian*	austriaco/-a
Belarus	**Bielorussia**[f]	*Belarusian*	bielorusso/-a
Belgium	**Belgio**[m]	*Belgian*	belga
Belize	**Belize**[m]	*Belizean*	beliziano/-a
Central America	**America Centrale**[f]	*Central American*	centroamericano/-a
Chile	**Cile**[m]	*Chilean*	cileno/-a
Costa Rica	**Costa Rica**[f]	*Costa Rican*	costaricano/-a
Denmark	**Danimarca**[f]	*Danish*	danese
Ecuador	**Ecuador**[m]	*Ecuadorian*	ecuadoriano/-a
Finland	**Finlandia**[f]	*Finnish*	finlandese
Greece	**Grecia**[f]	*Greek*	greco/-a
Guatemala	**Guatemala**[m]	*Guatemalan*	guatemalteco/-a
Haiti	**Haiti**[m]	*Haitian*	haitiano/-a
Honduras	**Honduras**[m]	*Honduran*	honduregno/-a
Hungary	**Ungheria**[f]	*Hungarian*	ungherese
India	**India**[f]	*Indian*	indiano/-a
Ireland	**Irlanda**[f]	*Irish*	irlandese
Lebanon	**Libano**[m]	*Lebanese*	libanese
Middle East	**Medio Oriente**[m]	*Middle Eastern*	mediorientale
Netherlands	**Paesi Bassi**[m] **Olanda**[f]	*Dutch*	olandese
Nicaragua	**Nicaragua**[m]	*Nicaraguan*	nicaraguense
North America	**Nord America**[m]	*North American*	nordamericano/-a
Norway	**Norvegia**[f]	*Norwegian*	norvegese
Peru	**Peru**[m]	*Peruvian*	peruviano/-a
Philippines	**Filippine**[f]	*Filipino*	filippino/-a
Romania	**Romania**[f]	*Romanian*	rumeno/-a
South Korea	**Corea**[f] **del Sud**	*South Korean*	surdcoreano/-a
Sweden	**Svezia**[f]	*Swedish*	svedese
Switzerland	**Svizzera**[f]	*Swiss*	svizzero/-a
Syria	**Siria**[f]	*Syrian*	siriano/-a
Thailand	**Tailandia**[f]	*Thai*	tailandese
Ukraine	**Ucraina**[f]	*Ukrainian*	ucraino/-a

United Kingdom	**Regno Unito**ᵐ	British	**britannico/-a** [1]
United States	**Stati Uniti**ᵐ	American	**statunitense** [2]
Venezuela	**Venezuela**ᵐ	Venezuelan	**venezuelano/-a**
Wales	**Galles**ᵐ	Welsh	**gallese**

[1] The term "**britannico**" is also used to refer to the citizens of *Great Britain* or "**Gran Bretagna.**"

[2] Although "**statunitense**" is the correct term to refer to someone from the US and "**americano**" refers to a male person from the American continent, the term "**americano**" is widely accepted referring to a male person from the US.

6. Transportation II

We continue to add more vocabulary related to transportation.

anchor	**ancora**ᶠ	ride (bike)	**passeggiata**ᶠ
bus stop	**fermata**ᶠ **dell' autobus**	ride (car)	**giro**ᵐ
chassis	**telaio**ᵐ	rush hour	**ora**ᶠ **di punta**
cobblestone	**ciottoli**ᵐ	sailing boat	**veliero**ᵐ
convertible (car)	**decappottabile**ᶠ	scratch	**graffio**ᵐ
curb sidewalk	**marciapiede**ᵐ **cordolo**ᵐ	seat	**sedile**ᵐ **posto**ᵐ **a sedere**
dashboard	**pannello**ᵐ	seat belt	**cintura**ᶠ **di sicurezza**
dent	**ammaccatura**ᶠ	ship	**nave**ᶠ
flat tire	**gomma**ᶠ **a terra**	shipwreck	**naufragio**ᵐ
fuel	**combustibile**ᵐ **carburante**ᵐ	speed bump	**dosso**ᵐ
glove compartment	**guantiera**ᶠ **portaoggetti**ᵐ	speed limit	**limite**ᵐ **di velocità**
gravel	**ghiaia**ᶠ	steering wheel	**volante**ᵐ **sterzo**ᵐ
hood (car)	**cofano**ᵐ	toll	**pedaggio**ᵐ
landing	**atterraggio**ᵐ	traffic jam	**imbottigliamento**ᵐ
lane	**corsia**ᶠ	traffic light	**semaforo**ᵐ
notice (warning)	**avviso**ᵐ	truck	**camion**ᵐ
pedestrian	**pedone**ᵐ	tunnel	**tunnel**ᵐ **galleria**ᶠ
postage stamp	**francobollo**ᵐ	undocumented	**non documentato**ᵐ
pothole	**buca**ᶠ	van	**furgone**ᵐ
railway	**ferrovia**ᶠ	warning	**avvertenza**ᶠ
rearview mirror	**specchietto retrovisore**ᵐ	wheel	**ruota**ᶠ

7. Nature II

Let us go over more vocabulary related to nature.

ash	**cenere**[f]	*mud*	**fango**[m]
bank (river)	**riva**[f] **sponda**[f]	*organ*	**organo**[m]
bay	**baia**[f]	*passage*	**passaggio**[m]
beauty	**bellezza**[f]	*path*	**percorso**[m] **sentiero**[m] **cammino**[m]
branch	**ramo**[m]	*peak*	**picco**[m] **cima**[f]
brook	**ruscello**[m]	*pearl*	**perla**[f]
bush	**cespuglio**[m]	*pollutant*	**inquinante**[m] **contaminante**[m]
carbon dioxide	**anidride carbonica**[f]	*pollution*	**inquinamento**[m] **contaminazione**[f]
cliff	**precipizio**[m]	*pond*	**stagno**[m]
darkness *gloom*	**buio**[m] **oscurità**[f]	*puddle*	**pozzanghera**[f]
dawn	**alba**[f]	*rainbow*	**arcobaleno**[m]
dew	**rugiada**[f]	*ranch*	**fattoria**[f]
dusk *nightfall*	**tramonto**[m]	*ravine*	**burrone**[m]
earthquake	**terremoto**[m] **sisma**[m]	*ray* *beam*	**raggio**[m]
eclipse	**eclisse**[f]	*reef*	**scogliera**[f]
environment	**ambiente**[m]	*rock*	**roccia**[f]
flood	**inondazione**[f] **diluvio**[m]	*seashell*	**conchiglia**[f]
fog	**nebbia**[f]	*slope*	**pendenza**[f]
forecast	**previsione**[f]	*soil*	**suolo**[m]
forest	**bosco**[m] **foresta**[f]	*sound*	**suono**[m]
frost	**gelo**[m]	*species*	**specie**[f]
fumes *smoke*	**fumo**[m]	*spectrum*	**spettro**[m]
galaxy	**galassia**[f]	*stick*	**bastoncino**[m]
gap	**spacco**[m] **divario**[m]	*stone*	**pietra**[f]

geology	**geologia**f	*storm*	**tempesta**f **tormenta**f
grove	**boschetto**m	*strength force*	**forza**f
heat	**calore**m	*sunrise*	**alba**f **sorgere**m **del sole**
heatwave	**ondata**f **di caldo**	*sunset*	**tramonto**m **(del sole)**
hemisphere	**emisfero**m	*surface*	**superficie**f
hill	**collina**f	*swamp*	**palude**f **pantano**m
horizon	**orizzonte**m	*thorn*	**spina**f
humidity	**umidità**f	*thunder*	**tuono**m
hurricane	**uragano**m	*trail*	**sentiero**m
hydrogen	**idrogeno**m	*trench*	**fosso**m
instinct	**istinto**m	*trunk (tree) log (tree)*	**tronco**m
jungle	**selva**f **giungla**f	*twilight*	**crepuscolo**m
leaf (tree)	**foglia**f	*vacuum*	**vuoto**m
lightning	**lampo**m	*valley*	**valle**m
marvel	**meraviglia**f	*vine*	**vite**f
mist	**foschia**f	*volcano*	**vulcano**m
molecule	**molecola**f	*waterfall*	**cascata**f
mountain range	**catena montuosa**f	*wave*	**onda**f

8. HEALTH II

We add more vocabulary related to health.

allergy	**allergia**f	*injection*	**iniezione**f
ambulance	**ambulanza**f	*microbe*	**microbo**m
antibiotic	**antibiotico**m	*migraine*	**emicrania**f
arthritis	**artrite**f	*operating room*	**sala operatoria**f
bandage	**benda**f	*outbreak*	**epidemia**f
bee sting	**puntura**f **d'ape**	*pandemic*	**pandemia**f
cholesterol	**colesterolo**m	*paralysis*	**paralisi**f
cough	**tosse**f	*pest*	**peste**f
cramp	**crampo**m	*plague*	**piaga**f
cream	**crema**f	*pneumonia*	**polmonite**f
diabetes	**diabete**m	*prescription*	**ricetta**f

diagnosis	**diagnosi**[f]	*pulse (health)*	**polso**[m] **pulsazione**[f]
dizziness	**vertigini**[f] **capogiro**[m]	*remedy*	**rimedio**[m]
dose	**dose**[f]	*rupture*	**rottura**[f]
drop	**goccia**[f]	*scar*	**cicatrice**[f]
emergency room	**pronto soccorso**[m]	*seizure*	**convulsioni**[f]
epilepsy	**epilessia**[f]	*shiver* *chill*	**brivido**[m]
first aid	**primo soccorso**[m]	*side effect*	**effetto collaterale**[m]
food poisoning	**intossicazione alimentare**[f]	*smallpox*	**varicella**[f]
fracture	**frattura**[f]	*sneeze*	**starnuto**[m]
germ	**germe**[m]	*stroke*	**ictus**[m]
heart attack	**infarto**[m]	*stitches*	**punti**[m] **suture**[f]
heart burn	**reflusso**[m]	*stuffy nose*	**naso chiuso**[m]
blood pressure	**pressione sanguigna**[f]	*sunstroke*	**insolazione**[f]
hygiene	**igiene**[f]	*syringe*	**siringa**[f]
immunity	**immunità**[f]	*vomit*	**vomito**[m]

9. FOOD III

We continue to add to our set of vocabulary related to food.

all-you-can-eat buffet	**buffet libero**[m]	*ginger*	**zenzero**[m]
asparagus	**asparago**[m]	*jam*	**marmellata**[f]
beet	**barbabietola**[f]	*layer*	**strato**[m]
bite	**boccone**[m]	*leftovers*	**avanzi**[m]
blackberry	**mora**[f]	*mushroom*	**fungo**[m]
carbohydrate	**carboidrato**[m]	*oat*	**avena**[f]
cashew	**anacardo**[m]	*peach*	**pesca**[f]
cauliflower	**cavolfiore**[m]	*peas*	**piselli**[m]
chewing gum	**gomma**[f] **da masticare**	*pine nut*	**pinolo**[m]
chickpea	**ceci**[m]	*plum*	**prugna**[f]
cookie	**biscotto**[m]	*potion*	**pozione**[f]
crust	**crosta**[f]	*pumpkin*	**zucca**[f]
dairy	**latticino**[m]	*quince*	**mela cotogna**[f]
date	**dattero**[m]	*radish*	**ravanello**[m]
fat	**grasso**[m]	*sausage*	**salsiccia**[f]
fig	**fico**[m]	*seed*	**seme**[m]

flour	farina^f	soy	soia^f
garlic	aglio^m	slice	fetta^f trancio^m
glucose	glucosio^m	spinach	spinaci^m
grain	chicco^m	starch	amido^m
green beans	fagiolini^m	turnip	rapa^f
harvest crop	raccolto^m	wheat	grano^m
hazelnut	nocciola^f	zucchini	zucchina^f

10. ANATOMY II

Below is some more advanced vocabulary related to anatomy:

armpit	ascella^f	lung	polmone^m
blood vessel	vaso sanguigno^m	nail	unghia^f
bone	osso^m	neck	collo^m
cell	cellula^f	nerve	nervo^m
chest	petto^m	reflex	riflesso^m
chin	mento^m	skeleton	scheletro^m
elbow	gomito^m	skull	cranio^m
dimple	fossetta^f	spine	colonna vertebrale^f
forehead	fronte^f	spleen	milza^f
hip	fianco^m	tear	lacrima^f
intestine	intestino^m	throat	gola^f
joint	articolazione^f	tongue	lingua^f
kidney	rene^m	vein	vena^f
liver	fegato^m	waist	vita^f

LEVEL VI: FLUENT

I. Introductory Topics & Grammar

Congratulations on reaching the fluent level. It must feel great to have achieved this accomplishment. At this level, all you need is to perfect a few concepts that are preventing you from achieving full fluency.

1. ORDINAL NUMBERS II

Ordinal numbers from 11 and beyond are formed by dropping the last vowel and adding "-**esimo**" at the end. Ordinal numbers between 11 and 19 are as follows:

undici	11	undicesimo/-a/-i/-e	11.° / 11.ª/ 11.ⁱ / 11.ᵉ
dodici	12	dodicesimo/-a/-i/-e	12.° / 12.ª/ 12.ⁱ / 12.ᵉ
tredici	13	tredicesimo/-a/-i/-e	13.° / 13.ª/ 13.ⁱ / 13.ᵉ
quattordici	14	quattordicesimo/-a/-i/-e	14.° / 14.ª/ 14.ⁱ / 14.ᵉ
quindici	15	quindicesimo/-a/-i/-e	15.° / 15.ª/ 15.ⁱ / 15.ᵉ
sedici	16	sedicesimo/-a/-i/-e	16.° / 16.ª/ 16.ⁱ / 16.ᵉ
diciassette	17	diciassettesimo/-a/-i/-e	17.° / 17.ª/ 17.ⁱ / 17.ᵉ
diciotto	18	diciottesimo/-a/-i/-e	18.° / 18.ª/ 18.ⁱ / 18.ᵉ
diciannove	19	diciannovesimo/-a/-i/-e	19.° / 19.ª/ 19.ⁱ / 19.ᵉ

Note that ordinal numbers are adjectives and must agree in gender and number with the noun. Here are some higher ordinal numbers:

venti	20	ventesimo/-a/-i/-e	20.° / 20.ª/ 20.ⁱ / 20.ᵉ
trenta	30	trentesimo/-a/-i/-e	30.° / 30.ª/ 30.ⁱ / 30.ᵉ
quaranta	40	quarantesimo/-a/-i/-e	40.° / 40.ª/ 40.ⁱ / 40.ᵉ
cinquanta	50	cinquantesimo/-a/-i/-e	50.° / 50.ª/ 50.ⁱ / 50.ᵉ
sessanta	60	sessantesimo/-a/-i/-e	60.° / 60.ª/ 60.ⁱ / 60.ᵉ
settanta	70	settantesimo/-a/-i/-e	70.° / 70.ª/ 70.ⁱ / 70.ᵉ
ottanta	80	ottantesimo/-a/-i/-e	80.° / 80.ª/ 80.ⁱ / 80.ᵉ
novanta	90	novantesimo/-a/-i/-e	90.° / 90.ª/ 90.ⁱ / 90.ᵉ
cento	100	centesimo/-a/-i/-e	100.° / 100.ª/ 100.ⁱ / 100.ᵉ

duecento	200	duecentesimo/-a/-i/-e	200.° / 200.ª / 200.ⁱ / 200.ᵉ
trecento	300	trecentesimo/-a/-i/-e	300.° / 300.ª / 300.ⁱ / 300.ᵉ
quattrocento	400	quattrocentesimo/-a/-i/-e	400.° / 400.ª / 400.ⁱ / 400.ᵉ
cinquecento	500	cinquecentesimo/-a/-i/-e	500.° / 500.ª / 500.ⁱ / 500.ᵉ
seicento	600	seicentesimo/-a/-i/-e	600.° / 600.ª / 600.ⁱ / 600.ᵉ
settecento	700	settecentesimo/-a/-i/-e	700.° / 700.ª / 700.ⁱ / 700.ᵉ
ottocento	800	ottocentesimo/-a/-i/-e	800.° / 800.ª / 800.ⁱ / 800.ᵉ
novecento	900	novecentesimo/-a/-i/-e	900.° / 900.ª / 900.ⁱ / 900.ᵉ
mille	1.000	millesimo/-a/-i/-e	1000.° / 1000.ª / 1000.ⁱ / 1000.ᵉ

❖ Numbers following the names of kings and queens are ordinal and, unlike in English, do not use the definite article before the number, e.g., "**Elisabetta Seconda**" *(Elizabeth the Second)*, "**Edoardo Terzo**" *(Edward the Third)*, "**Luigi Quattordicesimo**" *(Louis the Fourteenth)*, etc.

❖ Fractional numbers are identical to the ordinal numbers, e.g., "1/16 = **un sedicesimo**." If the numerator is larger than one, the denominator is expressed in plural, e.g., "3/4 = **tre quarti**."

❖ The collective numbers "**un paio**" *(a pair)* and "**una dozzina**" *(a dozen)* may also be used to describe quantities. The adjectives "**doppio**" and "**triplo**" are used for *"double"* and *"triple,"* respectively.

2. THE PAST INFINITIVE

The past infinitive is formed as follows:

> "**avere**" or "**essere**" + past participle

It is equivalent to the English combination of *"having"* followed by the past participle, e.g., *"having finished," "having eaten," "having seen,"* etc.

Let us consider the following two examples:

Penso di **guidare** molto.	*I think that I **drive** a lot.*
Crede di **cambiare** velocemente.	*He believes that he **changes** fast.*

Notice that both examples are in the present tense, and that the subject is the same in the main clause and the subordinate clause. In Italian, unlike in English where the subject is repeated, we use the infinitive preceded by "**di**" to avoid repeating the subject.

Now, consider the case when the subordinate clause in the two examples is in the past instead of the present. In this case, the past infinitive is used instead of the infinitive. For example:

Pensavo di **aver guidato** molto.	*I thought that I **had driven** a lot.*
Crede di **essere cambiato** velocemente.	*He believes that he **changed** fast.*

Notice that only the verb in the subordinate clause must be in the past to use the past infinitive, whereas the verb in the main clause can be in the present or in the past.

Another common use of the past infinitive in Italian is when there are two actions in the past and the subject is the same. For example:

Dopo **aver terminato** il suo lavoro, si è preso una settimana di ferie.	*After **having finished** his work, he took a week off.*
Gli è stato detto di lasciare il posto per **aver violato** le regole.	*He was told to leave the place for **having violated** the rules.*

We can also use the past infinitive in cases where we would normally use the infinitive in English, if the action referred to by the infinitive is in the past. For example:

Grazie per **aver**mi **invitato**.	*Thank you for **inviting** me.*
Mi dispiace di **essere andato** via prima ieri sera.	*I'm sorry for **leaving** early last night.*

Notice that the actions that the past infinitive refers to in both examples are understood to be in the past. Notice also that a pronoun can be attached to the end of "**avere**" or "**essere**."

The infinitive forms "**avere**" and "**essere**" are often shortened to "**aver**" and "**esser**," respectively, when used in the past infinitive in daily informal speech.

3. IMPERFECT SUBJUNCTIVE TENSE

The imperfect subjunctive, similar to the present perfect in the subjunctive, is used to express desires and wishes. However, these desires and wishes are often in the past or refer to unlikely events or possibilities, for example:

Se **fossi** in te, non andrei.	*If I **were** you, I wouldn't go.*

Conjugation

To form the stem of the verb needed for regular verb conjugation, we drop the final "**-re**" of the verb and attach the conjugation suffix. The suffixes are the same for the three types of verbs.

	-are ending parlare *(to speak)*	**-ere ending** vendere *(to sell)*	**-ire ending** partire *(to leave)*
io	parla**ssi**	vende**ssi**	parti**ssi**
tu	parla**ssi**	vende**ssi**	parti**ssi**
lui/lei	parla**sse**	vende**sse**	parti**sse**
noi	parla**ssimo**	vende**ssimo**	parti**ssimo**
voi	parla**ste**	vende**ste**	parti**ste**
loro	parla**ssero**	vende**ssero**	parti**ssero**

Irregular Verbs

Verbs that are irregular in the imperfect indicative are also irregular in the imperfect subjunctive. Here are the most common irregular verbs:

	io	**tu**	**lui/lei**	**noi**	**voi**	**loro**
bere *(to drink)*	bevessi	bevessi	bevesse	bevessimo	beveste	bevessero
dare *(to give)*	dessi	dessi	desse	dessimo	deste	dessero
dire *(to say/tell)*	dicessi	dicessi	dicesse	dicessimo	diceste	dicessero
essere *(to be)*	fossi	fossi	fosse	fossimo	foste	fossero
fare *(to do/make)*	facessi	facessi	facesse	facessimo	faceste	facessero
stare *(to stay/be)*	stessi	stessi	stesse	stessimo	steste	stessero

Uses of the Imperfect Subjunctive

Let us discuss the common uses of the imperfect subjunctive and check some examples:

1. Expressing Past Desires, Wishes, Feelings, Requests, and Recommendations.

Whereas the present subjunctive is used to express opinion, possibility, and feelings such as fear, doubt, hope, desire, etc., about something in the present or the future, the imperfect subjunctive can be used similarly, but when the hope, desire, feeling, etc. itself is in the past.

For example, using the present subjunctive, we can say:

| Voglio che tu **venga** a casa mia. | *I want you to **come** to my house.* |
| Mi rattrista che non mi **chiamino**. | *It makes me sad that they don't **call** me.* |

If that hope or desire occurred in the past, the imperfect subjunctive should be used:

| Volevo che tu **venissi** a casa mia. | *I wanted you to **come** to my house.* |
| Mi ha rattristato che non mi **chiamassero**. | *It made me sad that they didn't **call** me.* |

2. Unlikely or Hypothetical Conditional Statements.

As discussed previously, conditional statements that contain hypothetical or unlikely assumptions, such as *"if I were you," "if I were the president,"* and *"if I had a lot of money,"* use the imperfect subjunctive, for example:

| Se **fossi** in te, oggi non andrei in palestra. | *If I **were** you, I wouldn't go to the gym today.* |
| Se **avessi** molti soldi, comprerei un palazzo. | *If I **had** a lot of money, I would buy a palace.* |

4. PLUPERFECT INDICATIVE TENSE

The pluperfect tense, literally *the more than perfect*, describes the past before the simple past. If two actions took place in the past, the one that occurred before is often described in the pluperfect.

The pluperfect indicative is formed as follows:

"**avere**" or "**essere**" in the imperfect indicative + past participle

Depending on the verb, the pluperfect indicative uses the auxiliary "**avere**" or "**essere**" in the imperfect, which are conjugated as follows:

	"avere" in the imperfect indicative	"essere" in the imperfect indicative
io	avevo	ero
tu	avevi	eri
lui/lei	aveva	era
noi	avevamo	eravamo
voi	avevate	eravate
loro	avevano	erano

For example:

Prima che ci conoscessimo, non **ero** mai **stato** in Spagna.	*Before we met, I **had** never **been** to Spain.*
Quando sono andato a trovare mia madre, mia sorella **era** già **arrivata**.	*When I visited my mom, my sister **had** already **arrived**.*
Dopo che la sicurezza **aveva chiuso** la porta, la folla è tornata a casa.	*After the security **had closed** the door, the crowd went home.*

5. PLUPERFECT SUBJUNCTIVE TENSE

The pluperfect subjunctive is formed as follows:

"**avere**" or "**essere**" in the imperfect subjunctive + past participle

Depending on the verb, the pluperfect subjunctive uses the auxiliary "**avere**" or "**essere**" in the imperfect subjunctive, which are conjugated as follows:

	"avere" in the imperfect subjunctive	"essere" in the imperfect subjunctive
io	avessi	fossi
tu	avessi	fossi
lui/lei	avesse	fosse
noi	avessimo	fossimo
voi	aveste	foste
loro	avessero	fossero

The pluperfect in the subjunctive mood has different uses than the pluperfect in the indicative mood studied earlier. It is mostly used to describe an event that already happened in the past, but we wish it did not happen or happened differently, or we want to discuss what would happen if we hypothetically changed that past event.

We will discuss two examples in which the pluperfect subjunctive is used:

1. The pluperfect subjunctive can be used in conditional statements to convey the meaning of the impossible past, for example:

Se **avessi studiato** medicina, ...	If I **had studied** *medicine*, ...
Se mio nonno **non fosse morto**, ...	If *my grandfather* **hadn't died**, ...

The conditional statements above are usually followed by

❖ a verb in simple conditional, or

❖ *"would have"* + past participle

Se **avesse studiato** medicina, oggi **sarebbe** ricco.	If I **had studied** *medicine, I* **would be** *rich today.*
Se mio nonno **non fosse morto, avrei passato** del tempo con lui.	If *my grandfather* **hadn't died,** *I* **would have spent** *time with him.*

Another way to describe a hypothetical or impossible past is using the expression "**come se**," translated as *"as if,"* for example:

Parla come se **avesse studiato** medicina.	He talks as if he **had studied** *medicine.*
Pianse come se suo nonno **fosse morto.**	He cried as if his grandfather **had died.**

2. The other use of the pluperfect in the subjunctive is similar to that in the indicative mood. As studied earlier, the pluperfect in the indicative mood is used to describe the past before the simple past. If a feeling, doubt, or hope is added to the action described in the pluperfect, the subjunctive mood should be used. Let us look at the following examples for comparison:

a) Pluperfect in the indicative mood:

Eri andato in Spagna prima che ci conoscessimo.	*You **had been** to Spain before we met.*
Quando sono andato a trovare mia madre, mia sorella **era** già **arrivata**.	*When I visited my mom, my sister **had** already **arrived**.*

b) Pluperfect in the subjunctive mood:

Mi piaceva che tu **fossi** già **andato** in Spagna prima che ci conoscessimo.	*I was delighted that you **had** already **been** to Spain before we met.*
Quando sono andato a trovare mia madre, dubitavo che mia sorella **fosse arrivata**.	*When I visited my mom, I doubted that my sister **had arrived**.*

6. PASSIVE VOICE & IMPERSONAL "SI"

One way to describe something in the passive voice in Italian is by moving the noun acted upon to the beginning of the sentence to emphasize it and using a *"to be"* verb followed by the adjective or the past participle. For example:

Il tessuto è stato **realizzato** con materiale riciclato (dalla fabbrica).	*The textile was **made** from recycled material (by the factory).*
Il contratto sarà **firmato** (dalla società).	*The contract will be **signed** (by the company).*

The performer of the action in the above two examples, denoted by "**da ...**" (*by* ...), can be omitted because it is deemed not to be of great significance.

Impersonal "Si"

Another way to construct the passive voice in Italian is by using the *impersonal* "**si**." Expressions such as "**si dice**" *(it is said)*, "**si sa**" *(it is known)*, and "**si pensa**" *(it is thought)* are some frequently used examples of the impersonal "**si**."

An impersonal "**si**" construction uses one of the following formulas:

1. "**Si**" + third-person *transitive*[1] verb (sing. or plural) + noun (sing. or plural)

2. "**Si**" + third-person *intransitive*[2] verb (singular)

3. "**Si**" + third-person *copular*[3] verb (singular) + adjective (plural)

#1: Impersonal "Si" with Transitive Verbs (Passive "Si")

This type is also called the *passive* "**si**" because it replaces the standard passive voice discussed previously. This is the passive construction that you are likely to encounter in ads and commercials, or when the performer of the action is unknown or not as important. For example:

Si ricercano persone con esperienza.	*Wanted: people with experience.*
In Egitto, **si parla** l'arabo.	*In Egypt, they speak Arabic.*
Qui **si vendono** i cellulari.	*Cell phones are sold here.*
Al mattino **si consuma** la colazione.	*In the morning, one eats breakfast.*
Non **si sa** mai tutta la verità.	*You never know the whole truth.*

Notice that when a transitive verb is used to construct a passive "**si**" phrase, the verb can be in the *singular* or *plural* third-person

---

[1] A verb is *transitive* if it requires an object. For example, the verb *"to bring"* can only be transitive, because the meaning is not complete without an object, e.g., *"I bring."*

[2] A verb is *intransitive* if it does not require an object to complete the meaning, e.g., *"I sleep," "I laugh," "I run,"* etc.

[3] A *copular* verb does not make sense on its own. It simply links the subject to the adjective in a sentence, e.g., *"to be," "to seem," "to feel," "to become,"* etc. For example, in the sentence *"The weather seems nice,"* we use *"seems"* to link the subject *"the weather"* to the adjective *"nice."*

form depending on the following noun (the object in the active voice construction).

Sometimes there are two verbs, like in the case of modal verbs, e.g., **"dovere,"** **"potere,"** etc., or compound tenses that use an auxiliary, e.g., the present perfect tense.

In this case, only the first verb is conjugated following the noun in gender and number, whereas the second verb is in the infinitive. For example:

Si <u>può</u> praticare la <u>lingua</u> per diventare fluenti.	*One can practice the language to become fluent.*
Si <u>devono</u> seguire le <u>regole</u> della strada per evitare le multe.	*One must follow the traffic rules to avoid tickets.*
Si è mangiato questo solo in Italia.	*One ate this only in Italy.*

Notice that we always use the verb **"essere"** with impersonal **"si"** in compound tenses even if the verb is normally conjugated with **"avere."**

#2: Impersonal "Si" with Intransitive Verbs

In English, we sometimes make general statements or observations such as:

We *work better as a team.*

They *sleep early in the village.*

One *does not travel far alone.*

Notice that in these sentences, we used the subject pronouns *"we," "they,"* and *"one"* to convey a general meaning.

Furthermore, notice that the verbs *"to work," "to sleep,"* and *"to travel"* are *intransitive*, meaning that they do not need an object for the meaning to be complete.

In Italian, we can express such observations or statements using the impersonal **"si"** followed by the *singular* third-person conjugation of the verb.

The previous examples in English can be translated as follows:

We work better as a team.	**Si lavora** meglio in una squadra.
They sleep early in the village.	**Si dorme** presto al villaggio.
One does not travel far alone.	Non **si viaggia** lontano da soli.

As you can see, the verb is always *singular* regardless of any implicit assumptions about the subject, which is grammatically absent.

"Si" + third-person *intransitive* verb (always singular)

If there is another pronoun, e.g., a reflexive or object pronoun, in addition to the impersonal **"si,"** the other pronoun must come before the impersonal **"si,"** regardless of whether the verb is transitive or intransitive. For example:

Mi **si deve** prendere sul serio.	*One must take me seriously.*

If the reflexive pronoun is also **"si,"** the reflexive pronoun is changed to **"ci"** and placed before the impersonal **"si."** For example:

<u>Ci</u> **si diverte** in vacanza.	*People[1] have fun on vacation.*
<u>Ci</u> **si prepara** per gli esami.	*One prepares for the exams.*

---

[1] The translation as *"people"* is used generally in the same way that *"we," "they,"* or *"one"* are used to convey a general meaning.

Some verbs can be transitive in some contexts and intransitive in others if the object is absent. For example, the verb *"change"* in *"Technology has changed the world"* is transitive and *"the world"* is the object. However, the verb *"change"* in *"He changed a lot recently"* is intransitive because there is no object.

Let us take an example in Italian:

Si mangia bene in Italia.	*One **eats** well in Italy.*

| **Si mangiano** frutti di mare deliziosi in Italia. | *One **eats** delicious seafood in Italy.* |

In the first example, the verb "**mangiare**" *(to eat)* is intransitive; thus, it is always in singular form. In the second example, the verb is transitive; thus, it is in plural form following the plural noun "**frutti di mare**" *(seafood)*.

#3: Impersonal "Si" with Copular Verbs

A copular verb connects a subject to an adjective, adverb, noun, or phrase. The most common example is the verb *"to be."* Other examples of copular verbs in English include: *seem, feel, appear, look, become, taste, get, sound, turn, grow,* and *find.* For example, in the sentence *"The weather seems nice"* or *"The grass turned green,"* the verbs *"seem"* and *"turn"* do not make sense on their own because they do not complete the meaning. They simply link the subject to the adjective in each sentence. In Italian, there are such similar verbs like "**essere**" *(to be)*, "**sembrare**" *(to seem)*, "**sentirsi**" *(to feel)*, "**diventare**" *(to become)*, etc.

If a copular verb falls between the impersonal "**si**" and an adjective, the adjective must be in plural form. For example:

Si è <u>stanchi</u> dopo l'allenamento.	*One is tired after working out.*
Si è <u>felici</u> per il successo di un amico.	*One is happy for a friend's success.*
Si sembra <u>gioiosi</u> sulla spiaggia.	*It seems joyful on the beach.*
Ci si sente <u>strani</u> senza vita sociale.	*It feels strange without a social life.*

Notice that the adjective in each of the examples above is in plural form. This also applies to the past participles treated like adjectives including those of verbs that are normally conjugated with "**essere**." For example:

| **Si è** <u>morti</u> molto tempo prima dell'invenzione di Internet. | *One died long ago before the invention of the internet.* |
| A che ora **si è** <u>partiti</u> per arrivare in tempo? | *At what time has one left to arrive in time?* |

Notice that the past participles "**morti**" and "**partiti**" are treated like adjectives and are in plural form, because the verbs "**morire**" *(to die)* and "**partire**" *(to leave)* are normally conjugated with the auxiliary "**essere**."

7. IDIOMATIC PRONOMINAL VERBS

A pronominal verb is a verb that is accompanied by at least one pronoun. An example of pronominal verbs is reflexive verbs, which have the ending "-**si**" in the infinitive, indicating that the action is performed on oneself.

Not all pronominal verbs are reflexive. Some verbs simply change their meaning when attached to pronouns to form new idiomatic meanings that do not often make complete sense if translated literally into English.

Take, for example, the verb "**andare**" *(to go)*. If we attach the pronouns "**si**" and "**ne**" to the verb "**andare**," we obtain the pronominal verb "**andarsene**," which means *"to go away,"* often encountered in the command form "**Vattene!**" *(Go away!)*, that is: "**va**" + "**ti**" + "**ne**," or "**Andiamocene!**" *(Let's go!)*, that is: "**andiamo**" + "**ci**" + "**ne**."

Similarly, if we attach the pronouns "**ci**" and "**la**" to the verb "**avere**" *(to have)*, we obtain the pronominal verb "**avercela**," which means *"to be mad or angry."*

There are many similar idiomatic pronominal verbs in Italian. Some are formed by attaching one pronoun, while others are formed by attaching two pronouns. The pronouns attached can be reflexive such as "**si**," direct object such as "**le**" *(it)* and "**la**" *(them)*, or the special pronouns "**ci**" and "**ne**." Remember that the pronoun "**mi**," "**ti**," "**ci**," or "**vi**" is changed to "**me**," "**te**," "**ce**," or "**ve**," respectively, when followed by a second pronoun attached to it. One notable exception is when "**ci**" and "**si**" are used together to form "-**cisi**" at the end of a pronominal verb.

Unless the pronominal verb is in the infinitive or the imperative, the pronouns are placed in the same order before the conjugated verb. If the conjugation needs a past participle, as in the present perfect tense, the past participle takes the treatment of an adjective and must follow the ending pronoun in gender and number. Here is the conjugation of the pronominal verb "**farcela**" *(to make it or to succeed)* and "**prenderle**" *(to get it or to give a beating)* in the present perfect:

	farce**la**	prender**le**
io	ce l'ho fatt**a**	le ho pres**e**
tu	ce l'hai fatt**a**	le hai pres**e**
lui/lei	ce l'ha fatt**a**	le ha pres**e**
noi	ce l'abbiamo fatt**a**	le abbiamo pres**e**
voi	ce l'avete fatt**a**	le avete pres**e**
loro	ce l'hanno fatt**a**	le hanno pres**e**

The following table lists some of the most common idiomatic pronominal verbs:

Verb	Meaning	Example	
andarsene	*to leave a place or to go away*	**Andatevene!** Non voglio parlare.	*Go away! I do not want to talk.*
avercela	*to be mad or angry*	Non **avercela** con me!	*Don't be angry with me!*
cavarsela	*to manage a difficult situation*	**Se la** sono **cavata** da soli.	*They managed on their own.*
cercarsela	*to look for trouble*	**Ce la** siamo **cercata** da soli.	*We brought this on ourselves.*
farcela	*to make it or to succeed*	Sono rimasto sorpreso ma **ce l'ha fatta**.	*I was surprised but he made it.*
godersela	*to enjoy something*	**Se la gode** in questa atmosfera.	*He enjoys it in this atmosphere.*
intendersene	*to know a lot about something*	Lo lasci dire a chi **se ne intende!**	*Leave it to those who know best!*
mettercela	*to put all effort into something*	**Ce l'hanno messa** tutta in campo.	*They gave it their all on the field.*
piantarla	*to quit something*	Per favore! Ti ho detto di **piantarla**.	*Please! I told you to knock it off.*
prendersela	*to get angry*	Mio fratello sempre **se la prende** con me.	*My brother always gets angry with me.*

sbrigarsela	*to manage or to deal with*	La prossima volta, **se la sbrigherà** da solo.	*Next time, he'll* **handle it** *himself.*
sentirsela	*to feel like or have desire to*	Può partecipare quando **se la sente**.	*He can participate when he* **feels like it.**
smetterla	*to stop or quit something*	Devi **smetterla** di metterti in mostra.	*You need to* **stop** *showing off.*
spassarsela	*to have a blast*	**Me la** sono **spassata** in quel periodo.	*I* **had a blast** *during that period.*
tirarsela	*to show off*	**Se la tira** sempre tanto.	*He always* **shows off** *too much.*
trovarcisi	*to find oneself in*	**Mi ci** sono **trovato** per caso.	*I* **found myself there** *by accident.*
vedercisi	*to see oneself in*	Non **mi ci vedo** con loro.	*I don't* **see myself** *with them.*
vederne	*to see something of*	Non **ne vedo** il motivo.	*I don't* **see** *the reason* **of** *it.*
venirne	*to get to the bottom of*	Alla fine, **ne** sono **venuto** a conoscenza.	*Eventually, I* **came to** *know about it.*

8. DIMINUTIVES & AUGMENTATIVES

In Italian, diminutives and augmentatives are sometimes used to exaggerate descriptions or show certain emotions such as endearment or affection. Understanding some rules and familiarity with some vocabulary in this category will help you enhance your understanding of the Italian language and culture.

Diminutives

In the English language, we sometimes form the diminutive by suffixing *"-ie"* or *"-y,"* as in *"doggie"* for *"dog"* and *"kitty"* for *"kitten,"* indicating small size and sometimes the state or quality of being familiarly known, lovable, pitiable, or contemptible. Sometimes other suffixes are used, such as *"-ette"* in *"kitchenette"* and *"novelette,"* *"-let"* in *"booklet"* and *"droplet,"* and *"-ling"* in *"duckling"* and *"gosling"* *(a young goose).*

In Italian, the purpose of using the diminutive is often similar to that in English, although in a few cases, the diminutive may be used to express sarcasm or negativity.

Unfortunately, there are not always specific rules on which suffix to use for a particular word in Italian. However, we discuss the most common examples and hope that with practice you can continue to enrich your vocabulary in this area.

1. "-ino"

The suffix "-ino" is commonly used to form diminutives from masculine singular nouns and adjectives. Regular end-changes often apply for feminine and plural forms.

Let us take some examples of diminutives ending in "-ino":

ragazzo[m] *(boy)*	ragazz~~o~~	+	-ino	=	ragazzino[m] *(young or little boy)*
ragazza[f] *(girl)*	ragazz~~a~~	+	-ina	=	ragazzina[f] *(young or little girl)*
gatto[m] *(cat)*	gatt~~o~~	+	-ino	=	gattino[m] *(kitten)*
tazza[f] *(cup)*	tazz~~a~~	+	-ina	=	tazzina[f] *(small cup)*
mano[f] *(hand)*	man~~o~~	+	-ina	=	manina[f] [1] *(little hand)*
bello[m] *(beautiful)*	bell~~o~~	+	-ino	=	bellino[m] *(cute)*

---

[1] Remember that "mano" *(hand)* is a feminine noun although it ends with an "-o." Thus, it takes the suffix "-ina" instead of "-ino."

The above examples include nouns and adjectives. Some adverbs can also be used in diminutive forms. These usually use the "-ino" suffix. For example:

bene *(well)*	ben~~e~~	+	-ino	=	benino *(goodish)*
male *(badly)*	mal~~e~~	+	-ino	=	malino *(a little badly)*
presto *(soon)*	prest~~o~~	+	-ino	=	prestino *(a little soon)*
tanto *(much)*	tant~~o~~	+	-ino	=	tantino *(a little much)*
poco *(little)*	poc~~o~~	+	-ino	=	pochino *(a tiny bit)*
tardi *(late)*	tard~~i~~	+	-ino	=	tardino[m] *(a bit late)*

Sometimes "-ic-" or "-ol-" is inserted before the suffix, forming the modified suffixes "-icino" or "-olino," respectively. Here are some examples:

posto[m] *(place)*	post~~o~~	+	-ino	=	posticino[m] *(small place)*
libro[m] *(book)*	libr~~o~~	+	-ino	=	libriccino[m] *(booklet)*
topo[m] *(mouse)*	top~~o~~	+	-ino	=	topolino[m] *(little mouse)*
magro[m] *(thin)*	magr~~o~~	+	-ino	=	magrolino[f] *(skinny)*
cane[m] *(dog)*	cane	+	-ino	=	cagnolino[m] *(small dog)*

The suffix "**-ino**" is widely used when affectionately describing or talking about babies, e.g., "**faccino**" *(little face)*, "**manina**" *(little hand)*, etc.

2. "-etto"

Another common suffix used to form diminutives is "**-etto**." This suffix is often applied affectionately to names, especially female names, using the suffix feminine form "**-etta**," e.g., "**Lauretta**" (diminutive for "**Laura**"), "**Paoletta**" (diminutive for "**Paola**"). Let us take a look at some examples:

casaᶠ *(house)*	casa	+	-etta	=	casettaᶠ *(small house)*
poveroᵐ *(poor)*	povero	+	-etto	=	poverettoᵐ *(poor little guy)*
caneᵐ *(dog)*	cane	+	-etto	=	cagnettoᵐ *(small dog)*
borsaᶠ *(purse)*	borsa	+	-etta	=	borsettaᶠ *(small purse)*
piccoloᵐ *(small)*	piccolo	+	-etto	=	piccolettoᵐ *(shorty)*

3. "-ello"

The suffix "**-ello**" can also be used to form diminutives. Here are some examples:

alberoᵐ *(tree)*	albero	+	-ello	=	alberelloᵐ *(small tree)*
finestraᶠ *(window)*	finestra	+	-ella	=	finestrellaᵐ *(little window)*
cattivoᵐ *(bad)*	cattivo	+	-ello	=	cattivelloᵐ *(naughty)*

Sometimes "**-ic-**" or "**-er-**" is inserted before the suffix, forming the modified suffixes "**-icello**" or "**-erello**," respectively. Here are some examples:

campoᵐ *(field)*	campo	+	-icello	=	campicelloᵐ *(small field)*
fattoᵐ *(fact)*	fatto	+	-erello	=	fatterelloᵐ *(anecdote or minor event)*

4. "-uccio"

The suffix "**-uccio**" is sometimes used to form diminutives showing affection or endearment when used with proper nouns, e.g., "**Micheluccio**" (diminutive for "**Michele**"), "**Guiduccio**" (diminutive for "**Guido**"), "**Mariuccia**" (diminutive for "**Maria**"), etc. In other contexts, it may be used as a pejorative. Here are some examples of diminutives using the suffix "-uccio":

avvocato^m *(lawyer)*	avvocat~~o~~	+ -uccio	=	avvocatuccio^m *(inferior lawyer)*
caldo^m *(hot)*	cald~~o~~	+ -uccio	=	calduccio^m *(cozy)*
cappello^m *(hat)*	cappell~~o~~	+ -uccio	=	cappelluccio^m *(worn-out hat)*
casa^f *(house)*	cas~~a~~	+ -uccia	=	casuccia^f *(small cozy house)*
zio^m *(uncle)*	zi~~o~~	+ -uccio	=	ziuccio^m *(dear uncle)*

5. "-otto"

The suffix "-otto" is used to form diminutives. It is sometimes used to refer to baby animals. Here are some examples of diminutives that take the suffix "-otto":

giovane^m *(young)*	giovane	+ -otto	=	giovanotto^m *(young lad)*
aquila^f *(eagle)*	aquil~~a~~	+ -otto	=	aquilotto^m *(eaglet)*
tigre^f *(tiger)*	tigre	+ -otto	=	tigrotto^m *(tiger cub)*

Sometimes "-acchi-" is inserted before the suffix, forming the modified suffix "-acchiotto." Here are some examples:

lupo^m *(wolf)*	lup~~o~~	+ -acchiotto	=	lupacchiotto^m *(wolf cub)*
orso^m *(bear)*	ors~~o~~	+ -acchiotto	=	orsacchiotto^m *(bear cub or teddy bear)*
tigre^f *(tiger)*	tigre	+ -acchiotto	=	tigracchiotto^m *(tiger cub)*

6. "-uzzo"

Another less common suffix is "-uzzo," although is more common in some Southern regions of Italy. Examples include:

| pietra^f *(stone)* | pietr~~a~~ | + -uzza | = | pietruzza^f *(pebble)* |
| paglia^f *(straw)* | pagli~~a~~ | + -uzza | = | pagliuzza^f *(little straw)* |

We can also sometimes combine two diminutive suffixes, e.g., "casettina" *(very small house)*, "giovanottino" *(young lad)*.

Although these are not all the suffixes used to form diminutives in Italian, most other suffixes are either of mainly regional use or rarely encountered in daily life.

Augmentatives

Augmentatives are the opposite of diminutives. They indicate that something is large or intense, sometimes in an undesirable way. Augmentatives can apply to nouns and adjectives. In the English language, although not as versatile and common, augmentatives are formed by using prefixes rather than suffixes. You can think of the prefix *"super-"* in *"superpower"* and *"supernatural,"* the prefix *"mega-"* in *"megaphone"* and *"megastore,"* the prefix *"grand-"* in *"grandmaster"* and *"grandfather,"* the prefix *"over-"* in *"overgrown"* and *"overqualified,"* and the prefix *"arch-"* in *"archrival"* and *"archenemy."*

In Italian, we mainly use the suffix "**-one**," and in less common cases "**-ona**," to form augmentatives. It is common for many feminine nouns to change their gender to masculine and take the suffix "**-one**" to form the augmentative. To form the augmentative, the final vowel is dropped, and the suffix is added.

Let us take some examples:

ragazzo^m *(boy)*	ragazz~~o~~	+	-one	=	ragazzone^m *(very tall boy)*
casa^f *(house)*	cas~~a~~	+	-one	=	casone^m *(big house)*
libro^m *(book)*	libr~~o~~	+	-one	=	librone^m *(very large book)*
porta^f *(door)*	port~~a~~	+	-one	=	portone^m *(main gate or entrance)*
donna^f *(woman)*	donn~~a~~	+	-one	=	donnone^m *(very tall woman)*
sorella^f *(sister)*	sorell~~a~~	+	-ona	=	sorellona^f *(big sister)*

While these are the most common suffixes, there are some less-common suffixes, some of which may also have a pejorative or sarcastic connotation, such as "**-accione**" and "**-acchione**." For example:

buono^m *(good)*	buon~~o~~	+	-accione	=	bonaccione^m *(good-natured)*
matto^m *(mad)*	matt~~o~~	+	-acchione	=	mattacchione^m *(joker)*
furbo^m *(cunning)*	furb~~o~~	+	-acchione	=	furbacchione^m *(slick)*

Notice that the above examples are of singular nouns. The plural is often regular and formed by changing the ending to "**-i**" for masculine plural, e.g., **"casoni"** *(big houses)* and **"-e"** for feminine plural, e.g., **"sorellone"** *(big sisters).*

II. Vocabulary Building

Go over the vocabulary in this section. You could use Anki to study and memorize the new vocabulary efficiently.

1. VERBS VI

Below is a list of some important verbs that we need at this level:

English	Italian	Examples
acquire	acquisire	**Ha acquisito** l'appartamento senza problema l'anno scorso. *He acquired the apartment with no problems last year.*
adore worship	adorare	Mia figlia **adorava** sua nonna quando era piccola. *My daughter adored her grandma when she was young.*
align	allineare	Mi piace **allineare** correttamente i barattoli. *I like to align the jars correctly.*
ally	alleare(-si)	I governi **si sono alleati** tra loro per molti anni. *The governments allied with one another for many years.*
approve	approvare	Non posso **approvare** tali misure. *I can't approve of such measures.*
attack	attaccare aggredire	Il cane del mio vicino **attacca** sempre il postino. *My neighbor's dog always attacks the mailman.*
attend	assistere a	Se lo avessi saputo, **avrei assistito** alla riunione. *Had I known, I would've attended the meeting.*
behave	comportarsi	Spero che **ti comporterai** da gentiluomo. *I hope you will behave like a gentleman.*
betray	tradire	Non **tradire** la fiducia del tuo amico. *Don't betray your friend's trust.*
bless	benedire	Il sacerdote **ha benedetto** la coppia. *The priest blessed the couple.*
blush	arrossire	**È arrossito** dopo aver sentito la storia. *He blushed upon hearing the story.*
brag boast	vantarsi	Mi piacerebbe se non **si vantasse** di tutto. *I'd like him if he would not brag about everything.*
brake (vehicle)	frenare	Se non **avessi frenato** sarei caduto. *If I had not braked, I would have crashed.*
broadcast transmit	trasmettere	**Stanno trasmettendo** in diretta. *They are broadcasting live.*

bury	seppellire sotterrare	Abbiamo dovuto **seppellire** il pesce domestico. *We had to bury the pet fish.*
charge (fee)	fare pagare	**Fanno pagare** molto per i biglietti. *They charge a lot for tickets.*
check in	registrare fare il check-in	Ieri sera **ho fatto il check-in** in un hotel vicino. *I checked in at a nearby hotel last night.*
chop down	abbattere	**Stanno abbattendo** gli alberi nel parco. *They are chopping down the trees in the park.*
cite	citare	**Hanno citato** molte prove nelle loro ultime ricerche. *They cited a lot of evidence in their latest research.*
collapse	crollare	Quell'edificio sta per **crollare**. *That building is about to collapse.*
collect or raise (money)	raccogliere	**Stanno raccogliendo** fondi per la beneficenza. *They are raising money for the charity.*
collide	scontrarsi	Sono riusciti a evitare che si **scontrasse**. *They managed to avoid him colliding.*
commit	commettere	Non voleva **commettere** un crimine. *He didn't want to commit a crime.*
compose	comporre	**Ha composto** quella bellissima canzone. *She composed that beautiful song.*
compress	comprimere	Ho dovuto **comprimere** i file. *I had to compress the files.*
compromise	compromettere	Hanno deciso di **compromettere** alcune idee. *They decided to compromise some ideas.*
confuse	confondere	La sua spiegazione ci **ha confuso**. *His explanation has confused us.*
conquer	conquistare	Hanno cercato di **conquistare** quell'isola. *They tried to conquer that island.*
contain	contenere	Questo tubo può **contenere** un liquido pericoloso. *This tube may contain a dangerous liquid.*
contaminate	contaminare	Il fiume è **contaminato** dai rifiuti. *The river is contaminated by waste.*
contradict	contraddire	Non voglio **contraddir**ti. *I don't want to contradict you.*
correspond	corrispondere	I calzini non **corrispondono** allo stesso paio. *The socks don't correspond to the same pair.*
cram	stipare	Era **stipato** della mia roba. *It was crammed with my stuff.*
crease	piegare	**Piega** i bordi della carta. *Crease the edges of the paper.*
curse	maledire imprecare	Sai che non dovresti **imprecare**. *You know you shouldn't curse.*

damage harm	danneggiare nuocere	Stava molto attento a non **danneggiare** la vernice. *He was very careful not to **damage** the paint.*
dazzle	abbagliare	Lo spettacolo ti **abbaglierà**. *The show **will dazzle** you.*
defeat	sconfiggere vincere	Mi **ha sconfitto** in questo round. *He **defeated** me in this round.*
deliver turn in	consegnare	Lo **stanno consegnando** proprio ora. *They **are delivering** it right now.*
deny	negare	Nessuno dovrebbe **negare** l'acqua agli altri. *No one should **deny** water to others.*
deplete	esaurire	La guerra **ha esaurito** le risorse del paese. *The war **has depleted** the country's resources.*
detain	detenere trattenere	La polizia l'**avrebbe detenuto** comunque. *The police **would have stopped** him anyway.*
diagnose	diagnosticare	Il dottore sarà colui che mi **diagnosticherà**. *The doctor will be the one who will **diagnose** me.*
dig	scavare	**Stanno scavando** nella grotta. *They **are digging** in the cave.*
dive	immergersi[1] tuffarsi[1]	**Si tuffa** in acqua senza guardare. *He **dives** into the water without looking.*
dribble (soccer)	dribblare	L'attaccante **ha dribblato** tre difensori e ha segnato un gol. *The striker **dribbled** past three defenders and scored a goal.*
drip	gocciolare	Il rubinetto **gocciolava** mentre dormivano. *The faucet **was dripping** while they were asleep.*
drizzle	piovigginare	In questo momento **sta piovigginando**. *It **is drizzling** right now.*
drown	annegare	**Sarei annegato** senza il giubbotto di salvataggio. *I **would have drowned** without the life jacket.*
embellish	abbellire	**Abbelliscono** sempre le loro storie d'avventura. *They always **embellish** their adventure stories.*
emphasize	enfatizzare	Ho cercato di **enfatizzare** questo punto. *I tried to **emphasize** that point.*
engrave	incidere	**Hanno inciso** i loro nomi sull'anello prima del matrimonio. *They **engraved** their names on the ring before the wedding.*

---

[1] In general, "**immergersi**" refers to underwater swimming, whereas "**tuffarsi**" refers to the act of jumping into water.

enlarge extend	ampliare	**Ha ampliato** la stanza abbattendo quel muro. *She **extended** the room by knocking down that wall.*
enroll (school)	iscriversi	Devo **iscrivermi** il mese prossimo. *I have to **enroll** next month.*
entail implicate	comportare	Non sapeva cosa **avrebbe comportato**. *He didn't know what it **would entail**.*
equate (put on the same level)	equiparare uguagliare	Non possiamo **equiparare** le diverse idee e soluzioni. *We cannot **equate** the different ideas and solutions.*
evict	sfrattare	**Hanno sfrattato** l'intera famiglia il mese scorso. *They **evicted** the entire family last month.*
expel	espellere	Lo **avrebbero espulso** se l'avessero scoperto. *They **would have expelled** him if they'd found out.*
expose	esporre	**Esporrò** l'intera tesi. *I **will expose** the entire thesis.*
face confront	affrontare confrontare	Devi **affrontare** le tue paure. *You have to **face** your fears.*
fade	sbiadire svanire	La macchia è completamente **sbiadita**. *The stain completely **faded away**.*
faint	svenire	**È svenuto** quando ha visto il sangue dopo l'incidente. *He **fainted** when he saw blood after the accident.*
fall behind	rimanere indietro	**Rimarrà indietro** se non si sbriga. *He **will fall behind** if he doesn't hurry.*
feed	alimentare nutrire	Il mio vicino a volte **nutre** il mio gatto. *My neighbor sometimes **feeds** my cat.*
find out	scoprire	Sapevo che prima o poi lo **avrebbe scoperto**. *I knew he **would find out** sooner or later.*
fire dismiss	licenziare	Hanno dovuto **licenziare** molti dipendenti. *They had to **fire** many employees.*
fit	adattarsi	Penso che **si adatti** a quella stanza. *I think it **fits** in that room.*
flatter	lusingare adulare	**Lusinga** il capo perché gli dia un aumento. *He **flatters** the boss to give him a raise.*
flicker	tremolare	La luce **sta tremolando**. *The light **is flickering**.*
foil thwart	sventare frustrare	Il maltempo **ha sventato** i suoi piani. *The bad weather **thwarted** her plans.*
found	fondare	**Fonderanno** un'associazione per aiutare le persone. *They **will found** an association to help people.*
frown	accigliarsi	**Si accigliò** quando vide il dipinto. *He **frowned** when he saw the painting.*

get along	andare d'accordo	Le mie figlie non **vanno d'accordo**. *My daughters don't get along.*
get involved	farsi coinvolgere	È meglio non **farsi coinvolgere** in queste faccende. *It's best to not get involved in those matters.*
govern	governare	Abusava del potere quando **governava**. *He abused power when he governed.*
grab grasp seize	afferrare agguantare	**Afferra** l'ultimo prima che lo faccia qualcun altro. *Grab the last one before someone else does.*
grind	macinare	Devi **macinare** bene il pepe. *You have to grind the pepper well.*
hang	stendere appendere	Puoi **stendere** i vestiti? *Can you hang the clothes?*
hang on to	aggrapparsi a	Non dovresti **aggrapparti** al passato. *You shouldn't hang on to the past.*
harmonize	armonizzare	Ho cercato di **armonizzare** i colori. *I tried to harmonize the colors.*
have to do with	avere a che fare con	Questo **ha a che fare con** quello che è successo ieri. *This has to do with what happened yesterday.*
hesitate	esitare	Non dovresti **esitare** dopo aver iniziato. *You shouldn't hesitate after you've started.*
highlight stand out	distinguersi	Cercava sempre di **distinguersi**. *He'd always try to stand out.*
hire contract	assumere	**Assumerò** un falegname per questo. *I will hire a carpenter for that.*
house accommodate	alloggiare ospitare	**Ospiteranno** l'intera famiglia. *They will house the entire family.*
hurry rush	affrettarsi sbrigarsi	Puoi **sbrigarti**? *Can you hurry up?*
hurt	fare male ferire	Si è **fatto male** per caso. *He hurt himself by accident.*
hush	tacere	**Taci**, stiamo cercando di ascoltare! *Hush, we're trying to listen!*
impose	imporre	Hanno **imposto** una nuova legge di recente. *They imposed a new law recently.*
imprison	imprigionare incarcerare	Hanno **imprigionato** il criminale che ha commesso il crimine. *They imprisoned the felon who committed the crime.*
intend	avere intenzione di	**Ho intenzione di** iniziare una dieta. *I intend to start a diet.*
iron	stirare	Non mi piace **stirare** i vestiti. *I don't like to iron clothes.*

irrigate **water**	annaffiare irrigare	Se li **avessero annaffiati**, non sarebbero morti. *If they **had watered** them, they wouldn't have died.*
jump **hop**	saltare	Da bambini **saltavamo** ovunque. *We **would jump** everywhere when we were kids.*
kneel	inginocchiarsi	**Inginocchiati** per vedere sotto il bancone. ***Kneel down** to see under the counter.*
knock over	rovesciare	**Ha rovesciato** il vaso l'altro giorno. *He **knocked over** the vase the other day.*
lean on	appoggiarsi a	Si **appoggiava** sempre a me quando aveva il lavoro. *She always **leaned on** me when she had work.*
lease	affittare	I miei genitori **stanno affittando** la loro casa. *My parents **are leasing** their house.*
light **illuminate**	illuminare	Una lampada lì **illuminerebbe** l'intera stanza. *A lamp there **would light** the entire room.*
load	caricare	Mi aiuteresti a **caricare** la macchina? *Would you help me **load** the car?*
make fun of	prendere in giro burlare di	È spiacevole che tu lo **abbia preso in giro** in questo modo. *It's unpleasant that you **made fun of** him like this.*
manage **handle**	gestire	**Gestivo** sempre i soldi della casa. *I used to always **handle** the house's money.*
manifest	manifestare(-si)	Pensavo **si fosse manifestato** un fantasma. *I thought a ghost **had manifested**.*
manufacture	fabbricare	Lì **fabbricano** automobili. *They **manufacture** cars there.*
mar **spoil**	rovinare(-si) andare a male	Guarda! I pomodori **si sono rovinati** al sole. *Look! The tomatoes **spoiled** in the sun.*
meet up	incontrarsi ritrovarsi	**Ci incontreremo** in aula. *We **will meet up** in the classroom.*
murmur	mormorare	Riesco a **mormorare** solo quando ho sonno. *I only manage to **murmur** when I'm sleepy.*
nail **force in**	inchiodare	Ho dovuto **inchiodarlo** al muro. *I had to **nail** it to the wall.*
neglect	trascurare	**Trascuro** sempre le mie piante per sbaglio. *I always **neglect** my plants by accident.*
nourish **nurture**	nutrire	Dovresti **nutrirti** bene. *You should **nourish** yourself well.*
pack	impacchettare	Ho **impacchettato** tutto in cinque minuti. *I **packed** everything in five minutes.*
pamper **spoil**	coccolare viziare	**Coccolo** sempre il mio animale domestico. *I always **pamper** my pet.*

pave	pavimentare lastricare	**Stanno lastricando** la strada. *They are paving the street.*
penalize	penalizzare	Il lancio della spazzatura è **penalizzato** con multe. *Throwing trash is penalized with fines.*
perceive	percepire	Posso **percepire** il sarcasmo nella sua risposta. *I can perceive the sarcasm in his answer.*
pet stroke fondle	accarezzare	Il mio gatto ama essere **accarezzato**. *My cat loves being petted.*
pick up collect	raccogliere prendere	Puoi andare a **prendere** tua sorella? *Can you go pick up your sister?*
pinch	pizzicare	Non **pizzicar**mi! *Don't pinch me!*
please pander to	accontentare	È difficile da **accontentare**. *He is hard to please.*
pollute	inquinare	Non dovresti **inquinare** l'ambiente. *You shouldn't pollute the environment.*
portray	ritrarre	Penso che **abbiano ritratto** molto bene il suo personaggio nel film. *I think they portrayed her persona very well in the movie.*
pose (photo)	posare	Stanno già **posando** per la foto. *They are already posing for the photo.*
postpone	rinviare rimandare	**Hanno rinviato** l'evento a causa della pioggia. *They postponed the event because of the rain.*
praise	lodare elogiare	**Hanno lodato** la sua recitazione in quel film. *They praised her acting in that movie.*
pray	pregare	**Pregavano** ogni giorno. *They used to pray every day.*
predict	prevedere	Non **prevedono** mai correttamente il tempo. *They never correctly predict the weather.*
prescribe	prescrivere	Gli **hanno prescritto** delle vitamine per la malattia dell'ultimo anno. *They prescribed him some vitamins for his last year's illness.*
preserve	preservare	Il cibo **si preserva** meglio in frigorifero. *Food is preserved best in the fridge.*
press	premere pressare	**Avrebbe premuto** il pulsante per entrare. *He would have pressed the button to go in.*
pretend	fingere	Non **fingere** di dormire. *Don't pretend to be asleep.*
prevail	prevalere	I colori freddi **prevalgono** nel dipinto. *Cold colors prevail in the painting.*

prohibit ban	vietare proibire	L'anno scorso il governo **ha proibito** alcune importazioni. *The government **prohibited** certain imports last year.*
promote	promuovere	L'azienda **ha promosso** il suo nuovo prodotto per mesi. *The company **promoted** its new product for months.*
provide	fornire	Le banane **forniscono** molto potassio. *Bananas **provide** a lot of potassium.*
put together	mettere insieme	**Ha messo insieme** tutti i materiali e ha avviato il progetto. *He **put together** all the materials and started the project.*
rally behind	radunarsi dietro	**Si sono radunati dietro** il presidente nella sua ultima campagna. *They **rallied behind** the president in his last campaign.*
ransack	saccheggiare frugare	**Hanno saccheggiato** l'intero posto quando sono entrati. *They **ransacked** the entire place when they broke in.*
rape **violate**	violentare	Il sospetto è stato accusato di **aver violentato** qualcuno. *The suspect was accused of **raping** someone.*
recruit	reclutare	Ci si aspetterebbe che **reclutassero** più persone. *One would expect them to **recruit** more people.*
refine	affinare raffinare	Devi **affinare** la tua ricerca su Internet. *You have to **refine** your search on the internet.*
register **sign up**	registrare(-si)	Sapevo che avresti dovuto **registrarti** per entrare. *I knew you'd need to **register** to get in.*
regret	rimpiangere pentirsi	**Rimpiangerei** di averlo perso per tutta la vita. *I **would regret** missing it all my life.*
rehearse	provare fare le prove di	Hanno dovuto **provare** lo spettacolo molte volte. *They had to **rehearse** the play many times.*
remove	rimuovere togliere	Cercherò di **rimuovere** immediatamente quella macchia. *I'll try to **remove** that stain immediately.*
rescue	salvare	Lo **avresti salvato** se fossi stato lì. *You **would have rescued** him had you been there.*
restart **reboot**	riavviare	**Riavvierò** il computer. *I **will restart** the computer.*
restore **(order or** **connection)**	ristabilire	**Ristabiliremo** la pace per prevenire i conflitti. *We **will restore** peace to prevent conflicts.*

restore (repair)	restaurare	**Ho restaurato** i vecchi mobili. *I restored the old furniture.*
resume	riprendere	**Riprenderanno** i negoziati domani. *They will resume the negotiations tomorrow.*
reverberate	riverberare(-si)	Il rumore **si riverbera** in tutta la casa. *The noise reverberates through the entire house.*
reward	ricompensare premiare	Lo **avrebbero premiato** per il suo lavoro. *They would have rewarded him for his work.*
rise	salire aumentare	I prezzi **sono aumentati** molto lo scorso anno. *Prices rose a lot last year.*
risk	rischiare	Non vorrei che **rischiasse** tutto il suo stipendio. *I wouldn't want him to risk all his salary.*
rot decay	marcire	**Marcirà** se non lo usi presto. *It will rot if you don't use it soon.*
run out	esaurire	È difficile **esaurire** i risparmi. *It's hard to run out of savings.*
run over	investire	Lo **avrebbe investito** se non avesse corso. *It would have run him over if he hadn't run.*
sacrifice	sacrificare	A volte devi **sacrificare** un po' del tuo tempo. *Sometimes you have to sacrifice a bit of your time.*
sadden	rattristare	La notizia della morte di suo zio lo **ha rattristato**. *The news of his uncle's death saddened him.*
scorn	disprezzare sdegnare	**Disprezza** sempre sua nuora. *She always scorns her daughter-in-law.*
scrap (car)	rottamare	**Rottamano** le vecchie auto lì. *They scrap old cars there.*
scribble doodle	scarabocchiare	I bambini **scarabocchiano** molto. *Children scribble a lot.*
scrub	strofinare	**Strofinerò** i piatti dopo cena. *I will scrub the dishes after dinner.*
seal	sigillare	**Sigilleranno** la busta. *They will seal the envelope.*
shake	agitare scuotere	**Agita** molto bene la bottiglia. *Shake the bottle very well.*
sharpen	affilare	Devi **affilare** bene i tuoi coltelli da cucina. *You have to sharpen your kitchen knives well.*
shove tuck	spingere	**Spingeranno** tutto questo nel bagagliaio? *They will shove all that into the trunk?*
shovel	spalare	**Spalavano** sempre la neve quando vivevano lì. *They always shoveled the snow when they lived there.*
sigh	sospirare	**Sospiro** ogni volta che vedo mio nonno. *I sigh every time I see my grandfather.*

sin	peccare	L'uomo credeva che **avessero peccato**. *The man believed that they **had sinned**.*
skimp	lesinare	**Hanno lesinato** sulle decorazioni quando si sono trasferiti. *They **skimped** on the decorations when they moved in.*
skip over	saltare	È riuscito a **saltare** più di un anno. *He managed to **skip over** a year.*
slap	schiaffeggiare	**Ha schiaffeggiato** il cattivo sulla scena del crimine. *He **slapped** the villain at the crime scene.*
slide **slip**	scivolare	**Sta scivolando** come può. *He **is sliding** the way he can.*
smash **crush**	schiacciare	Lo **avrebbe schiacciato** se non si fosse mosso. *It **would have crushed** him if he hadn't moved.*
sneak	intrufolarsi	Siamo riusciti a **intrufolarci** nel posto. *We managed to **sneak** into the place.*
snore	russare	Il mio cane **russa** molto forte. *My dog **snores** very loudly.*
soak **drench**	inzuppare	Ho inzuppato i fagioli secchi per cinque ore. *I **soaked** the dry beans for five hours.*
sow	seminare	**Seminerò** i semi in primavera. *I **will sow** the seeds in spring.*
specify	specificare	**Ha specificato** esattamente quale classe fosse. *He **specified** exactly what classroom it was.*
spill **shed**	rovesciare versare	Il tè **si sarebbe rovesciato** se non avessi fermato la tazza. *The tea **would have spilled** if I hadn't stopped the cup.*
splash	schizzare	L'inchiostro **è schizzato** accidentalmente sul muro. *The ink **splashed** on the wall by accident.*
sponsor	sponsorizzare patrocinare	Penso che sia una grande idea **sponsorizzarli**. *I think it's a great idea that you **sponsor** them.*
spread **(extend)**	stendere	Devi **stendere** le lenzuola sul materasso. *You have to **spread** the bed sheets over the mattress.*
spread **(propagate)**	diffondere(-si)	Le malattie **si diffondono** molto rapidamente. *Diseases **spread** very quickly.*
squander **fritter**	sperperare sprecare	Smettila di **sperperare** i tuoi soldi. *Stop **squandering** your money.*
squeeze	spremere	Devi **spremere** bene i limoni. *You have to **squeeze** the lemons well.*
stain **taint**	macchiare	**Macchiavo** sempre i miei vestiti con il cibo. *I used to always **stain** my clothes with food.*

stamp	timbrare	Devi **timbrare** il pacco. *You have to **stamp** the package.*
stir	mescolare agitare	Puoi **mescolare** lo stufato, per favore? *Can you **stir** the stew, please?*
stray **get lost**	perdersi	**Si sarebbe perso** senza la mappa. *He **would have gotten lost** without the map.*
stretch	allungare(-si)	**Mi allungo** sempre quando mi sveglio. *I always **stretch** when I wake up.*
stun	stordire	Il forte rumore mi ha **stordito** mentre leggevo. *The loud noise **stunned** me as I was reading.*
stutter	balbettare	**Ho balbettato** molto durante quel discorso. *I **stuttered** a lot during that speech.*
summarize	riassumere	Devo **riassumere** i testi di questi libri. *I have to **summarize** the texts in these books.*
support **back up**	sostenere appoggiare	Puoi **sostenere** tuo fratello? *Can you **support** your brother?*
suppress	sopprimere	**Hanno soppresso** molti temi dello spettacolo di ieri sera. *They **suppressed** many themes from the show last night.*
surrender **give up**	arrendersi	**Arrenditi** così vinco questo round! ***Give up** so I win this round!*
surround **encircle**	circondare	**Lo avrebbero circondato** se avessero potuto. *They **would have surrounded** him if they could.*
survey **poll**	sondare	**Hanno sondato** un centinaio di persone la scorsa settimana. *They **surveyed** a hundred individuals last week.*
swallow	ingoiare	Devi **ingoiare** le tue medicine. *You have to **swallow** your medication.*
swell	gonfiare(-si)	Il mio piede **si è gonfiato** molto velocemente dopo la partita. *My foot **swelled** up really fast after the game.*
take for **granted**	dare per scontato	**Dava per scontato** che avrebbe vinto quella gara. *He **took for granted** that he'd win that race.*
tangle	aggrovigliare(-si)	I miei capelli **si sono aggrovigliati** mentre li pettinavo ieri sera. *My hair **got tangled** while I was styling it last night.*
tear **rip**	strappare	Il mio cane **strappava** tutti i fogli che vedeva. *My dog **would rip** all the papers he saw.*
terrorize **terrify**	terrorizzare	Quando ero bambino, le bambole mi **terrorizzavano**. *When I was a child, dolls **terrified** me.*

threaten	minacciare	Non andrebbe bene se **minacciasse** i suoi figli. *It wouldn't be okay if he **threatened** his children.*
thunder	tuonare	**Sta tuonando** adesso. *It **is thundering** now.*
tickle	fare il solletico a	I suoi genitori **facevano il solletico** ai figli. *His parents used to **tickle** their kids.*
toast	brindare	**Brindiamo** al tuo successo! *Let's **toast** to your success!*
touch	toccare	Mi **avrebbe toccato** il viso se non mi fossi mosso. *It **would have touched** my face if I hadn't moved.*
transfer	trasferire	**Trasferirò** i soldi direttamente sul tuo conto. *I **will transfer** the money directly into your account.*
trigger	innescare	Quel movimento **ha innescato** una valanga. *That movement **triggered** an avalanche.*
twinkle	scintillare	Le stelle **scintillano** e i pianeti no. *Stars **twinkle** and planets don't.*
uncover	scoprire	Qualcuno un giorno **scoprirà** il mistero. *Someone **will uncover** the mystery one day.*
unleash	scatenare	**Hanno scatenato** il drago quando è iniziata la guerra. *They **unleashed** the dragon when the war started.*
waste	sprecare	**Stai sprecando** le risorse. *You **are wasting** the resources.*
watch over	sorvegliare vigilare	**Sorveglia** il forno in modo che non bruci. ***Watch over** the oven so that it doesn't burn.*
withdraw retreat	ritirare(-si)	La tartaruga **si ritirò** nel suo guscio quando mi vide. *The turtle **withdrew** into its shell upon seeing me.*
withdraw (money)	ritirare	**Ritirerà** denaro dalla banca. *He **will withdraw** money from the bank.*
wrinkle	stropicciare raggrinzire	Fai attenzione a non **stropicciare** i vestiti. *Be careful not to **wrinkle** your clothes.*
yawn	sbadigliare	Non **sbadigliare** in pubblico. *Don't **yawn** in public.*

2. ADJECTIVES VI

Below is a list of some important adjectives that we need at this level:

English	Italian	Examples
abnormal	anomalo anormale	Questo formaggio ha un colore **anomalo**. *This cheese has an **abnormal** color.*

advocate (supporter)	sostenitore difensore	È un **sostenitore** dei diritti dei bambini. *He's an **advocate** for children's rights.*
affectionate	affettuoso	Mio nonno è molto **affettuoso**. *My grandfather is very **affectionate**.*
agricultural	agricolo	È diventato interessato al lavoro **agricolo**. *He's become interested in **agricultural** work.*
anxious	ansioso	Il mio gatto diventa **ansioso** nel parco. *My cat gets **anxious** in the park.*
appetizing	appetitoso	Quella bistecca sembra molto **appetitosa**. *That steak looks very **appetizing**.*
arctic	artico	Non mi piacciono questi freddi **artici**. *I don't like these **arctic** colds.*
attached (file)	allegato	Puoi trovare il file **allegato** alla mail. *You can find the file **attached** to the mail.*
audacious	audace	Ha finito per essere molto **audace**. *She ended up being very **audacious**.*
bankrupt	in bancarotta	Entro la fine del mese, sono **in bancarotta**. *By the end of the month, I'm **bankrupt**.*
bent	piegato	La forcella è finita **piegata**. *The fork ended up **bent**.*
broken down (vehicle)	in panne	La macchina era a casa perché era **in panne**. *The car was at home because it had **broken down**.*
cheerful	allegro	L'insegnante è molto **allegro** con i bambini. *The teacher is very **cheerful** with the children.*
chemical	chimico	Attenzione alle reazioni **chimiche**. *Be careful with **chemical** reactions.*
civilian	civile	Lasciò l'esercito e tornò a essere un **civile**. *He left the army and went back to being a **civilian**.*
compassionate	compassionevole	È molto **compassionevole** con gli animali. *He's very **compassionate** with animals.*
corny	banale	Mi ha scritto una poesia **banale**. *He wrote me a **corny** poem.*
creepy	inquietante strisciante	Con quella maschera sembra **inquietante**. *With that mask he looks **creepy**.*
crispy	croccante	Mi piace il mio toast molto **croccante**. *I like my toast very **crispy**.*
crowded	affollato	Il cinema era troppo **affollato**. *The cinema was too **crowded**.*
deceased	deceduto defunto	Apparteneva al mio **defunto** nonno. *It belonged to my **deceased** grandfather.*
deceptive	ingannevole	Quella pubblicità era **ingannevole**. *That advertisement was **deceptive**.*
devoid of	privo di	Questa regione è **priva di** materia prima. *This region is **devoid of** raw material.*

disabled	disabile	Quel parcheggio è per persone **disabili**. *That parking space is for **disabled** people.*
dissatisfied	insoddisfatto	Ero **insoddisfatto** del servizio. *I was **dissatisfied** with the service.*
elementary	elementare	È **elementare** saper cucinare. *It's **elementary** to know how to cook.*
empty-handed	a mani vuote	È venuto **a mani vuote**. *He came **empty-handed**.*
even & odd	pari e dispari	Hanno ordinato le cose in **pari e dispari**. *They ordered the things in **evens and odds**.*
expected	previsto atteso	Era un risultato **previsto**. *It was an **expected** result.*
fierce	feroce	Il leone allo zoo sembra **feroce**. *The lion at the zoo looks **fierce**.*
giant	gigante	Hanno un elefante **gigante** in questo zoo. *They have a **giant** elephant in this zoo.*
gigantic	gigantesco	La montagna era **gigantesca**. *The mountain was **gigantic**.*
gratifying	gratificante	È **gratificante** fare opere di beneficenza. *It is **gratifying** to do charity work.*
greedy	avido goloso	Stai lontano dalle persone **avide**. *Stay away from **greedy** people.*
hasty	frettoloso affrettato	Era molto **frettoloso** per andarsene. *He was very **hasty** to leave.*
hollow	cavo	Quell'albero è **cavo**. *That tree is **hollow**.*
homeless roofless	senzatetto	Era un giovane **senzatetto**. *He was a **homeless** young man.*
hooked	agganciato	È **agganciato** al muro. *It's **hooked** to the wall.*
impolite	scortese maleducato	Il cameriere era un po' **scortese**. *The waiter was a bit **impolite**.*
in a hurry	di fretta	Lei andava **di fretta** per arrivarci. *She was **in a hurry** to get there.*
in open-air outdoors	all'aperto	È consentito fumare **all'aperto**. *Smoking is allowed **outdoors**.*
indebted	indebitato	È stato molto **indebitato** per un anno. *He was very **indebted** for a year.*
inebriated	ubriaco	Era **ubriaco** ieri sera. *He was **inebriated** last night.*
inner internal	interno interiore	La mia voce **interiore** mi dice di non farlo. *My **inner** voice tells me not to do it.*
juristic	giuridico	Gli piace molto l'ambito **giuridico**. *He really likes the **juristic** scope.*

last	ultimo	Abbiamo preso l'**ultimo** autobus. *We took the **last** bus.*
led by	guidato da	Erano **guidati dal** più anziano di loro. *They were **led by** the oldest one of them.*
lower	inferiore	Il suo labbro **inferiore** si è gonfiato. *His **lower** lip got swollen.*
loyal	leale fedele	Ho molti amici **fedeli**. *I have a lot of **loyal** friends.*
lurking **stalking**	in agguato	Il mio cane è **in agguato** nel patio. *My dog is **lurking** on the patio.*
mature **ripe**	maturo	Quell'avocado non è ancora **maturo**. *That avocado isn't **ripe** yet.*
merciful	misericordioso	Era molto **misericordioso** con la multa. *He was very **merciful** with the fine.*
needy	bisognoso	Ci sono molte persone **bisognose** qui. *There are many **needy** people here.*
negligible	trascurabile insignificante	La quantità di zucchero che ha è **trascurabile**. *The amount of sugar it has is **negligible**.*
newcomer	nuovo arrivato	In realtà, è un **nuovo arrivato** in classe. *Actually, he is a **newcomer** to the class.*
ongoing **in progress**	in corso	Lo schermo dice che il download è **in corso**. *The screen says the download is **in progress**.*
opponent **adversary**	avversario	Era un buon **avversario** nel gioco. *He was a good **opponent** in the game.*
ostentatious	ostentato	Quella villa è molto **ostentata**. *That mansion is very **ostentatious**.*
outstanding	eccezionale	È sempre stato uno studente **eccezionale**. *He's always been an **outstanding** student.*
overcrowded	sovraffollato	Lo stadio era **sovraffollato**. *The stadium was **overcrowded**.*
overlooking **(building)**	con vista su affacciato su	Mi piacciono le case **con vista su**lla spiaggia. *I like houses **overlooking** the beach.*
overweight	in sovrappeso	L'esercizio fisico è molto utile per le persone **in sovrappeso**. *Exercise is very useful for **overweight** people.*
overwhelming	travolgente	L'aroma era **travolgente**. *The aroma was **overwhelming**.*
pending	di attesa	È ancora in stato **di attesa**. *It's still in **pending** status.*
poisonous	velenoso	Quella pianta è molto **velenosa**! *That plant is very **poisonous**!*
predicted	previsto predetto	Il finale era **previsto**. *The ending was **predicted**.*

profitable	redditizio	È un affare piuttosto **redditizio**. *It's a pretty **profitable** business.*
rear	posteriore di dietro	La luce **posteriore** non funziona. *The **rear** light isn't working.*
reluctant	riluttante	Cucinava, anche se era **riluttante** a farlo. *He cooked, although he was **reluctant** to do so.*
replete with full of	pieno di	L'armadietto è **pieno di** tazze. *The cabinet is **replete with** mugs.*
reputable respectable	rispettabile	L'ho preso da un fornitore **rispettabile**. *I got it from a **reputable** provider.*
rooted	radicato	Ha una cultura molto **radicata**. *He has a deeply-**rooted** culture.*
rotten	marcio putrido	Metà delle uova erano **marce**. *Half of the eggs were **rotten**.*
rough	grezzo ruvido	Quella carta vetrata è molto **ruvida**. *That sandpaper is very **rough**.*
royalty (king)	regalità	La mia vicina dice che discende dalla **regalità**. *My neighbor says she descends from **royalty**.*
seasonal	stagionale	Quel lavoro è solo **stagionale**. *That job is just **seasonal**.*
second-hand	di seconda mano	Vendono vestiti **di seconda mano** qui. *They sell **second-hand** garments here.*
secure safe	sicuro	I soldi saranno al **sicuro** qui. *The money will be **safe** here.*
shallow (water)	poco profondo	La piscina è molto **poco profonda**. *The pool is very **shallow**.*
sharp (knife)	affilato	Lo tagli con un coltello **affilato**. *You cut it with a **sharp** knife.*
slippery	scivoloso	Stai attento! Il pavimento è **scivoloso** lì. *Be careful! The floor is **slippery** there.*
smooth	liscio	La superficie è venuta molto **liscia**. *The surface came out very **smooth**.*
sold out	esaurito	I biglietti erano **esauriti**. *The tickets were **sold out**.*
stranded	incagliato	Lo hanno trovato **incagliato** su un'isola. *They found him **stranded** on an island.*
stray	randagio	Ho trovato un gatto **randagio**. *I found a **stray** cat.*
stubborn	ostinato testardo	A volte sono un po' **testardo**. *Sometimes I'm a bit **stubborn**.*
stuck	bloccato incollato	Il cane è rimasto **bloccato** nel buco. *The dog was **stuck** in the hole.*

subsequent	susseguente successivo	Seguirò i passaggi **successivi**. *I will follow the subsequent steps.*
tanned	abbronzato	È tornata **abbronzata** dalle vacanze. *She came back tanned from her vacation.*
terrified terrorized	terrorizzato	Il film mi ha lasciato **terrorizzato**. *The movie left me terrified.*
tidy	in ordine ordinato	Mi piace tenere **in ordine** la mia scrivania. *I like to keep my desk tidy.*
tied	legato	Le carote vengono **legate** insieme. *The carrots come tied together.*
tiny	minuscolo piccolo	Ha comprato una **piccola** casa. *She bought a tiny house.*
trustworthy	affidabile fidato	Questo assegno sembra **affidabile**? *Does this check look trustworthy?*
unexpected	inaspettato imprevisto	Ho avuto una visita **inaspettata**. *I had an unexpected visit.*
unpleasant	sgradevole spiacevole	Rilasciava un odore molto **sgradevole**. *It released a very unpleasant smell.*
unscathed	illeso indenne	È sopravvissuto all'incidente **illeso**. *He survived the accident unscathed.*
upper	superiore	È nel cassetto **superiore**. *It's in the upper drawer.*
upstairs	di sopra	Lo trovi nel bagno al piano **di sopra**. *You can find it in the upstairs bathroom.*
waterproof	impermeabile	La giacca era **impermeabile**. *The jacket was waterproof.*
widespread	diffuso	Ormai è una tendenza **diffusa**. *Now it's a widespread trend.*

3. CONCEPTS & BEHAVIORS

A more abstract topic is related to *concepts and behaviors*, or "**i concetti e i comportamenti**." The table below covers some related vocabulary:

ability *capacity*	**capacità**^{f}	*legacy*	**eredità**^{f}
affection	**affetto**^{m}	*legend*	**leggenda**^{f}
anxiety	**ansia**^{f}	*leisure*	**ozio**^{m}
apology	**scusa**^{f} **apologia**^{f}	*luxury*	**lusso**^{m} **lussuria**^{m}
applause	**applauso**^{m}	*mentality*	**mentalità**^{f}

attitude	**atteggiamento**^m **attitudine**^f	*mercy*	**misericordia**^f **pietà**^f
birth	**nascita**^f	*mischief*	**malizia**^f **dispetto**^m
certainty	**certezza**^f	*mood*	**umore**^m [1]
chance (accident)	**casualità**^f	*motive*	**motivo**^m
charm	**fascino**^m **incanto**^m	*myth*	**mito**^m
choice	**scelta**^f **opzione**^f	*nap*	**pisolino**^m **sonnellino**^m
comfort	**comodità**^f	*nightmare*	**incubo**^m
common sense	**buon senso**^m **senso comune**^m	*novelty*	**novità**^f
compliment (praise)	**complimento**^m	*nuisance*	**fastidio**^m
concern	**preoccupazione**^f	*objective*	**oggettivo**^m
contrast	**contrasto**^m	*opportunity chance*	**opportunità**^f
courage	**coraggio**^m	*pat*	**colpetto**^m
courtesy	**cortesia**^f	*perspective outlook*	**prospettiva**^f
craziness	**pazzia**^f	*pinch*	**pizzico**^m
cycle	**ciclo**^m	*plagiarism*	**plagio**^m
death	**morte**^f **fallimento**^m	*praise*	**lode**^f
deception	**inganno**^m	*prejudice*	**pregiudizio**^m
deterioration	**deterioramento**^m	*pride*	**orgoglio**^m
difficulty	**difficoltà**^f	*privilege*	**privilegio**^m
disrespect	**mancanza**^f **di rispetto**	*promise*	**promessa**^f
dream	**sogno**^m	*purpose*	**proposito**^m
ethnicity	**etnia**^f	*race (ethnicity)*	**razza**^f
ease	**facilità**^f **agio**^m	*rage*	**furia**^f **collera**^f
encouragement	**incoraggiamento**^m	*randomness*	**aleatorietà**^f **casualità**^f
fable	**favola**^f	*reach*	**portata**^f **raggiungimento**^m

---

[1] For instance, "**essere di buon umore**" means *"to be in a good mood"* and "**essere di cattivo umore**" means *"to be in a bad mood."*

failure	**fallimento**^m	*recognition* *acknowledgment*	**riconoscimento**^m
fate	**fato**^m **destino**^m	*refusal*	**rifiuto**^m
focus	**fuoco**^m **concentrazione**^f	*Renaissance*	**Rinascimento**^m
feeling	**sentimento**^m	*respect*	**rispetto**^m
foolishness	**stoltezza**^f	*responsibility*	**responsabilità**^f
freedom *liberty*	**libertà**^f	*rest* *remainder*	**resto**^m
friendship	**amicizia**^f	*rhythm*	**ritmo**^m
gender *sex*	**genere**^m **sesso**^m	*scientific research*	**ricerca scientifica**^f
goal (aim)	**obiettivo**^m **meta**^f	*self-esteem*	**autostima**^f
goodwill	**buona volontà**^f	*shadow*	**ombra**^f
greed	**avidità**^f	*silence*	**silenzio**^m
glance *gaze*	**sguardo**^m **occhiata**^f	*snore*	**russamento**^m
habit	**abitudine**^f	*solidarity*	**solidarietà**^f
hatred	**odio**^m	*solitude* *loneliness*	**solitudine**^f
heaviness	**pesantezza**^f	*slap*	**schiaffo**^m
hobby	**passatempo**^m	*slavery*	**schiavitù**^f
homage *(tribute)*	**omaggio**^m	*spirit*	**spirito**^m
hope *expectation*	**speranza**^f	*spite* *grudge*	**rancore**^m
hunch (feeling)	**intuizione**^f	*stupidity*	**stupidità**^f
hypothesis	**ipotesi**^f	*subtlety*	**sottigliezza**^f
idiocy	**idiozia**^f	*suggestion*	**suggerimento**^m
impulse	**impulso**^m	*sympathy*	**simpatia**^f
inequality	**ineguaglianza**^f	*term*	**termine**^m
intelligence	**intelligenza**^f	*thirst*	**sete**^f
interchange	**scambio**^m	*thought* *thinking*	**pensiero**^m
joy	**gioia**^f **allegria**^f	*tip* *gratuity*	**propina**^f
knowledge	**conoscenza**^f	*virtue*	**virtù**^f
language	**lingua**^f **linguaggio**^m	*weakness*	**debolezza**^f

laughter	risata^f	wisdom	saggezza^f
leadership	guida^f direzione^f	whisper	sussurro^m
learning	apprendimento^m	yawn	sbadiglio^m

4. ECONOMY & BUSINESS

The economy is "**l'economia**" in Italian, and *business* is "**gli affari.**" Some important vocabulary is in the following list:

achievement	raggiungimento^m traguardo^m	index	indice^m
acquaintance	conoscenza^f	industrial waste	rifiuti industriali^m
advantage	vantaggio^m	installment	rata^f quota^f
agriculture	agricoltura^f	interest	interesse^m
apprenticeship	apprendistato^m	internship	tirocinio^m
asset	risorsa^f bene^m	investment	investimento^m
auction	asta^f	investor	investitore^m
audit	verifica^f	living standard	tenore^m di vita
banknote	banconota^f	loan	prestito^m
bankruptcy	bancarotta^f	machine	macchina^f
barter	permuta^f	mailing list	lista postale^f
benefit	beneficio^m	making decisions	prendere decisioni^f
birthrate	tasso^m di natalità	management	gestione^f direzione^f
brainstorming	pioggia^f di idee	maternity leave	congedo^m di maternità
branch office	succursale^f	member	membro^m
bubble	bolla^f	merchandise	merce^f mercanzia^f
budget	bilancio^m	mismanagement	cattiva gestione^f
business	affari^m	money exchange	cambio valuta^m
challenge	sfida^f	mortgage	ipoteca^f
charity	carità^f	on my own	per conto mio
chart	grafico^m	over-the-counter	da banco^m
committee	comitato^m	phase	fase^f
commitment	impegno^m	pile	mucchio^m pila^f

company	impresa^f compagnia^f	*priority*	**priorità^f**
coin	moneta^f	*process*	**processo^m**
consumer	consumatore^m	*procrastination*	**procrastinazione^f indugio^m**
consumption	consumo^m	*profits*	**profitti^m guadagni^m**
contract	contratto^m	*progress*	**progresso^m**
cost-of-living	costo^m della vita	*public holiday*	**giorno festivo^m festa nazionale^f**
credit	credito^m	*quality*	**qualità^f**
cubicle	cubicolo^m	*range*	**gamma^f**
currency	valuta^f	*ratio*	**proporzione^f**
customer service	servizio clienti^m	*reminder*	**promemoria^m ricordo^m**
deadline	scadenza^f termine^m data limite^f	*resignation*	**dimissioni^f rassegnazione^f**
dealership	concessionario^m	*resource*	**risorsa^f**
debt	debito^m	*retail (sales)*	**vendita^f al dettaglio**
decline	declino^m diminuzione^f	*reward*	**ricompensa^f**
development	sviluppo^m	*rise*	**salita^f ascesa^f**
digit	cifra^f	*scale*	**scala^f**
dollar	dollaro^m	*scrap*	**rottame^m scarto^m**
done deal	affare fatto^m	*skill*	**abilità^f**
employment	impiego^m	*sponsor*	**promotore^m garante^m**
entrepreneurship	imprenditoria^f	*staff personnel*	**personale^m**
excess	eccesso^m	*stage step*	**tappa^f**
exchange rate	tasso^m di cambio	*statistics*	**statistica^f**
executive	esecutivo^m	*street value*	**valore^m di strada**
expenses	spese^f	*stress*	**stress^m**
expertise	competenza^f	*strike*	**sciopero^m**
exports	esportazioni^f	*success*	**successo^m riuscita^f**
fair (exhibition)	fiera^f	*supplier*	**fornitore^m**

finances	**finanze**f	supplies	**forniture**f **provviste**f
fixed schedule	**orario fisso**m	supply and demand	**domanda**f **e offerta**f
flea market	**mercato**m **delle pulci** **mercato**m **di strada**	surplus (goods)	**eccedenza**f
fortune	**fortuna**f	surplus (money)	**eccedenza**f
franchise	**franchigia**f	talent	**talento**m
fund	**fondo**m	tax	**tassa**f
Gross Domestic Product (GDP)	**Prodotto**m **Interno Lordo (PIL)**	trade	**commercio**m
growth	**crescita**f	unemployment	**disoccupazione**f
guarantee	**garanzia**f	unemployment benefits	**sussidio**m **di disoccupazione**
headquarters	**sede**f **quartier generale**m	unfinished business	**affare**m **inconcluso** **affare**m **in sospeso**
hierarchy	**gerarchia**f	wealth	**ricchezza**f
high season	**alta stagione**f	wholesale	**vendita**f **all'ingrosso**
human development	**sviluppo civile**m	windmill	**mulino**m
imports	**importazioni**f	workday	**giornata lavorativa**f
income revenue	**entrata**f	workshop	**officina**f

5. FAMILY II

We continue to add more to our vocabulary related to the family.

ancestor	**antenato**m	orphan	**orfano**m
brother-in-law	**cognato**m	parents	**genitori**m
clan	**clan**m	single	**celibe**m **nubile**f
cousins	**cugini**m	sister-in-law	**cognata**f
divorce	**divorzio**m	spouse partner	**coniuge**m,f
divorced	**divorziato**m **divorziata**f	tribe	**tribù**f
engagement	**fidanzamento**m	trouble hardship	**difficoltà**f

father-in-law	**suocero**^m	*twins*	**gemelli**^{m 1}
grandparents	**nonni**^m	*visitor*	**visitatore**^m
link (tie or bond)	**legame**^m **vincolo**^m	*vow (marriage)*	**voto**^m
marital status	**stato civile**^m	*wedding*	**matrimonio**^m **nozze**^f
marriage	**matrimonio**^m	*widow*	**vedova**^f
married	**sposato**^m **sposata**^f	*widower*	**vedovo**^m
mother-in-law	**suocera**^f	*will* *testament*	**testamento**^m

[1] We use "**gemelli omozigoti**" to refer to identical twins, and "**gemelli eterozigoti**" to refer to non-identical twins.

6. PEOPLE III

We add more vocabulary related to people that we encounter in our daily life.

acrobat	**acrobata**^{m,f}	*hero*	**eroe**^m **eroina**^f
alien	**alieno**^m	*homeless people*	**senzatetto**^m
altercation	**alterco**^m **lite**^f	*interpreter*	**interprete**^{m,f}
aristocrat	**aristocratico**^m	*janitor*	**inserviente**^m **custode**^m
astronaut	**astronauta**^{m,f}	*knight*	**cavaliere**^m
baker	**panettiere**^m	*laborer*	**operaio**^m
beggar	**mendicante**^m	*manager*	**dirigente**^m **direttore**^m
blacksmith	**fabbro**^m	*mechanic*	**meccanico**^m
bully	**bullo**^m	*messenger*	**messaggero**^m
captain	**capitano**^m	*miner*	**minatore**^m
caretaker	**custode**^m	*news anchor*	**presentatore**^m
chemist	**chimico**^m	*nurse*	**infermiere**^m **infermiera**^f
clown	**pagliaccio**^m	*painter*	**pittore**^m
cowboy	**cowboy**^m	*peasant*	**paesano**^m **contadino**^m
crew (plane)	**equipaggio**^m	*peer*	**pari**^m
dwarf	**nano**^m	*physiotherapist*	**fisioterapista**^{m,f}

farmer	**contadino**^m	*pirate*	**pirata**^m
feature characteristic	**caratteristica**^f	*plumber*	**idraulico**^m
feature trait	**tratto**^m	*postman*	**postino**^m
firefighter	**pompiere**^m	*prisoner*	**prigioniero**^m
flight attendant	**assistente**^{m,f} **di volo**	*scholar*	**studioso**^m **erudito**^m
freelancer	**libero professionista**^m	*servant*	**servo**^m **servitore**^m
gesture	**gesto**^m	*shepherd*	**pastore**^m
greeting	**saluto**^m	*slave*	**schiavo**^m
guard	**guardia**^f	*tailor*	**sarto**^m
hairdresser	**parrucchiere**^m **parrucchiera**^f	*witch*	**strega**^f

7. WAR

War, or "**la guerra**," is another important topic in any language. Some related vocabulary is presented in the table below:

agreement	**accordo**^m	*marshal*	**maresciallo**^m
ally	**alleato**^m	*military*	**militare**^m
ambush	**imboscata**^f	*morale*	**morale**^f
armor	**armatura**^f	*mourning (grief)*	**lutto**^m
army	**esercito**^m	*needs*	**bisogni**^m **necessità**^f
atomic bomb	**bomba atomica**^f	*order (command)*	**ordine**^m
attack	**attacco**^m **attentato**^m	*pact*	**patto**^m
balance equilibrium	**equilibrio**^m	*panic*	**panico**^m
barrier	**barriera**^f	*parade*	**parata**^f
battle	**battaglia**^f	*peace*	**pace**^f
blast or gust (air)	**scoppio**^m	*poison*	**veleno**^m
bow (weapon)	**arco**^m	*population*	**popolazione**^f
bullet	**proiettile**^m	*poverty*	**povertà**^f
burden	**fardello**^m	*prison*	**prigione**^f
burial	**sepoltura**^f	*relief*	**sollievo**^m
cemetery	**cimitero**^m	*result outcome*	**risultato**^m

chaos *mess*	**caos**^{m} **disordine**^{m}	*revenge*	**vendetta**^{f} **rivincita**^{f}
circumstances	**circostanze**^{f}	*rocket*	**razzo**^{m}
collapse	**collasso**^{m}	*ruins*	**rovine**^{f}
conqueror	**conquistatore**^{m}	*sacrifice*	**sacrificio**^{m}
conquest	**conquista**^{f}	*sadness* *sorrow*	**tristezza**^{f}
consequences	**conseguenze**^{f}	*shelter*	**rifugio**^{m} **riparo**^{m}
control	**controllo**^{m}	*shipwreck*	**naufragio**^{m}
corpse	**cadavere**^{m}	*shooting*	**ripresa**^{f} **sparatoria**^{f} **tiro**^{m}
crying	**pianto**^{m}	*shortage*	**scarsità**^{f} **carenza**^{f}
dagger	**pugnale**^{m}	*siege*	**assedio**^{m}
damage	**danno**^{m} **danneggiamento**^{m}	*spear*	**lancia**^{f}
depletion (resources)	**esaurimento**^{m}	*support*	**appoggio**^{m} **supporto**^{m}
despair	**disperazione**^{f}	*sword*	**spada**^{f}
disaster	**disastro**^{m}	*tank*	**tanica**^{f}
effort	**sforzo**^{m}	*tomb* *grave*	**tomba**^{f}
enemy	**nemico**^{m}	*theft*	**furto**^{m}
famine	**carestia**^{f}	*tragedy*	**tragedia**^{f}
fatality	**fatalità**^{f}	*trap*	**trappola**^{f}
genocide	**genocidio**^{m}	*treason*	**tradimento**^{m}
gun	**pistola**^{f}	*trigger*	**grilletto**^{m}
homeland	**patria**^{f}	*triumph*	**trionfo**^{m}
hunger	**fame**^{m}	*troop*	**truppa**^{f}
infrastructure	**infrastruttura**^{f}	*veteran*	**veterano**^{m}
killing	**uccisione**^{f}	*victory*	**vittoria**^{f}
lack of	**mancanza**^{f} **di**	*volunteer*	**volontario**^{m}
loss	**perdita**^{f}	*warrior*	**guerriero**^{m}
march	**marcia**^{f}	*weapon*	**arma**^{f}
marine	**marina**^{f}	*zone*	**zona**^{f}

8. MEDIA II

Here is more vocabulary related to media and entertainment:

art	**arte**^f	*mainstream*	**corrente principale**^f
band (music)	**banda**^f	*mania*	**mania**^f
broadcast	**emissione**^f **trasmissione**^f	*masterpiece*	**capolavoro**^m
broadcasting station	**stazione**^f **di trasmissione**	*maze*	**labirinto**^m
cards deck	**mazzo**^m **di carte**	*media coverage*	**copertura mediatica**^f
cartoon	**cartoni animati**^m	*New Year's Day*	**Capodanno**^m
celebrity	**celebrità**^f	*New Year's Eve*	**vigilia**^f **di Capodanno**
circus	**circo**^m	*noise*	**rumore**^m
comment remark	**commento**^m	*orchestra*	**orchestra**^f
concert	**concerto**^m	*painting*	**dipinto**^m **pittura**^f
craftsmanship	**artigianato**^m	*plot (movie)*	**trama**^f
criticism	**critica**^f	*poem*	**poema**^m **poesia**^f
crossword	**cruciverba**^m	*poster*	**poster**^m
debate	**dibattito**^m	*protagonist*	**protagonista**^{m,f}
dice	**dado**^m	*rehearsal*	**saggio**^m
drum	**tamburo**^m	*review (movie or book)*	**recensione**^f
entertainment	**intrattenimento**^m	*riddle*	**enigma**^m
exhibition	**esposizione**^f	*scene (movie)*	**scena**^f
fairy	**fata**^f	*script (movie)*	**copione**^m
fame	**fama**^f	*shock*	**shock**^m
fantasy	**fantasia**^f	*show performance*	**prestazione**^f
fireworks	**fuochi**^m **d'artificio**	*spectacle*	**spettacolo**^m
fun	**divertimento**^m	*stage (platform)*	**scenario**^m
gazette	**gazzetta**^f	*subtitle*	**sottotitolo**^m
headline	**titolo**^m **di testa**	*symphony*	**sinfonia**^f
image	**immagine**^f	*tattoo*	**tatuaggio**^m
journalism	**giornalismo**^m	*trend*	**tendenza**^f
magic	**magia**^f	*tune melody*	**melodia**^f

9. RELIGION II

We add more vocabulary related to *religion*.

believer	**credente**^{m,f}	*nun*	**suora**^f

blessing	benedizione^f	pilgrim	pellegrino^m
Christmas Eve	vigilia^f di Natale	pilgrimage	pellegrinaggio^m
curse	maledizione^f	priest	sacerdote^m prete^m
Easter	la Pasqua^f	rabbi	rabbino^m
Good Friday	il Venerdì Santo^m	ritual	rituale^m rito^m
mass	messa^f	Scripture	la Scrittura^f
monk	monaco^m	sect	setta^f

10. SPORTS II

More vocabulary related to sports is in the table below:

ball boy	raccattapalle^m	parachute	paracadute^m
bat (baseball)	bastone^m	performance	rendimento^m
betting	scommessa^f	physiotherapy	fisioterapia^f
bullfight	corrida^f	post (soccer)	palo^m
commentator	commentatore^m	practice	pratica^f
competition	competizione^f	prize	premio^m
contest	concorso^m	rivalry	rivalità^f
cycling	ciclismo^m	running track	pista^f da corsa
defender	difensore^m difenditrice^f	score	punteggio^m
diving	immersione^{f 1} tuffo^{m 1}	skydiving	paracadutismo^m
draw (random selection)	sorteggio^m	sled sledge	slitta^f
fencing	scherma^f	stretching	stiramento^m
friendly match	partita amichevole^f	team	squadra^f
header	testata^f	throw-in (soccer)	calcio laterale^m
helmet	casco^m elmetto^m	tournament	torneo^m
horse riding	equitazione^f	trophy	trofeo^m
midfielder (soccer)	centrocampista^m	whistle	fischietto^m
on the bench	in panchina^f	wrestling	lotta^f

[1] In general, "**immersione**" refers to underwater swimming, whereas "**tuffo**" refers to the act of jumping into water.

REFERENCES

The following is a list of references that we found useful in writing this book:

Sagar-Fenton, Beth & McNeill, Lizzy (2018). How many words do you need to speak a language? Retrieved from https://www.bbc.com/news/world-44569277

Nation, Paul & Waring, Robert (1997). Vocabulary Size, Text Coverage, and Word Lists, by Paul Nation and Robert Waring. Retrieved from https://www.lextutor.ca/research/nation_waring_97.html

Francis, W. N., Kucera, H., Kučera, H., & Mackie, A. W. (1982). Frequency analysis of English usage: Lexicon and grammar. Houghton Mifflin.

Nation, Paul. (2019). 4000 Essential English Words 1-6. Compass Publishing.

Foreign Service Institute (FSI)
https://www.state.gov/foreign-language-training/

Anki Webpage
https://apps.ankiweb.net/

Vermeer, Alex. (2017). Anki Essentials v1.1: The complete guide to remembering anything with Anki [Kindle edition].

Danesi, Marcel. (2016). Complete Italian Grammar (2nd edition). McGraw Hill.

Battista, J. L. (2014). Essentials of Italian Grammar. Harvard University Press.

Petrunin, Mikhail. (2018). Comparative Grammar of Spanish, Portuguese, Italian, and French. McGraw Hill.

Lawless Italian website.
https://www.lawlessitalian.com/

ThoughtCo website.
https://www.thoughtco.com/

Italian Bello website.
https://italiano-bello.com/en/

Italian Pills website.
https://italianpills.com/

APPENDIX

Appendix A. Coupon Code for Free Flashcards

The Anki flashcards that accompany this book are available for free until December 31, 2023. Once you download the cards and back them up with the Anki account you create, the cards do not expire.

To download the free flashcards that accompany this book:

1. Visit the ADROS VERSE EDUCATION website at: https://www.adrosverse.com/books-and-flashcards/
2. Add the product "**Italian: Level I - Basic**" Anki Flashcards to the *Shopping Cart*.
3. Go to the *Shopping Cart* and use the following Coupon Code:

$$\boxed{\text{AMZNAVEIT2}}$$

4. Proceed to *Checkout* and place your order.
5. Download the flashcards in ".zip" format and extract the ".apkg" files.

Appendix B. Verb Tenses and Conjugation Charts

We provide two useful cheat sheets that give you an overall perspective of most moods and verb tenses in Italian.

The two sheets are available **in color** in pdf format on the resources page of our website at https://www.adrosverse.com/resources/

The first cheat sheet is the Verb Conjugation Chart, which is structured as a comprehensive reference for the reader.

The second sheet dives into the irregular verbs of each tense, where applicable. Besides the imperative mood, we cover the irregular verbs in four tenses in the indicative: the present, the absolute past, the imperfect, the simple future; two in the subjunctive, that is, the present subjunctive and the imperfect subjunctive, and the past participle irregulars which are used in many tenses including: present perfect, pluperfect, and conditional perfect.

We recommend that you keep these two sheets handy by printing them out or having them available separately on your desk or electronic device.

VERB CONJUGATION CHART

CONDITIONAL

CONDITIONAL PERFECT

Io avrei parlato (I would have spoken)

Depending on the verb, the auxiliary "avere" or "essere" is used

	"avere"	"essere"	
io	avrei	sarei	
tu	avresti	saresti	
lui/lei	avrebbe (or)	sarebbe	+ past participle
noi	avremmo	saremmo	
voi	avreste	sareste	
loro	avrebbero	sarebbero	

SIMPLE CONDITIONAL

Io parlerei (I would speak)

The stem is formed by dropping the final "e" of the verb and change the final "-ar" to "-er" in the case of "-are" verbs., i.e., "parlere"

	-are	-ere	-ire (I)	-ire (II)
io	-ei	-ei	-ei	-ei
tu	-esti	-esti	-esti	-esti
lui/lei	-ebbe	-ebbe	-ebbe	-ebbe
noi	-emmo	-emmo	-emmo	-emmo
voi	-este	-este	-este	-este
loro	-ebbero	-ebbero	-ebbero	-ebbero

INDICATIVE

FUTURE PERFECT

Io avrò parlato (I will have spoken)

Depending on the verb, the auxiliary "avere" or "essere" is used

	"avere"	"essere"	
io	avrò	sarò	
tu	avrai	sarai	
lui/lei	avrà (or)	sarà	+ past participle
noi	avremo	saremo	
voi	avrete	sarete	
loro	avranno	saranno	

SIMPLE FUTURE

Io parlerò (I will speak)

The stem is formed by dropping the final "e" of the verb and change the final "-ar" to "-er" in the case of "-are" verbs., i.e., "parlere"

	-are	-ere	-ire (I)	-ire (II)
io	-ò	-ò	-ò	-ò
tu	-ai	-ai	-ai	-ai
lui/lei	-à	-à	-à	-à
noi	-emo	-emo	-emo	-emo
voi	-ete	-ete	-ete	-ete
loro	-anno	-anno	-anno	-anno

SUBJUNCTIVE

PRESENT

che io parli (that I speak)

The stem is formed from the present ind. "io" form, i.e., "io parlare" for all forms except "noi" and "voi"

	-are	-ere	-ire (I)	-ire (II)
io	-i	-a	-a	-a
tu	-i	-a	-a	-a
lui/lei	-i	-a	-a	-a
noi	-iamo	-iamo	-iamo	-iamo
voi	-iate	-iate	-iate	-iate
loro	-ino	-ano	-ano	-ano

Io parlo (I speak)

The stem is formed from the infinitive, i.e., "parlare"

	-are	-ere	-ire (I)	-ire (II)
io	-o	-o	-o	-isco
tu	-i	-i	-i	-isci
lui/lei	-a	-e	-e	-isce
noi	-iamo	-iamo	-iamo	-iamo
voi	-ate	-ete	-ite	-ite
loro	-ano	-ono	-ono	-iscono

PRESENT PERFECT

che io abbia parlato (that I have spoken)

Depending on the verb, the auxiliary "avere" or "essere" is used

	"avere"	"essere"	
io	abbia	sia	
tu	abbia	sia	
lui/lei	abbia (or)	sia	+ past participle
noi	abbiamo	siamo	
voi	abbiate	siate	
loro	abbiano	siano	

Io ho parlato (I have spoken)

Depending on the verb, the auxiliary "avere" or "essere" is used

	"avere"	"essere"	
io	ho	sono	
tu	hai	sei	
lui/lei	ha (or)	è	+ past participle
noi	abbiamo	siamo	
voi	avete	siete	
loro	hanno	sono	

PROGRESSIVE TENSES

Progressive tenses are formed by adding the proper conjugation of the verb "stare" to the gerund.

Present Progressive:	Io sto parlando (I am speaking)
Past Progressive:	Io stavo parlando (I was speaking)
Future Progressive:	Io starò parlando (I will be speaking)
Conditional Progressive:	Io starei parlando (I would be speaking)

ABSOLUTE PAST

Io parlai (I spoke)

The stem is formed from the infinitive, i.e., "parlare"

	-are	-ere	-ire (I)	-ire (II)
io	-ai	-ei/-etti	-ii	-ii
tu	-asti	-esti	-isti	-isti
lui/lei	-ò	-é/-ette	-ì	-ì
noi	-ammo	-emmo	-immo	-immo
voi	-aste	-este	-iste	-iste
loro	-arono	-erono/-ettero	-irono	-irono

IMPERFECT

che io parlassi (that I spoke)

The stem is formed by dropping the final "-re", i.e., "parlare"

	-are	-ere	-ire (I)	-ire (II)
io	-ssi	-ssi	-ssi	-ssi
tu	-ssi	-ssi	-ssi	-ssi
lui/lei	-sseva	-sseva	-sseva	-sseva
noi	-ssimo	-ssimo	-ssimo	-ssimo
voi	-ste	-ste	-ste	-ste
loro	-ssero	-ssero	-ssero	-ssero

Io parlavo (I spoke)

The stem is formed by dropping the final "-re", i.e., "parlare"

	-are	-ere	-ire (I)	-ire (II)
io	-vo	-vo	-vo	-vo
tu	-vi	-vi	-vi	-vi
lui/lei	-va	-va	-va	-va
noi	-vamo	-vamo	-vamo	-vamo
voi	-vate	-vate	-vate	-vate
loro	-vano	-vano	-vano	-vano

PLUPERFECT

che io avessi parlato (that I had spoken)

Depending on the verb, the auxiliary "avere" or "essere" is used

	"avere"	"essere"	
io	avessi	fossi	
tu	avessi	fossi	
lui/lei	avesse (or)	fosse	+ past participle
noi	avessimo	fossimo	
voi	aveste	foste	
loro	avessero	fossero	

Io avevo parlato (I had spoken)

Depending on the verb, the auxiliary "avere" or "essere" is used

	"avere"	"essere"	
io	avevo	ero	
tu	avevi	eri	
lui/lei	aveva (or)	era	+ past participle
noi	avevamo	eravamo	
voi	avevate	eravate	
loro	avevano	erano	

IRREGULAR VERBS

PRESENT INDICATIVE TENSE

1. Completely Irregular Verbs
andare: vado, vai, va, andiamo, andate, vanno
avere: ho, hai, ha, abbiamo, avete, hanno
bere: bevo, bevi, beve, beviamo, bevete, bevono
essere: sono, sei, è, siamo, siete, sono
dare: do, dai, dà, diamo, date, danno
dire: dico, dici, dice, diciamo, dite, dicono
dovere: devo/debbo, devi, deve, dobbiamo, dovete, devono/debbono
fare: faccio, fai, fa, facciamo, fate, fanno
potere: posso, puoi, può, possiamo, potete, possono
sapere: so, sai, sa, sappiamo, sapete, sanno
stare: sto, stai, sta, stiamo, state, stanno
scegliere: scelgo, scegli, sceglie, scegliamo, scegliete, scelgono
uscire: esco, esci, esce, usciamo, uscite, escono
volere: voglio, vuoi, vuole, vogliamo, volete, vogliono

2. Add a "g" to the stem of the verb in the "io" and "loro" forms
salire: salgo, sali, sale, saliamo, salite, salgono
rimanere: rimango, rimani, rimane, rimaniamo, rimanete, rimangono
venire: vengo, vieni*, viene*, veniamo, venite, vengono
tenere: tengo, tieni*, tiene*, teniamo, tenite, tengono
Note that the "venire" and "tenere" also change the stem in the "tu" and "lui/lei" forms from "ven-" and "ten-" to "vien-" and "tien-," respectively.

3. Minor Stem Changes
appaire: appaio, appari, appare, appariamo, apparite, appaiono
morire: muoio, muori, muore, moriamo, morite, muoiono
sedere: siedo, siedi, siede, sediamo, sedete, siedono
udire: odo, odi, ode, udiamo, udite, odono

4. Orthographic Changes
Add an "h" in "tu" & "noi" forms: "-care": e.g., cherchi/cherchiamo.
"-gare": e.g., paghi/paghiamo
Drop one "i" in "tu" & "noi" forms: "-ciare": e.g., baci/baciamo. "-giare":
e.g., mangi/mangiamo, "-gliare": e.g., tagli/tagliamo

5. Contracted Infinitive Verbs ("-rre" Ending)
"-arre":
trarre (tra-), contrarre (contra-), disttrarre (distra-), sottrarre (sottra-)
e.g., trarre (tra-): traggo, trai, trae, traiamo, traete, traggono
"-orre":
porre (pon-), comporre (compon-), esporre (espon-), imporre (impon-)
e.g., porre (pon-): pongo, poni, pone, poniamo, ponete, pongono
"-urre":
tradurre (traduc-), condurre (conduc-), produrre (produc-)
e.g., tradurre (traduc-): traduco, traduci, traduce, traduciamo, traducete,
traducono

PRESENT SUBJUNCTIVE TENSE

1. "-are" verbs conjugated like "-ere" & "-ire" verbs
andare: vada, vada, vada, andiamo, andiate*, vadano
fare: faccia, faccia, faccia, facciamo, facciate, facciano
*The "voi" form "andiate" is irregular
2. "-are" verbs conjugated like "-ere" & "-ire" verbs
avere (abbi-): abbia, abbia, abbia, abbiamo, abbiate, abbiano
dare (di-): dia, dia, dia, diamo, diate, diano
essere (si-): sia, sia, sia, siamo, siate, siano
sapere (sappi-): sappia, sappia, sappia, sappiamo, sappiate, sappiano
stare (sti-): stia, stia, stia, stiamo, stiate, stiano
Note that the "voi" form drops an "i" to avoid the double "i" sound
3. Contracted Inf. verbs are conjugated like "-ere" & "-ire" verbs
trarre: tragga, tragga, tragga, traiamo, traiate, traggano
porre: ponga, ponga, ponga, poniamo, poniate, pongano
tradurre: traduca, traduca, traduca, traduciamo, traduciate, traducano
Note that the "voi" form uses stem from infinitive with "-iate" ending
4. Same orthographic changes applied to verbs ending in "-care," "-gare," "-ciare," "-giare," and "-gliare" in the present indicative tense are applied here to maintain the proper pronunciation.

ABSOLUTE PAST

Many irregular verbs, most of which are "-ere" verbs:
avere, bere, cadere, chiedere, chiudere, conoscere, correggere, dare,
decidere, dire, discutere, essere, fare, leggere, mettere, nascere,
perdere, piacere, prendere, ridere, sapere, scegliere, scendere,
scrivere, stare, vedere, venire, vincere, volere

FUTURE INDICATIVE TENSE

1. Stem formed by dropping final "e" & the vowel before final "r"
andare (andr-): andrò, andrai, andrà, andremo, andrete, andranno
avere (avr-): avrò, avrai, avrà, avremo, avrete, avranno
cadere (cadr-): cadrò, cadrai, cadrà, cadremo, cadrete, cadranno
dovere (dovr-): dovrò, dovrai, dovrà, dovremo, dovrete, dovranno
potere (potr-): potrò, potrai, potrà, potremo, potrete, potranno
2. Stem of some short "-are" verbs does not chnage "-ar" to "-er"
dare (dar-): darò, darai, darà, daremo, darete, daranno
fare (far-): farò, farai, farà, faremo, farete, faranno
stare (star-): cadrò, cadrai, cadrà, cadremo, cadrete, cadranno
3. Stem replaces the consonant & vowel preceding the final "r" with an extra "r" to form "rr-" ending stem
tenere (terr-): terrò, terrai, terrà, terremo, terrete, terranno
volere (vorr-): vorrò, vorrai, vorrà, vorremo, vorrete, vorranno
venire (verr-): verrò, verrai, verrà, verremo, verrete, verranno
4. Completely Irregular Verbs
essere (sar-): sarò, sarai, sarà, saremo, sarete, saranno
bere (berr-): berrò, berrai, berrà, berremo, berrete, berranno
5. Same orthographic changes applied to verbs ending in "-care," "-gare," "-ciare," "-giare," and "-gliare" in the present indicative tense are applied here to maintain the proper pronunciation.

SIMPLE CONDITIONAL TENSE

Same irregular verbs as in the future indicative tense.

IMPERATIVE INDICATIVE TENSE

Most common irregular verbs:
bere: bevevo, bevevi, beveva, bevevamo, bevevate, bevevano
dare: davo, davi, dava, davamo, davate, davano
dire: dicevo, dicevi, diceva, dicevamo, dicevate, dicevano
essere: ero, eri, era, eravamo, eravate, erano
fare: facevo, facevi, faceva, facevamo, facevate, facevano
stare: stavo, stavi, stava, stavamo, stavate, stavano

IMPERATIVE SUBJUNCTIVE TENSE

Most common irregular verbs:
bere: bevessi, bevessi, bevesse, bevessimo, beveste, bevessero
dare: dessi, dessi, desse, dessimo, deste, dessero
dire: dicessi, dicessi, dicesse, dicessimo, diceste, dicessero
essere: fossi, fossi, fosse, fossimo, foste, fossero
fare: facessi, facessi, facesse, facessimo, faceste, facessero
stare: stessi, stessi, stesse, stessimo, steste, stessero

IMPERATIVE

1. Singular Informal (i.e., "tu" form)
essere (sii), andare (vai/va'), avere (abbi), dire (di'), fare (fai/fa'), stare
(stai/sta')
2. Singular Formal (i.e., "Lei" form)
essere (sia), andare (vada'), avere (abbia), dare (dia), dire (dica), fare
(faccia), stare (stia), uscire (esca), venire (venga)
3. Plural Informal (i.e., "voi" form)
essere (siate), avere (abbiate)
4. Plural Formal (i.e., "Loro" form)
essere (siano), avere (abbiano)

PAST PARTICIPLE

accendere (acceso), aprire (aperto), bere (bevuto), chiedere (chiesto),
chiudere (chiuso), coprire (coperto), correre (corso), cuocere (cotto),
decidere (deciso), dire (detto), discutere (discusso), dividere (diviso),
fare (fatto), friggere (fritto), leggere (letto), mettere (messo), morire
(morto), nascere (nato), offendere (offeso), perdere (perso/perduto),
piangere (pianto), porre (posto), ridere (riso), rimanere (rimasto),
risolvere (risolto), rompere (rotto), soddisfare (soddisfatto), scegliere
(scelto), scendere (sceso), scrivere (scritto), soffrire (sofferto),
spegnere (spento), stare (stato), tradurre (tradotto), vedere
(visto/veduto), venire (venuto), vincere (vinto), vivere (vissuto)

Appendix C. Soccer Vocabulary

Football or *soccer* is incredibly popular in Italy. It is quite useful to familiarize yourself with the vocabulary associated with **"il calcio."**

armband	**fascia**^f **bracciale**^m	*left-back*	**terzino sinistro**^m
assist	**assistenza**^f	*locker rooms*	**spogliatoi**^m
assistant referee	**assistente**^m **dell'arbitro**	*manager*	**direttore tecnico**^m
bench	**panchina**^f	*midfield*	**centrocampo**^m
bicycle kick	**rovesciata**^f	*midfielder*	**centrocampista**^{m,f}
captain	**capitano**	*nutmeg*	**tunnel**^m
central defender	**difensore centrale**^m	*offside*	**fuorigioco**^m
champion	**campione**^m	*own goal*	**autogol**^m
championship	**campionato**^m	*pass*	**passaggio**^m
championship title	**titolo**^m **di campione**	*penalty kick*	**calcio di rigore**^m
chance	**occasione**^f	*penalty area*	**area**^f **di rigore**
clearance	**disimpegno**^m	*penalty shootout*	**calci di rigore**^m
coach	**allenatore**^m **coach**^m	*playing field*	**campo**^m **terreno**^m
comeback	**rimonta**^f	*possession*	**possesso**^m
corner kick	**calcio d'angolo**^m	*post (goal)*	**palo**^m
corner flag	**bandierina**^f	*red card*	**cartellino rosso**^m
crossbar	**traversa**^f	*referee*	**arbitro**^m
cup	**coppa**^f	*right-back*	**terzino destro**^m
defender	**difensore**^m	*score*	**punteggio**^m
defensive wall	**barriera difensiva**^f	*shin guards*	**parastinchi**^m **schinieri**^m
dive	**tuffo**^m	*shot*	**calcio**^m
dribble	**palleggio**^m	*soccer ball*	**pallone**^m **da calcio** **palla**^f **da calcio**
equalizer	**gol**^m **del pareggio**	*soccer match*	**partita**^f **di calcio**
extra time	**tempi supplementari**^m	*soccer player*	**calciatore**^m **giocatore**^m **di calcio**
fans	**tifosi**^m **di calcio appassionati**^m **di calcio**	*soccer team*	**squadra**^f **di calcio**
flag	**bandiera**^f	*sportsmanship*	**sportività**^f **spirito sportivo**^m
forward	**attaccante**^{m,f}	*stadium*	**stadio**^m

foul	fallo^m	stands	spalti^m tribuna^f
free kick	calcio di punizione^m	stoppage time injury time	tempi^m di fermo
goal (score)	gol^m	studs	tacchetti^m
goal (structure)	porta^f	substitute player	sostituto^m
goal kick	calcio di rinvio^m	tackle	placcaggio^m
goalkeeper	portiere^m	throw-in	rimessa^f
halftime	intervallo^m metà partita^f	tie draw	pareggio^m
handball (soccer)	fallo di mano^f	touchline	linea laterale^f
hat trick	tripletta^f	jersey	maglia^f
header	colpo^m di testa	victory	vittoria^f
injury	lesione^f	whistle	fischio^m
kickoff	calcio d'inizio^m	World Cup	mondiale^m
kit	kit^m	yellow card	cartellino giallo^f

In addition to the vocabulary above, the following verbs come in handy when you want to watch or describe soccer in Italian:

English	Italian	Examples
to attack	attaccare	La squadra ha perso, anche se **ha attaccato** fino all'ultimo minuto. *The team lost, although they **attacked** until the last minute.*
to bump into	urtare	**Ha urtato** l'altro giocatore per sbaglio. *He **bumped into** the other player by accident.*
to clear	respingere	**Ha respinto** la palla fuori dall'area di rigore. *He **cleared** the ball outside the penalty area.*
to defeat	sconfiggere	La squadra è stata **sconfitta**. *The team was **defeated**.*
to defend	difendere	Il portiere **difende** la porta. *The goalie **defends** the goal.*
to dive (pretend)	tuffarsi	Non mi piacciono i giocatori che **si tuffano** tutto il tempo. *I don't like players who **dive** all the time.*
to eliminate	eliminare	**Hanno eliminato** molte squadre forti per raggiungere la finale. *They **eliminated** many strong teams to reach the final.*

to head	colpire di testa	**Colpisce di testa** molto bene. He **heads** the ball very well.
to lose	perdere	Se continuano a giocare così, **perderanno**. If they keep playing that way, they **will lose**.
to mark	marcare	Questo difensore è noto per **marcare** molto bene gli attaccanti. This defender is known for **marking** strikers very well.
to prevail	prevalere	La squadra è riuscita a **prevalere** negli ultimi minuti. The team managed to **prevail** in the last minutes.
to qualify	qualificarsi	**Si sono qualificati** per le semifinali. They **qualified** for the semifinals.
to recover	riprendersi recuperare	Ci vorranno due settimane per **riprendersi** dalla stagione. He will take two weeks to **recover** from the season.
to referee	arbitrare	Penso che **abbia arbitrato** bene oggi. I think he **refereed** well today.
to run	correre	Quel giocatore **corre** molto nel gioco. That player **runs** a lot in the game.
to score	segnare	**Hanno** appena **segnato** un altro gol. They've just **scored** another goal.
to simulate **to feign**	simulare	L'arbitro gli ha mostrato un cartellino giallo per **aver simulato** un infortunio. The referee showed him a yellow card for **feigning** injury.
to stretch	allungare	Devi **allungare** prima di giocare sul campo. You have to **stretch** before playing on the field.
to substitute	sostituire	**Sostituirà** il giocatore principale. He will **substitute** for the main player.
to tackle	placcare	**Ha placcato** il giocatore senza preavviso. He **tackled** the player without a warning.
to tie **to equalize**	pareggiare	Alla fine, **hanno pareggiato** la partita. In the end, they **tied** the game.
to volley	lanciare	Riuscì a **lanciare** la palla all'attaccante. He managed to **volley** the ball to the striker.
to warm up	scaldarsi	**Si scalderanno** prima di giocare. They **will warm up** before playing.

Appendix D. Acronyms and Abbreviations

Acronyms, initialisms, and abbreviations are common in Italian. Here, we summarize some basic rules and list some common examples.

Acronyms and Initialisms

Acronyms and initialisms are both utilized to shorten a phrase by using the first letter of each word. The difference between an acronym and an initialism is that the former is pronounced as one word, e.g., "NASA" and "LASER," whereas the latter is pronounced as separate letters, e.g., "ATM" and "UN."

In most cases, we follow the same rules to form acronyms and initialisms in Italian. For example:

United Nations	UN	**O**rganizzazione delle **N**azioni **U**nite	ONU
International Monetary Fund	IMF	**F**ondo **M**onetario **I**nternazionale	FMI
World Health Organization	WHO	**O**rganizzazione **M**ondiale della **S**anità	OMS
Non-Governmental Organization	NGO	**O**rganizzazione **N**on **G**overnativa	ONG
Value Added Tax	VAT	Imposta sul **V**alore **A**ggiunto	IVA

Abbreviations

An abbreviation is a shortened version of a word or phrase. It uses the initial part of a word or a combination of the initial and final parts and is often characterized by a period at the end.

Examples of such abbreviations are titles and professions, such as:

Sig./Sig.ra	signor/signora	*Mr./Mrs.*
Sig.na	signorina	*Miss*
Dtt./Dtt.sa	dottor/dottoressa	*Dr.*
Prof./Prof.ssa	professor/professoressa	*Prof.*
Ing.	ingegnere	*Eng.*

The months of the year are abbreviated as follows:

January	genn.	July	luglio
February	febbr.	August	ag.
March	mar.	September	sett.
April	apr.	October	ott.
May	magg.	November	nov.
June	giugno	December	dic.

Notice that the months of "**giugno**" *(June)* and "**luglio**" *(July)* are not abbreviated.

The days of the week are often abbreviated using a single letter as follows:

Mon.	Tue.	Wed.	Thur.	Fri.	Sat.	Sun.
lunedì	martedì	mercoledì	giovedì	venerdì	sabato	domenica
lun.	mar.	mer.	gio.	ven.	sab.	dom.
L	Ma	Me	G	V	S	D

The *Before Christ (BC)* era is referred to as "**avanti Cristo**," and is abbreviated as "**a.C.**" The *Common Era (CE)* is often referred to as "**dopo Cristo**," and is abbreviated as "**d.C.**"

The four cardinal directions are abbreviated as "**N**" for "**nord**" *(north)*, "**S**" for "**sud**" *(south)*, "**E**" for "**est**" *(east)*, and "**O**" for "**ovest**" *(west)*. The four ordinal directions are abbreviated as "**NE**" for "**nordest**" *(northeast)*, "**NO**" for "**nordovest**" *(northwest)*, "**SE**" for "**sudest**" *(southeast)*, and "**SO**" for "**sudovest**" *(southwest)*.

Abbreviation of Plural Nouns

One notable exception to abbreviation in Italian is the doubling of the letters in the abbreviation of some plural nouns. For example:

Traffic Police	**V**igili **U**rbani	VV. UU.
Posts and Telegraphs	**P**oste e **T**elegrafi	PP. TT.
Royal Highnesses	**A**ltezze **R**eali	AA. RR.

Notice that this rule does not apply to all plural nouns, and there are many exceptions.

INDEX- ITALIAN

cagnetto, 270
cagnolino, 269
calamaro, 194
calci di rigore, 306
calciatore, 306
calcio, 42, 106, 131, 158, 299, 306
calcio d'angolo, 306
calcio d'inizio, 307
calcio di punizione, 307
calcio di rigore, 306
calcio di rinvio, 307
calcolare, 154
calcolatrice, 160
calcolo, 68
caldo, 43, 69, 139, 140, 165, 172, 231, 251, 271
calduccio, 271
calendario, 203
calligramma, 40
calmare, 66
calmo, 155, 236
calore, 251
calvo, 240
calze, 205
calzini, 205, 236, 274
cambiamento, 197, 242
cambiare, 65, 86, 123, 124, 255, 256
cambio, 292, 293
camera, 36, 157
cameriera, 49
cameriere, 49, 200, 286
camerino, 205
camicetta, 205
camicia, 46, 52, 69, 115, 205, 243
camino, 157
camion, 113, 249
camioncino, 112
cammello, 246
camminare, 66, 214
cammino, 250
campagna, 113, 247, 280
campanello, 150
campeggio, 113, 203
campicello, 270
campionato, 158, 306
campione, 306
campo, 131, 159, 213, 245, 267, 270, 306, 308
Canada, 72
canadese, 44, 72
canale, 40, 157
cancellare, 66, 186
candela, 203
candidato, 247
cane, 30, 53, 62, 77, 152, 185, 196, 230, 232, 234, 269, 270, 273, 282, 283, 287, 288
canguro, 246
canna, 246
cannella, 149
cannuccia, 190, 204

canovaccio, 105, 158
canta, 182
cantante, 49, 200
cantare, 106, 231
cantina, 157
canzone, 274
caos, 297
capace, 194, 207
capacità, 155, 289
capanna, 203
capelli, 70, 76, 109, 186, 205, 231, 283
capire, 66, 104, 133
capirsi, 171
capitale, 53, 109
capitano, 295, 306
capitolo, 189
capo, 76, 110, 152, 200, 244, 276
Capodanno, 298
capogiro, 252
capolavoro, 298
cappello, 115, 271
cappelluccio, 271
cappotto, 63, 115
capra, 246
caramelle, 104, 108, 197
caratteristica, 296
carboidrato, 252
carbone, 203
carburante, 249
cardigan, 243
carenza, 297
carestia, 297
carezza, 246
carica, 247
caricamento, 160
caricare, 86, 191, 278
caricatore, 160
carino, 110, 142, 190
carità, 292
caritatevole, 240
carne, 114, 154, 169, 229
caro, 68, 184, 240
carota, 114, 289
carriera, 116
carta, 116, 203, 236, 274, 288
carte, 298
cartella, 231
cartellino, 193, 306, 307, 308
cartello, 112
cartoni animati, 298
casa, 46, 61, 68, 69, 70, 78, 79, 80, 82, 89, 96, 105, 108, 124, 131, 137, 143, 145, 147, 151, 157, 163, 167, 169, 178, 202, 213, 224, 228, 233, 238, 241, 244, 258, 259, 270, 271, 272, 278, 281, 285, 289
casa di campagna, 203
cascata, 251
casco, 299
case, 69

casetta, 270
casettina, 271
caso, 70, 199, 201
casone, 272
cassa, 116
casseruola, 157
cassetto, 289
cassiere, 200
castello, 107
castigare, 189
castigo, 201
castoro, 246
casualità, 290
casuccia, 271
catena, 116
catena montuosa, 251
cattedrale, 39, 41
cattivello, 270
cattivissimo, 166
cattivo, 68, 133, 139, 164, 165, 166, 189, 243, 270, 282, 292
cattolicesimo, 156
cattolico, 39, 41, 156
catturare, 192, 231
causa, 202, 240
causare, 192
cautela, 235
cauto, 238, 240
cauzione, 201
cavalcare, 149
cavaliere, 295
cavallo, 70, 77, 149
cavarsela, 267
caviglia, 191
cavità, 40
cavo, 156, 160, 286
cavolfiore, 252
cavolo, 204
ceci, 252
cedere, 127, 237
ceduto, 127
celare, 231
celebrare, 150
celebrità, 107, 233, 298
celibe, 75, 294
cellula, 253
cellulare, 91, 92, 135, 152, 160, 197, 262
Celsius, 230
cemento, 117
cena, 30, 107, 158, 281
cenare, 66, 105
cenere, 250
centesimo, 116, 254
centimetro, 202
centinaio, 283
cento, 53, 254
centomila, 53
centrale, 37, 40, 198, 306
centro, 80, 114, 117, 237
centro commerciale, 79, 237
centroamericano, 248
centrocampista, 299, 306
centrocampo, 306

cera, 204
cercare, 68, 70, 71, 85, 100, 106, 107, 109, 112, 150, 151, 193, 194, 231, 234, 236, 238, 239, 242, 274, 275, 277, 280
cercarsela, 267
cerchio, 202
cero, 203
certamente, 144
certezza, 290
certi, 167
certificare, 41
certificato, 149
certificazione, 188
certo, 131, 144, 183
cervello, 76
cervo, 246
cesareo, 230
cespuglio, 250
cessare, 150
cesso, 127
cesta, 157
cestino, 157, 203, 242
cesto, 68
cetriolo, 110, 204
che, 63, 98, 99, 100, 182, 219, 221
che cosa, 63
che ora, 265
check-in, 274
chi, 30, 63, 98, 99, 100, 193, 209
chiamare, 64, 79, 103, 169, 224, 226, 258
chiamarsi, 125, 170
chiaramente, 164
chiarificare, 231
chiarimento, 116
chiarire, 231
chiaro, 163, 164, 178
chiave, 48, 63, 79, 105, 106, 157, 159, 179, 213, 220
chicco, 232, 253
chiedere, 96, 99, 104, 125, 211, 218
chiesa, 156
chiesto, 125
chilo, 102
chilometro, 202
chimica, 116
chimico, 285, 295
China, 72
chiodo, 203
chiosco, 117
chirurgia, 200
chirurgico, 154
chirurgo, 193
chissà, 129
chiudere, 65, 125, 211
chiunque, 132, 220, 221
chiuso, 37, 68, 125, 128, 252, 259
chiusura, 202
ci, 95, 206, 207

INDEX- ENGLISH

Made in United States
Troutdale, OR
02/28/2025

29395351R00197